OUR NEW MASTERS

Also Published In

Reprints of Economic Classics

By THOMAS WRIGHT

The Great Unwashed [1868]

Some Habits and Customs of the Working
Classes [1867]

OUR
NEW MASTERS

BY

THOMAS WRIGHT
THE JOURNEYMAN ENGINEER

[1873]

𝕂

REPRINTS OF ECONOMIC CLASSICS

AUGUSTUS M. KELLEY · PUBLISHERS
NEW YORK 1969

First Edition 1873

(London: Strahan & Co., *56 Ludgate - Hill*, 1873)

Reprinted 1969 by

AUGUSTUS M. KELLEY · PUBLISHERS

New York   New York   10010

Library of Congress Catalogue Card Number

69 - 20019

PRINTED IN THE UNITED STATES OF AMERICA

by SENTRY PRESS, NEW YORK, N. Y. 10019

OUR NEW MASTERS

" Books will speak plainly when counsellors blanch ; therefore it is good to be conversant in them, specially the books of such as themselves have been actors upon the stage."—BACON.

" Meantime, the questions, Why are the working classes discontented ; what is their condition, economical, moral, in their houses, and their hearts, as it is in reality, and as they figure it to themselves to be ; what do they complain of ; what ought they and what ought they not to complain of ?—these are measurable questions. On some of these any common mortal, did he but turn his eyes to them, might throw some light."—CARLYLE.

OUR NEW MASTERS

By THOMAS WRIGHT

("THE JOURNEYMAN ENGINEER")

AUTHOR OF "SOME HABITS AND CUSTOMS OF THE WORKING CLASSES,"
"THE GREAT UNWASHED," ETC., ETC.

STRAHAN & CO.

56, LUDGATE HILL, LONDON

1873

PREFACE.

THE greater part of the present work has already been before the public in the shape of articles in *Fraser's Magazine* and the *Contemporary Review,* which are now reprinted by the kind permission of their respective publishers. I think it due, however, alike to readers and myself to state that the work is not a mere collection of magazine articles brought together just because there happens to be enough of them to make up a volume. The book was planned as a book from the first; the fact that the bulk of it readily lent itself to publication in magazine form was a mere accident. This explanation applies to the whole of the book, with the exception of one article—the one, namely, on "The English Working Classes and the Paris Commune." That article was not originally intended to form part of this work—was not thought of when the general idea of the work was conceived. It arose incidentally out of a private correspondence; and on its first appearance—in *Fraser* for July, 1871—was doubtless better "timed" than it is just now. Still, the main part of it has lost nothing of whatever value it may have had as a statement of working-class views upon an important social question, and I have therefore ventured to add it to the present volume.

I have taken Mr. Lowe's phrase as a fitting and expressive title for a book dealing with the working classes and their views, as they stand in these latter days, when those classes are, potentially at any rate, the New Masters of the political and social situation. When, on the passing of the bill that gave the last extension of the franchise, Mr. Lowe said, "Let us educate our New Masters!" he did more than merely add another to the already tolerably lengthy list of synonyms for the working classes. He indicated a policy—the policy of the future; a policy which it must be evident to all thinking minds it will be imperatively necessary for those having the direction of the national policy to adopt. The key-note struck by Mr. Lowe was largely taken up. "Our New Masters" became *the* topic of the day. They formed the theme of newspaper and magazine articles, platform speeches, and parliamentary debates. On all hands they were treated as "objects of interest," on many hands as objects of flattery; were told that they were all-powerful, and begged to be merciful as they were strong. Such of the New Masters as took note of all this, looked on amazed ; and to the more intelligent and thoughtful among them the most wonderful feature of the whole matter was the ignorance respecting the class in question made manifest in the course of this abundant writing and speaking. They saw that in many things the New Masters were unknown, in others very much mis-known; that their views upon questions in which they were intimately concerned were apparently undreamt of in the philosophy of those setting up as exponents and advisers; while views which they did not hold were freely fathered upon them. Seeing how matters stood on this point, it occurred to me that a volume by one of the New Masters, setting forth what manner of men they were, how their class was composed, what views they really did and did not entertain on the more prominent "questions of the day," and wherein lay their strength and weakness, might be of some practical utility—might afford a little *useful* information to those of other classes who have to deal with or legislate for " Our New Masters." Having the opportunity of putting my idea before some whose opinions carry weight with the public, I did so; and finding that they were of opinion that such a work was required, and *would* be likely to prove useful to those seeking to understand the New Masters, I wrote the book, and, having written it, I can only hope that it may in some degree fulfil its intended mission.

Here and there in the course of the work I have ventured to *express* opinions. Such expressions of opinion will of course only be received for what they may be considered worth, and are open to any criticisms or contradictions that it may be thought proper to bestow upon them. But, as a rule, it will be found that in giving working-class opinions upon topics in which the class are concerned, we merely *state* them ; and, whatever may be thought of the rightness or wrongness of those opinions, it may, at any rate, be depended upon that they are fairly stated, and are the opinions actually held by working men.

Deptford,
    January, 1873.

CONTENTS.

———•———

PART I.

PART II.

THE COMPOSITION OF THE WORKING CLASSES.

"If a house be divided against itself, that house cannot stand."—MARK iii. 25.

PEOPLE in the upper and middle ranks of society, who, from taking an active and friendly interest in the welfare of the working classes, are anxious to understand them, often ask how those who have a practical acquaintance with the classes in question account for or reconcile a variety of matters in connection with them, which seem to throw doubt upon or are inconsistent with each other. The half-surprised, half-distrustful feeling which gives rise to such questioning is, as things stand, a very natural one. Judged by the contradictory character of some of their actions and opinions—or, to speak strictly, some of the actions and opinions generally attributed to them—the working classes must to others appear not only an unreasonable body, but an incomprehensible one also. For instance, the allegation that republicanism is the political creed of the working classes, may sound, we won't say more strange than true, but at any rate *curious*, to those who weigh the assertion in conjunction with the facts, that while the working classes have in their hands ample means whereby to send members to Parliament to advocate their political views, the House of Commons does not number a single expressly republican member— and yet the assertion *is* true.

This and many other *seeming* contradictions are easily explainable. The reason—and the blame, if there is blame—of them lies rather with others than the working classes themselves. Though they *speak* of the working classes, most people in other grades of society *think* only of a working class—a class comprehending species as well as genus, and capable of being generalized by being individualized in the person of that great and well-known character of the day, "the working man." A more material error than this there could scarcely be, and it would be strange, indeed, if to those labouring under it the working classes did not appear in an incomprehensible light. That it is a most prevalent error need not be specially demonstrated here. A glance through newspaper leaders and parliamentary and other speeches bearing upon topics in which the working class are concerned, will give abundant proof that such is the case, even if we put aside such evidence as self-examination upon the part of our readers might afford.

The working classes are not a single-acting, single-idea'd body. They are practically and plurally *classes*, distinct classes, classes between which there are as decisively marked differences as there are between any one of them and the upper or middle classes. And this explains many of the inconsistencies that are laid to the charge of the classes in the aggregate. The proceedings of a section are taken to be those of the whole, and presently when another section does something of an entirely opposite nature puzzled or indignant lookers-on exclaim : " There, my masters, is inconsistency for you ! What can be done with or for a body like this ? " Of the various " questions of the day," those more directly affecting the working classes are admittedly among the most pressing and important, and to the efficient dealing with such questions we think that two essential preliminaries are—firstly, a realisation of the fact that " the working classes " are literally classes, and not merely a class; and secondly, a general idea of the distinctive characteristics of at least the chief of those classes. Holding this belief, we are naturally of opinion that an account of the composition of the working classes, founded upon knowledge gathered from within them, by one of themselves, may have an attraction for, and possibly be of some slight use to, the many outside those classes who take an interest in them, and the great social questions in which they are concerned. It is at any rate in the hope that such may be the case, that we come to the subject proper of the present paper, as indicated in its title.

Taken literally, the phrase " the working classes " would include large numbers of all ranks of society, but in the popular and generally accepted sense—and that is the sense in which we wish to deal with it—it may be taken as broadly meaning the artisan and manual labouring classes, excluding even clerks and shopmen, who, though no better paid, and in other respects less advantageously situated than artisans, are yet ranked apart from and above the latter class, on the ground that they follow " genteel occupations." With this much premised, " the working man " becomes a partially admissible figure of speech. The working man as in contra-distinction to the man who does not work, or as distinct from the employing, or genteelly-employed man, can be easily understood. In this simple sense the phrase is self-explanatory, but when used, as it generally is, as a synonym for the working classes, it not only loses definiteness, but becomes an altogether misleading generalization. As such a generalizing synonym, it has for years past been in the mouths of all manner of men in connection with the discussion of the social and political problems of the age. Yet if a score of those professing to be the friends, to understand, and speak in the name of this assumedly representative individual were asked to define him, it would be found that each definition attributed to him some qualification in antagonism with one or more of those given to him by the others; while, could the attributes of all the definitions be combined, they would go to produce such a monster as happily for itself the world ne'er saw. As a stock phrase, or a rallying battle or party cry, " the working man " is sufficiently well-sounding; but as a matter of fact there is no wholly typical working man. Putting aside mere individual traits as outside the scope of our present purpose, there are characteristics marking considerable sections, which are altogether inapplicable to others. What would be true of the mechanic as " the working man," would not be true of the labourer in the same character. There is an educated and really intelligent section, and an uneducated and ignorant section; a political section (broken up again into several sub-sections), and a non-political section; a trade-unionist, and a non-trade-unionist section; a sober, steady, saving section, and a drunken, unsteady, thriftless section; and with the labour market habitually overstocked, there is fast arising a sectional difference of mode of life and feeling between the regularly and irregularly employed classes. Between all these sections there is difference, and in most instances antagonism of feeling. Between the artisan and the unskilled labourer a gulf is fixed. While the former resents the spirit in which he believes the followers of " genteel occupations " look down upon him, he in his turn looks down upon the labourer. The artisan creed with regard to labourers is, that the latter are an inferior class, and that they should be made to know and kept in their place. In the eyes alike of unionist and non-unionist mechanics, any clever or ambitious labourer who shows a desire to get out of his place, by attempting to pick up or creep into " the trade " to which he is attached as an unskilled assistant, is guilty of deadly sin, and deserving of the abhorrence of all right-thinking members of the craft. In the same way artisans' wives hold the wives of labourers to be of a lower social grade, and very often will either not "neighbour" with them at all, or else only in a patronising way.

On the other hand, the labourer looks upon the mechanic with much the same feeling that mechanics in general look upon many of those above them in the social scale. The mechanic is, as a rule, somewhat of a clever fellow, and he knows that by his daily labour he contributes to the national wealth and well-being, and has a more or less full belief in the doctrine so often preached to him that the working class are practically the sole creators of all national wealth. With this knowledge and belief in his mind he sees others whom he holds to be his inferiors in intelligence, usefulness, and everything else save some accident of birth or fortune, obtaining a far larger share of the substantial advantages of labour-created wealth than falls to his share. This state of things he holds to be wrong in the abstract and an injustice to him individually; a perversion of what ought to be. As a result he comes to entertain—either consciously or unconsciously—levelling doctrines, but like most other levellers he would only level down. Now the labourer is also a leveller, and as he too would likewise level down, his levelling ideas apply to the mechanic as well as to others; indeed more pointedly to him than to others. Many labourers have brighter natural parts than *some* mechanics; perhaps than the very mechanic at whose command they are. Most of them are of opinion that they have at least equal natural parts to the general run of mechanics, and that with the same opportunities they would have been as good or it may be better men—as skilful as craftsmen, as intelligent as members of society. Their lack of opportunity in regard to the acquisition of education or a trade, they argue, is visited upon them as a fault, while it is really a misfortune. Why, they ask, should they be regarded as the inferior of the mechanic, and be subject to him? Why, to come to more substantial things, should they whose work is harder and more disagreeable than that of the mechanic, be so much worse paid that they must perforce live in less comfortable homes, fare and dress more coarsely, and have less of all money-costing pleasures of life? To them it seems that there is no *necessary* or just Wherefore to these Whys. They see, in the existing state of affairs, undeserved wrong

to themselves individually and as a class, and a proof that
society is ill-constructed and in need of reconstruction.
It may be a law of nature that in all societies there shall
be a class of hewers of wood and drawers of water to
their social brethren. The history of mankind hitherto
is in favour of such a supposition, but the hewers and
drawers are very decidedly of opinion that the hewing and
drawing should be divided among all classes, or that otherwise the hewing and drawing class should be rewarded in
a manner that would enable them to command the good
things of life to an extent that would be equitably com-
pensatory to them for the degree in which the hard
things of life fell upon them. Coming most in contact
with the mechanic class, they, as we have said, apply
these ideas pointedly to them. The mechanic knows this;
knows that the labourer's notion of a radical reconstruction of the social system would involve the swamping
of his comparative social superiority, and to this extreme
inclusiveness of the levelling idea he objects. He cannot
" see the beauty" of the idea when made operative *upon*
him, as he can when made operative for him. In the
same way the workman—whether labourer or mechanic
—who may have a house of his own, or money in the
bank, knows that the idea with regard to the "redis-
tribution of property" of those who have neither house
nor money, would include in the total to be redistributed
his savings, as well as the millions of a Rothschild, or the

lands of a Westminster or a Bute ; a view of the question which the better-off workman is inclined to consider as too much of a good thing. Thus though artizans and labourers, well-off and ill-off workmen, may broadly and theoretically hold the same article of political belief, and to outsiders appear to be " all of a bunch," they are really divided, are mutually distrustful, and afraid of acting unitedly ; the one fearing that they may be dragged down, the other that they may be made tools of.

That many even of the uneducated among the working classes are endowed with a considerable degree of the quality generally spoken of as " shrewd common sense," is well known, and in comparing them with others it should also be borne in mind that their lack of education is their misfortune, not their fault. But with all due allowance made on this score, and speaking in a spirit the reverse of unkindly, it must be confessed that the ignorance, and—if we may be allowed the expression —uninformed-ness characteristic of a large proportion of the uneducated section, is so great and dense, and extends to such simple every-day matters, that to more or less educated men who are habitually brought into contact with it, it becomes irritating and seems contemptible. This is of course a wrong feeling upon the matter, but at present we are not speaking to extenuate but to explain. It may be " pity 'tis true," but it *is* true that no one has so impatient a contempt for the uneducated

working man as has the educated working man. This
feeling is not concealed; the uneducated men naturally
resent it, and so arises another bar to the unity which
would be strength to the working classes. The educated
workman holds the uneducated one to be responsible for a
low general estimate of the working classes being taken
by other classes, and he thinks it a matter of right that
the other should be ruled by him in all matters of opinion,
and indeed that he should scarcely presume to have an
opinion at all. This idea the uneducated man regards as
a piece either of self-seeking or "cheek," and in a mere
spirit of opposition to it—if there is no other ground of
difference—will act in antagonism to the views of his
educated fellow.

The political section of the working classes is, as we
have already mentioned, broken up into various sub-
sections. The views of one sub-section may, in comparison
with the extremer views of most of the others, be called
conservative; but a conservative working man in the
generally understood sense of the term, "the conservative
working man" who sometimes figures on paper as a member of a "constitutional association," is, if not an absolute
myth, a very infinitesimal reality. In the course of a
tolerably extensive experience, we have met with very
few who would admit that they were even nominally of
this type, and none who would admit it save under cross-
examination, and in a shamefaced manner, or the purity

of whose conservatism did not labour under suspicion ; who were not in the employ of, or otherwise dependent upon, or desirous of, the favour of some active and pronounced " gentleman member " of the particular " constitutional association " to which they belonged, or who did not bear the reputation among the fellow-workmen who had the best opportunities of knowing them, of being just the kind of men who would be likely to join *any* association that gave poor and accommodating members tickets for " banquets" at which baronets, colonels, and county members are the speakers, and the number of working-men banqueters bears about the same proportion to county gentry as did the one halfpenny worth of bread to the "intolerable deal of sack " in Falstaff's tavern bill. In short, though Conservative " organs " parade him as a type of a class, " the conservative working man " is *nil* for all practical purposes of estimating the composition of the working classes. The *creed* of the political section of the working classes is *at present* republicanism, or ultra-liberalism broadening down towards republicanism. It is on the question of the best means for gaining their end that they divide into sub-sections. One set says :—We must go in for a republic ; we shall do no good till we get it. Another—Our fight must be against capital. As things stand, it is practically lord of all, and till it falls we cannot rise. Another—What we want is working men in parliament, and we shall never be able to achieve anything for

ourselves till we have got them. And another—It is
mere waste and misdirection of energy to make home
politics the first consideration ; that the one thing really
needful is an international combination of the working
classes throughout the world. Of course, each sub-section
is strongly of opinion that their view alone is *the* correct
one, and is intolerant of the views of the others, except as
secondary to theirs. But they are unanimous upon one
point—to wit, that the non-political section are less true,
dutiful, and deserving members of their general brotherhood than they are, and they are given to expressing this
belief in rather hectoring fashion. This assumption of
superiority is of course resented, and, moreover, the
charge of class apathy is retorted by a counter one, of
personal self-seeking. Many of the non-political justify
themselves by saying that they do not see that they would
gain anything by " bothering " themselves with politics,
and they argue as a corollary from this that the others
would not interest themselves in politics did they not
believe they saw some prospect of special personal gain to
be obtained by such means.

Between trade-unionist and non-unionist workmen there
is, generally speaking, a certain degree of coolness and
suspicious watchfulness which leads to divided ideas and
action. The unionists are almost of necessity more or less
cliqueish, and this leads to non-unionist cliqueism. There
are—to use a paradoxical expression—unions of non-

unionists; exclusively non-union, as well as exclusively union workshops. That some trade-unions are seriously faulty, and even the best of them not faultless, is no doubt true; but still, so far as regards the larger, better, and more representative ones, it may safely be said that very few men qualified to become members of them refrain from doing so on the ground of conscientious objections to features of their constitution. The great majority of the non-unionist members of trades having well-organised unions, are either men who are not eligible for admission by reason of their not being considered up to the union standard of skill, or men who, being in regular employment, and having good prospects of remaining in it, decline to join the union on the ground that, as they are not likely to stand in need of its out-of-work pay, they do not see why they should subscribe to its funds for the benefit of others. The first kind are regarded—not only by the unionists, but by the more skilful non-unionists also—with somewhat of an evil eye, as being likely to bring down the trade—that is, the rate of wages in it. The others are by the unionists considered ignobly selfish; men without brotherly sympathy, and therefore little deserving of the sympathy of others should evil days come upon them. On the other hand, the non-unionists are of opinion that the unionists are unjustifiably and offensively dictatorial, and too much given to meddling and wire-pulling; and the general result is another and serious bar to that unity and feeling of mutual confidence by which the working classes might achieve so much ; for want of which they achieve so little.

That the drunkards, and too liberal drinkers, among the working classes are so numerous as to constitute a considerable section, is unfortunately but too well known a fact. Between them and the sober men there are decided differences of opinion. The sober men, generally speaking, despise the drunken ones, and in many instances look upon them as enemies, on the ground that their proceedings have the effect of giving a degraded aspect to the whole body, and that their sins are often visited upon the whole body, in the shape of workshop regulations, and other things which, though necessary and just as applied to drunkards, become harsh in respect to others. But while this is the opinion of others, the drinkers regard themselves as being simply "jolly good fellows," or at the very worst, "nobody's enemy but their own," and look upon those who censure them as prigs—men so lost to all proper feeling and sense of jolly-good-fellowship as to be capable of lending their aid to measures, the tendency of which would be in the language of jolly-good-fellowship to "rob a poor man of his beer"—men, consequently, against whom it behoves all jolly good fellows to be on their guard.

Between the steady and the unsteady section of the working classes, and between the saving, forethoughtful section, and that which in a too literal sense takes no heed for the morrow, there is much the same difference of opinion and distrustfulness. And this, of course, serves to further break up the working classes, and to show that "the working man," as an all-typical generalization, cannot but be inadequate and misleading.

With the chief of their antagonistic sections, together with their respective characteristics, and points of difference thus indicated, the working classes may, we think, for the convenience of a proximate generalization, be broadly divided into three "schools," of which representative members may be bodied forth. First comes the old school—the school in which the largest percentage of the lack of education, prejudice, and feeling of class-antagonism that stand in the way of the self-elevation of the working classes is to be found ; a school that was once the predominating one, and, though now a declining, is still a large and influential one. The members of it, like the members of other old schools, are given to speak of it as the *good* old school, and the time of its supremacy as the good old time. Though, seeing that the period in question was anterior to the passing of most of the laws at present in force for the protection of labour, other divisions of the working classes are disposed to look back to it as rather a bad old time. A majority of the old school are middle-aged, or more than middle-aged men, but this is not necessarily the case. Though it may sound somewhat paradoxical, it is a fact that there are many young men in the old school—men who, though young in years, are

"old school" in feeling and opinion. The man of this
school is pleased to regard himself as "rough and tough,"
and other working men as, comparatively speaking, effete.
He is chary of admitting anything good in things "new-
fangled," and still stoutly retains a belief in ideas that are
generally looked upon as exploded. As, for instance, in
the self-satisfactory and once almost universally accepted
doctrine that an Englishman is as good as three French-
men (or any other foreigners) ; that in fighting he could
"lick" them ; in the peaceful contests of labour "work
their heads off." He has a considerable contempt for
mere "book learning," or perhaps it would be more
accurate to say, for what he conceives to be the excessive
importance attached to education nowadays. He believes
in an elementary knowledge of the three R's, but is inclined to regard any attempt upon the part of a working
man to go beyond that as affectation and evidence of a
desire to set himself above his class—a sin not lightly
forgiven by the old school. His reading is generally
limited to the criminal records, and social and political
philippics, of his weekly newspaper ; which latter, though
often sound enough in substance, have nevertheless an
injurious effect upon him, as by their violent invective
and utter one-sidedness they pander to, and perpetuate,
his class prejudices. Moreover, they so flatter him—as
"the working man," the "brawny son of toil," the only
real creator of wealth, and so forth—that he turns a deaf

ear to all would-be advisers, who will not flatter, and all the more readily falls a prey to those who flatter in order to fleece. He is inclined to condemn as idlers all who, in the course of their avocations, do not need to soil their hands or pull their coats off. He regards himself as the Ishmael of modern society—the man upon whom all other classes seek to prey. And, holding this opinion, he deems that it behoves him to be watchful of others, to guard against their too close approach, and be scantily civil to them.

But if the workman of the old school has many faults, he has also many good qualities. He has plenty of "bottom" in him. He is of a self-reliant, self-helpful, independent spirit, and has none of those demi-semi genteel ideas and ways that are sometimes to be found among other sections of the working classes, and that make those afflicted by them so contemptible in the eyes of others. He dresses and lives plainly, and sees that his wife and family do the same. In his opinion a few pounds in the bank are better than a lot of fine clothes, and if he is ordinarily fortunate he *will* have money in the bank, and not unfrequently he is the proprietor of the house in which he lives. He is upright in his dealings, will stand by his friend and his class, and even when not individually affected by the matter in hand, is prepared to make the greatest personal sacrifices in support of the view of the working classes upon any principle affecting the welfare of the general body.

Gradually growing from the old school — from the explosion of old ideas ere they had engrained themselves in comparatively young minds, and the influence of new institutions, experiences, and knowledge—has arisen a division of the working classes which may be styled the school of the day. In point of numbers this is the greatest of the several schools, but still it is not preponderatingly great—not so great as to justify the putting up of its typical man as *the* working man, nor yet so great but that it would be swamped, both in numbers and influence, by a combination of the old school and the other leading school to be presently adverted to. It is not so " pronounced " a school as the old school, for though it has distinguishing traits, it has also important characteristics that are common to other schools. For instance, it is inclined to take the Ishmael view of itself—to believe that the hand of every other class is against it, and that therefore it becomes a self-defensive duty upon its part to have its hand against every other class. It, too, believes that all the best and truest political wisdom, honesty, and courage of the country are centred in those newspapers which profess themselves the " organs " of the working classes ; and it has been so vitiated by the persistent flattery of those " organs," that again, like the old school, it will accept no friendship but that which flatters. And from this cause it lends too ready and credulous an ear to those " friends of the working man " who do flatter them

—who would fain persuade them that, like the king, they can do no wrong—who make a trade of their friendship, and, flattering to live, live to flatter. On the whole, however, the man of this school is a decided improvement upon the men of the schools that have gone before. His general views are much broader and more cosmopolitan. He has got rid of some of the more offensive phases of what the old school are pleased to consider John Bullism. He does not believe it to be a law of nature that one Englishman is equal to several foreigners, or that the exercise of the manufacturing arts is a right divine of England alone. While he is of opinion that the extent and importance of foreign competition is designedly exaggerated by those whose interests are identified with capital, he concedes that it is a material fact of sufficient magnitude to be taken into account as one of the elements of the relations between capital and labour. In the face of it, he not only admits that the once generally—and by the old school still—despised foreigner is a man and a brother, but is anxious to be on friendly terms with him, and to co-operate with him upon labour and other specially working-class questions. Nay, on one point he is even willing to take pattern by him, to avail himself, would the State afford him the means, of that technical education, the machinery for acquiring which foreign governments have been wise and liberal enough to organize for the benefit of their working populations. Without having any very clear or definite idea of what constitute the much-talked-of "rights" of labour, he is firmly impressed with the notion that some of them are withheld by those having might upon their side. On the other hand, he is perfectly willing to grant that capital too may have rights—in the abstract. But he thinks that at present it has all its rights, and more. Though prepared, if need be, to take part in strikes, he regards them with a doubtful eye; looks upon them as a last instead of a first resource—as in any case an undesirable means even to a good end, and things, if possible, to be avoided. He prefers arbitration as a means of settling disputes, and in this regard it is only fair to him to say that he has shown greater earnestness and sincerity in attempting to establish courts of arbitration than has been displayed upon the side of capital.

Though comparatively little educated himself, he does not make light of education. On the contrary, he sets a high value upon it, and while regretting his own deficiencies, strives to give his children better educational opportunities than have fallen to his own lot. He takes a more or less warm and active interest in politics and in questions of social progress, and has an earnest though vague longing for a better state of things than now exists, and is ever willing to support this or that "movement" which he believes or is assured will lead to the desired improvement in the constitution of society. But at the same time he labours under a certain bitterness of spirit at finding how little actual material benefit has accrued to his class from even such of those movements as have been prosecuted to a successful end.

Naturally influenced by the tendencies of the times, he is more given to amusements, holiday-making, and dress, than the man of the old school—more perhaps than is altogether good for him. But with all due allowance of his faults, he is, upon the whole, a favourable style of man. A man meaning well, inclining to improvement—as a husband and father affectionate, as a neighbour and workfellow staunch and kindly.

The third school among the working classes is the one that may be spoken of as the " coming " or rising school. Numerically it is smaller than either of the other two schools, and it is also less demonstrative, and from these reasons is much less well known to the outer public. Still it is a large and influential school, and in the natural progress of events it is daily increasing, and is in all probability destined to become a predominating one in a greater degree than either of the other two have ever been or are likely to be. It is a natural development from the other schools. It has reaped the riper and later benefits of institutions that they have helped to establish, and of the general advances of the age; of increased facilities of home and foreign intercommunication, beneficial legislation, improved political status, and extended education.

The man of this school is necessarily a young man—
too young as yet, generally speaking, to exhibit that stern
persistent interest in the great questions affecting the
working classes that many men of the other schools show.
Still he does think of such questions, and time, while
making him fitter to deal with them, will also deepen his
interest in them. If superficially, he is at any rate tolerably widely educated—widely, that is, in comparison with
the other schools. He is the man who has availed himself
of the plentiful and diversified means of education now
within the reach of all; not only of the elementary and
technical means, but also of the—in many respects still
more important—supplementary means, the wide-spread-
ing press, public libraries, and cheap standard literature.
He knows what the *Times*, the *Saturday*, and the *Pall
Mall*, as well as *Reynolds'*, *Lloyd's*, and the *Beehive* have
to say upon working-class questions, and he does not take
it for granted that in regard to such questions all the
right must be upon the working-class side, all the wrong
on the side of those who hold different views. Nor does
he take it as an understood thing that a working man
must of necessity be a good man; a man of aristocratic
birth a bad one. He has little class prejudice, his
knowledge being more extensive than that of the men
of the other working-class schools; his sympathies are as
a consequence broader. He admits that there are bad as
well as good members among the working, as among other

classes; and while he believes that a good deal is yet due from the governing to the working classes, he knows, and has no˙ desire to conceal, that much *self*-improvement is needed among the latter body—improvement that will tend to eradicate the intemperance, ignorance, and bigotry that unhappily still largely prevail among them—improvement, without which improvement coming from the outside will be of but little avail.

He is not led away by Utopian ideas ; does not believe in social panaceas. But he does believe in "sweetness and light" and in the elevating effects of culture. Believes that education, abundant and easily accessible literature, and the resources of modern science, have already placed means within the reach of the working classes which, rightly appreciated and used by them, would diffuse a far higher and more general happiness among them than is to be found at present. Believes that a time may—probably will—come, when self-organized, self-supporting "Working Men's Clubs" will supersede the public-house, intelligent social intercourse the "booz-ing" and horse-play of the tap-room ; a time when a choicely-filled little bookcase will be an ordinary article of furniture in working-class homes, and working men generally acquainted with (through their works)—

> " The great of old,
> The dead but sceptred sovereigns who still rule
> Our spirits from their urns ; "

a time, in short, when mental culture will give such sweetness and light to the home and social life of the bulk of the working classes as, combined with the material improvement in their condition that—with education and knowledge thus advancing—may be reasonably expected from national progress in other matters, will make their lot one that to a *cultivated* mind will leave little room for envy.

The man of this school believes in liberty and fraternity, but not in equality. He knows that there is no natural equality, and is inclined to think that—

> " Beneath the sun
> The many still must labour for the one :
> 'Tis nature's doom ;"

that there must always be a working class, but that there is no necessary reason why they should not be as happy—perhaps happier—than the classes who do not work. And for the bringing about of such possible happiness he looks to a general and individual improvement *in* the working classes even more than to legislative action.

The man of the rising school has of course his faults, and the most prominent of them are unfortunately of such a character that, by their irritating action upon the men of the other schools, they stand as much in the way of the unity of the working classes as does the intolerant spirit of the other schools. Under existing circumstances he is inclined to be too egotistical and self-assured. He is given to drawing comparisons in his own favour between himself and the men of the other schools; to being hard upon their educational shortcomings, and on the strength of his superiority on this point, letting it be seen that he assumes a general superiority.

Though so generally spoken of, thought of, and legislated for as a single and unanimous body, any part of which characteristically represented, and might be taken as speaking for, the whole—though so generally regarded in this light, the working classes really are, as we hope we have shown, divided and subdivided; and not only that, but divided into antagonising sections. They are as a house divided against itself. To use the point of the old fable, they are a *number*, but not a *bundle*, of sticks. Their strength is wasted and made ineffective by want of coherence. Though all schools and sections of them have broad interests in common, they are so divided in feel ing as to be incapable of united action even for a common object. That they will in time become more united is tolerably certain; education is spreading, and ideas are enlarging among them, though slowly. In the meantime they stand divided in the manner we have attempted to describe, and those who would understand the working classes, or deal effectively with the great questions affecting them, must not only realise the fact that they are a divided body, but must also study their composition.

ON THE CONDITION OF THE WORKING CLASSES.

"There must be something wrong. A full-formed horse will in any market bring from twenty to as high as two hundred Friedrich's-d'or; such is his worth to the world. A full-formed man is not only worth nothing to the world, but the world could afford him a round sum would he simply engage to go and hang himself. Nevertheless, which of the two was the more cunningly-devised article, even as an engine! Good heavens! A white European man, standing on his two legs, with his two five-fingered hands at his shackle-bones and miraculous head on his shoulders, is worth, I should say, from fifty to a hundred horses!"—CARLYLE'S "Sartor Resartus."

"Man now presides
In power, where once he trembled in his weakness;
Science advances with gigantic strides;
But are we aught enriched in love and meekness?
Aught dost thou see, bright star! of pure and wise
More than in humbler times graced human story;
That makes our hearts more apt to sympathise
With heaven, our souls more fit for future glory,
When earth shall vanish from our closing eyes,
Ere we lie down in our last dormitory?"
WORDSWORTH.

TO those who understand its true significance, and see how wide and important are its bearings, it must be evident that the subject of the condition of the working classes is in this country fast becoming an Aaron's rod among the questions of the day. Its tendency is to swallow up the rest, for the complexion to which most others come at last is—How will they affect the working classes? It is a subject that in one way or another commands a good deal of attention, and gives rise to a considerable amount of theorizing, debating, and spasmodic action in the application of supposed panaceas for the remedy or removal of some particular evil, the consequences of which, after being long borne by those first concerned, are at length affecting other classes. But the degree of notice bestowed upon it, great as it undoubtedly is, is by no means commensurate with either its absolute or relative importance, nor is it of that minute and constantly watchful kind necessary to give a thorough understanding of the matter. So far as the constitutional powers that be are concerned, such notice as they give to it is almost invariably forced upon them, and that only after years of urging, and when there are symptoms of a dangerous impatience upon the part of those who have had to urge so long in vain. The working classes have been distinctly told, in words as well as by acts, that, at all events where they are concerned, the function of Government is not paternal. When artisans, who through no fault of their own had been out of work so long that they and their wives and children were starving, petitioned Government to assist them to emigrate, they were told that Government had no money for such a purpose—that it would be unfair to ratepayers to apply any portion of their money in that way. Yet there were items of expenditure in the financial returns of that year which we fancy most ratepayers would have regarded as far less justifiable or judicious than would have been a grant to enable starving workpeople to emigrate to home colonies, where there was good reason for believing they could earn a comfortable livelihood. A sensitive mind might easily have imagined that insult was added to injury in the refusal of the assistance asked for. In discussing the matter one noble lord—unconscious, we are quite willing to believe, that he was practically repeating the piece of grim mockery embodied in the saw : " Live, old horse, and you'll get grass "—said, " Let us keep them [the petitioning workmen] at home ; we shall need them when trade revives."

Though only one voice spoke so openly to this effect, workmen—not only those immediately interested, but the class generally—believe that this was substantially the meaning and motive of the refusal. Trade, they said, in effect, among themselves, and the interests of the " we's " of the governing and capital possessing classes, are to be considered before our sufferings. We and our wives and children must linger on half-starved, and wholly miserable, till the revival of trade, no matter how long that may be, because we shall be wanted when it does come— be wanted to help to keep down wages to the hand-to-mouth level that prevents all but a fortunate few among us, those who, by reason of their good fortune in finding constant employment, stand less in need of it, from making any adequate provision either for tiding over a time of want of work in something like decency and independence, or removing to countries in which labour is more highly paid, and want of work does not recur with the pauperising frequency and severity that it does in England. Such was the tenor of the remarks of working men upon the words of " the noble lord " when they were published in the parliamentary debates. They read, marked, and learned the words at that time, and have since been inwardly digesting them.

In a manufacturing country in which reckless speculation has eliminated the element of steadiness from business, and brought trade to be an alternation between " flushes " and " crashes," with long " spells " of slack time intervening,—in a country in this condition it *may* be sound political economy, and good statecraft, to look upon unemployed workmen merely as a description of manufacturing " plant," and aim at keeping them on hand, their sufferings here and prospects of doing better elsewhere notwithstanding. But it cannot be a matter for surprise that the working classes should be of opinion that such a national principle deals hard measure to them. They do believe that it is both hard and harsh, and, though it may be presumptuous, some of them even go so far as to argue that it is *not* good policy. So firm is their impression that the transfer to another country of English labour and artisan talent enriches that country, that they take it as understood that it would be a piece of stupidly unjust expectation to ask the State to assist workmen to emigrate to any other than British possessions. Their idea is that our colonies could be made to comfortably absorb the overflow of the home labour market, with benefit alike to the emigrating workmen and the colonies, and by consequence—and no very indirect consequence— the mother-country, whose working classes being relieved of some of their superabundant members would have better chances of *regular* employment, and whose market for her manufactures would be widened by the necessarily increased demands of the colonies. Though patriotism is now a good deal out of fashion, there *was* in this idea of working men a feeling of patriotism mingling with the other considerations prompting the idea. They would have liked to feel that while bettering themselves they were still contributing to England's greatness in helping to make her colonies great; and that though thousands of miles away, they were still bound to her, and virtually part of her. But statesmen, as we know, did not take the same view of the matter. They declined to assist the "unemployed" to emigrate to our colonies, and the feeling of the working classes has undergone a change so far as the patriotic sentiment is concerned. They say, speaking in bitterness of spirit, " Our country has shown that it has no true national regard for us; and that being the case, we don't see that we are called upon to any longer cherish a regard for her." Whatever they may become, the British colonies are not the best *ready-made* markets for English artisan labour. English mechanics who emigrate at their own expense mostly go to foreign countries—the greater number of them to America ; and any person who had the same opportunities as the present writer of seeing letters from such emigrated workmen, to friends and mates in England, would be forced to the same conclusion with him, namely, that the Irish emigrants were not the only ones that looked back to England with feelings the reverse of respectful and affectionate. Not that the sentiments of English workmen who have sought homes in the great Transatlantic republic are for a moment to be confounded with Fenianism. They have no desire to make war upon England, and their sympathies would be with her if any other country made war upon her, but socially they " crack up " the country of their adoption as in contrast to England. They say that the position and chances of the working man are substantially better there than here, and working men more thought of. They speak evil of dignities, and scoff at institutions that English workmen are called upon to honour, and are conventionally supposed to delight to honour. They refer to " the old country " contemptuously, and use " old " in the sense of effete, antiquated, and worn out; and they advise all who can to leave it, and go to a land in which there is really a prospect of " wealth for honest labour."

In some of these letters there is probably a too hasty generalization from isolated facts, and others lie open to a suspicion of being what is vulgarly called " bounceable," but there can be no doubt that the spirit that prompts their general tone is unfavourable to England, and one that has been engendered *in* England. "England's greatness" has been ascribed to a variety of causes: to her constitution, to her rank, to her talent, and, according to a popular pictorial treatment of the subject, to her liberal distribution of the Bible. But, as a matter of fact, few we think will dispute that much of her greatness has been due to the muscle, skill, and patriotic good-will of her working class. Taking this to be the case, it may be truly said that her greatness is departing—chiefly because Government has failed to give a just degree and wise manner of attention to the condition of the working classes.

On the question of Commons Preservation—the importance of which to the working class will be manifest as we come to speak further of their condition—Government takes the side of the enclosing individuals rather than of the people, though the almost invariable decisions of judges go to show that law as well as right is upon the side of the latter. The domestic legislation needed to give something of " sweetness and light," and which *could* give sweetness and light, to the homes of working classes, has yet to be inaugurated. In short, we think that more than enough has been said to show that so far as Government is concerned the subject of the condition of the working classes does not receive anything like the attention to which its importance entitles it, and which it would be well, both for those classes and the country at large, it should have. So large a subject is it, that only Government could hope to deal with it in adequate fashion. The efforts of private and amateur reformers to grapple with it—for it is generally with an admitted necessity for reform in it that it is noticed—are scarcely ever of a comprehensive character, generally being confined to an attempt to establish some supposed cure-all—teetotalism, co-operation, Sunday observance, or the like.

If the condition of the working classes was as carefully watched and thoroughly understood as it should be, there would be no room for doubt on the point of its being a most hard and unsatisfactory one, and one, moreover, tending to bring about a collapse of the country's greatness. At present there is both doubt and dispute upon it. Many persons, and among them some whose utterances carry weight on the ground that they *ought* to have knowledge on such subjects, assert—though generally more by implication than directly—that the condition of the working classes is as satisfactory as the circumstances of the case will admit of its being; that it is upon the whole so admirable as to be a matter for national congratulation; and that those who say to the contrary are ingrates, croakers, and maligners of the working classes. It need scarcely be said that the working classes themselves are not of those who hold this comforting view, and as little need it be mentioned that those who do entertain it have facts and figures to offer in support of it. What view is there nowadays on behalf of which facts and figures cannot be offered? But there are facts and facts. "False facts," says Dr. Darwin in his "Descent of Man," "are highly injurious to the progress of science;" and we think it may be safely said that they are still more injurious to the progress of truth and knowledge in regard to social problems, and the facts by which it is sought to demonstrate the accuracy of the view we speak of are of the false-fact, or perhaps we had better say the half-fact, order. They are units of a series of facts that can only be fairly applied as a series, and when used isolatedly they become practically false, though still verbally true. Working men when they complain of their lot—and indeed very often when they do not complain of it—are told that the times are, and for generations have been, progressive; and that the working classes have of necessity participated in the beneficial results of such progress, and must consequently be in a better position than they could have been in before such results had been achieved. They are told to bear in mind how wonderfully steam and machinery have economised labour, and increased the range and capabilities of manufacturing production; and how rail-

ways and ocean steamers have facilitated travelling, and
the export and import of all manner of food and goods.
They are reminded that they possess a cheap press, cheap
literature, and cheap education, and enjoy the advantages
of many important concessions in things political; and as
a sort of stock climax, they are bidden to consider that
the working classes in the present time have, as every-day
comforts and conveniences, things which even as luxuries
were beyond the reach of the Plantagenet kings. This
line of argument is now somewhat antiquated, and it has
been subjected to a good deal of scornful ridicule; but it
still flourishes, and is constantly in the mouths of those
well-meaning "friends of the working man," who yet
talk believingly of the good fortune of being born " a
happy English child," and "the happy homes of England," and who regard working men as being in point of
intellect and understanding mere overgrown children,
and in addressing them talk down to what they conceive
to be their level. The fallacy of the deduction made from
these arguments by those who use them has been frequently
exposed, and the matter is merely dwelt upon here because
it forms a good illustration of the false-fact system of
dealing with the question of the condition of the working
classes. The facts taken singly are literally true, and
their general tendency to improve the condition of the
labouring classes incontestable *as far as it goes*. Their
falsifying effect arises from the attempt to make the

inferences from them go too far—from, as we have said, taking them out of the series of which they form a part, and the other portions of which neutralise the conclusions attached to them, in the fashion under consideration. That for centuries past the times have been continuously progressive in the development of physical science, and the practical application of it to purposes of every-day life, is most true. It is equally true that the working classes, as part of society at large, have shared in the advantages of this progress, and enjoy means of comfort and physical happiness that were beyond the reach of any class in former generations. No one denies this. But it does not follow from it, as those who resort to this line of argument would wish to be inferred, as a self-evident corollary, that the present condition of the working classes is a good one. This mode of arguing on the subject is simply evasive. Where difference of opinion exists respecting the condition of the working classes, the questions raised are not whether this age is "progressive," the nineteenth century "enlightened," and the existing generation "highly civilized;" but whether the state of the labouring population is not absolutely bad, a disgrace to our boasted-of enlightenment, and a satire upon our much-talked-of progress; and secondly, whether, while all else has been progressing, the working classes, as regards their material well-being, have really made anything like a proportionate progress. To the first of these

questions the *whole* facts of the case emphatically answer
—It is bad. Only on the second point is there the
slightest room for doubt, and even the most favourable
consideration of the circumstances bearing upon it must,
we think, lead to the answer—Proportionate progress?
No. Indeed those best qualified by investigation to give
judgment upon the point are uniformly of opinion that
the present condition of the working classes shows an
absolute decline when put in comparison with the state of
things obtaining in the Middle Ages. Mr. Thornton, in
his work on " Over-Population and its Remedy," goes
very carefully and elaborately into this question. He
gives numerous wage-tables and other statistical details,
which leave no room for any other conclusion than the
one he draws from them, namely, that the condition of
the English labouring population during the centuries
immediately following the establishment of the Anglo-
Saxon kingdom was substantially superior to what it is at
the present day. After commenting on the ignorance of
those who, in the face of such information as he adduces,
gravely argue " that the English peasantry of the Middle
Ages were less comfortably situated than their living
descendants, because they used barley instead of wheaten
bread, ate off wooden platters, never knew the luxury of a
cotton shirt or of a cup of tea, and slept on straw pallets
within walls of wattled plaster "—after commenting on
this he winds up by saying : " Although ruder means

were employed to supply the wants of nature, every want was abundantly satisfied, which is far indeed from being the case at present."

Professor Thorold Rogers, in his "History of Agriculture and Prices in England," comes, after very diligent research and comparison, to the same conclusion; and the reviewer of that book in the *Athenæum* remarks : " In so far as Mr. Rogers demonstrates that the working men of the fourteenth century were upon the whole far better paid and fed than the labourers of modern England, he merely supports a view which in these latter years has been generally accepted by historical students." Mr. Mill takes a similar view, and Hallam and Froude in their histories incidentally confirm it. The Middle Ages rather than " the enlightened nineteenth century " would appear to have been the real golden age of the English working classes, though even then things were not constantly in the golden state. There were " spells " of hard times— times when, through the failure of crops or the operations of capitalists, the price of provisions was so enhanced, that in the language of an act of Henry VIII. (quoted in the first chapter of Froude's " England "), intended to restrain the action of some capitalists whose proceedings were supposed to have this injurious effect, many poor persons in the realm were " so discouraged with misery and poverty, that they fell daily to theft, robbery, and other inconveniences, or pitifully died of hunger." But deductions have been made for these drawbacks in arriving at the conclusion that the workmen of the thirteenth and fourteenth centuries were, upon the whole, better off than those of the present generation. Hallam, who goes into the subject at considerable length (in the second part of the ninth chapter of "The Middle Ages"), and with an avowed desire to think the best of modern times that a sense of impartiality will admit, says : " But after every allowance of this kind (bad harvests and the like), I should find it difficult to resist the conclusion that, however the labourer has derived benefit from the cheapness of manufactured commodities, and from many inventions of common utility, he is much inferior in ability to support a family than were his ancestors four centuries ago."

To occupy space in showing that, however we may have progressed in other matters, there has, during a period of four centuries, been—to say the least of it—no tangible and decisive improvement in the condition of the working classes, will, to those who have a proper acquaintance with the subject, seem a work of supererogation ; and yet it may not be altogether so, seeing how many of those who wish working men to accept them as teachers and advisers, are, so to speak, triumphantly ignorant of the fact. In any case, however, we have gone over this ground less with a view to demonstrating the fact itself, than to showing that working men are acquainted with it.

Pastors, and masters, patrons of mechanics' institutions, and others whom working men may not safely contradict, or who address them from positions that put contradiction out of the question, tell them differently, and the men listen, and under the influence of "speechifying," perhaps applaud, but in their cooler moments they "larf, they du," among themselves, at the notion that they are supposed to believe that they are infinitely better off than previous generations of their class. The better educated among them are up in the evidence of the case, and the general body of them have a single argument which is conclusive to their mind, despite any amount of talk about the unprecedented glories of "the age we live in." They know but too well the present condition of their class, and they reason from that knowledge that the class could not have been much worse off at *any* time, or the members of it would not have been able to keep body and soul together. And if there has been no absolute improvement in the condition of the working classes, there has certainly been no improvement in it relatively to other grades of society. Never was the contrast between rich and poor so great, and to the poor so stinging, as it is at the present time. We have been making vast and continuous material progress for centuries past, but it is the rich who have reaped the fruits of it; the direction of it has been such that the rich have generation after generation grown richer, and the poor by contrast poorer.

To many this matter of the comparative condition of the working classes of this age, and past ages, may appear a simple controversial question; but it has one important practical bearing—the one we have had in view in going into it—namely, the opinion upon it of the working classes. If they could believe that, however hard their lot might be, it was still better than that of those who had gone before them; that they had participated in, as well as contributed to, the material improvements of the age, and were, in common with other persons and things of the age, in a progressively improving way—if they could believe this they could be, and would be, patient and hopeful under present evils. But they know that it is not so—that the contrary is the case; and the knowledge makes them impatient, and it may be unjust—puts bitterness and hatred towards society in their hearts.

But whether the working classes as a body are, or are not, better off than their ancestors who lived in the Middle Ages, is, after all, a question of very secondary importance compared with this: Is their existing condition a good, or even a tolerable one? Let us look at this point. In the first place, what would be a fairly good condition of the working classes? We think this. That every man who was willing and able to work should be able to obtain employment at such wages and with such a degree of constancy as would enable him, by judicious management, to secure for himself and those depending upon him a sufficiency of plain food, and clothing, and a dwelling with—say—the same sanitary conveniences and air-space per person as a model prison cell; and to make provision during a working life of from forty to five-and-forty years for passing the remainder of his days without the necessity of hard work; not so much with a view to his mere personal ease, as to the contingency of his being no longer able to find a market for his labour, by reason of the physical deterioration that age and so many years of wear and tear must bring.

The above is not, we think, an unreasonably high standard; and yet, compared with the existing state of affairs, it sounds quite Utopian. Such a condition would satisfy the working classes, and make them a contented race. It would make life more than barely tolerable to all, while it would still leave room for men of more than average ability and perseverance to rise to higher social standards. That their general body cannot attain to it, the working classes hold to be a grievance and a wrong. They believe (whether rightly or wrongly is, of course, an open question) that there is nothing in the *natural* order of things that makes their present so much lower standard of condition inevitable, or the better one necessarily unattainable. Though the suffering falls upon them, the blame, in their opinion, attaches to an unjust constitution of society, and those who benefit by its injustice; and while they suffer, they brood and "feed fat a grudge" against society—a grudge that may some day break out in most disastrous action.

It is making a liberal allowance on the favourable side of the matter, to say that not more than one in twenty of the working classes get within the standard of comfort we have sketched—who have always a sufficiency of food and clothing, and a decent and healthy home; and who, when too old to find employment in a market in which employers have a choice of younger men, can maintain themselves without having to seek public charity, or becoming dependent upon relatives who, being themselves in straitened circumstances, generally regard such dependence as a burden, and make it very bitter. There is room for a certain number of the class to achieve such a position, and some do achieve it; but no individual workman can, at the outset of his career, be sure that, by the utmost exertion and willingness upon his part, he will win such a position—all platitudes about the success, commanding powers of industry and perseverance, notwithstanding. Chance, as well as character and qualifications, has a part in deciding who shall be the fortunates of the working classes, and this uncertainty is, in itself, an evil—an ever-standing anxiety to the more steady and thoughtful, and a cause of recklessness in others. Mr. Mayhew, the author of " London Labour and London Poor," treating of the subject of low wages, says: " It is calculated by those who have the best means of knowing, that out of 5,000,000 operatives in this country, one-third only are fully employed, or occupied their whole time; one-third partially employed, or occupied but half their time; and the remaining third unemployed, or obtaining a day's work or job occasionally through the illness or absence of others." This, of course, could only have been a proximate calculation, and it may be that it was an over-estimate on the dark side; but, apart from any citation of figures, working men know from practical experience that a large proportion of their class can only be employed in a more or less casual manner. In manufacturing establishments there is, as a rule, a set of hands who are virtually regarded as a staff, and who, so long as the works are kept open, will be retained in employment. As a rough estimate, these may be set down as ten per cent. of the number of workmen the place is capable of employing, and in very slack times * they will be all who are in work, the other ninety per cent. being unemployed. This is the extreme case of slackness, and the state of affairs

* Such times, for instance, as those which befell the Thames shipbuilding districts in 1866-7, when after some years of unparalleled briskness, the shipbuilding trade in those quarters came to a standstill. Yard after yard was closed, and thousands of workmen thrown out of employment. In the long-continued dulness that ensued savings were spent—as the post office savings-bank officials could testify—and those gone, clothing and household furniture had to be parted with to keep the wolf from the door; so that many who up to that time had made considerable progress in laying aside a provision for old age had to commence life afresh again in that respect when they once more got into work.

varies from that up to the " full-handed " standard characteristic of a " flush " of trade. The calculations of observant working men—which, though founded upon experience, are, of course, only broadly proximate—are that a
" flush " of trade, and the slack time that has been found
to follow it with an invariableness that practically amounts
to a law of reaction, occur within a period of seven years;
that the gradual rise from the average to the flush condition occupies a year, and the flush lasts six months ; and
that the decline down to slackness also takes a year, and
the slack lasts six months. During the other four out of
the seven years, things will be in the average state, which
is from ten to twenty per cent. below the " full-handed "
condition ; for even in ordinary times there are considerable fluctuations, hands being habitually discharged or
" shopped " as the passing exigencies of work may require.
Taking it that during a flush *all* working men were
employed—and that is certainly allowing too much—there
still remains the consideration that at all other times there
must be some greater or lesser number of men out of
work. In this floating or extra working population a
man, from no fault of his own, may have to remain all his
life, and some in it suffer far more of its evils than others.
That a manufacturing country should be in a position to
contract and expand its operations, is necessary and beneficial ; but unless, at the same time, the pay of the operatives is such as to enable them as a body to provide for

the times of enforced idleness consequent upon this condition, the general benefit to the country is gained at the expense of suffering and privation to them, as is the case in England at present. The country does progress in a certain sense. Wealth accumulates, but men decay; and there are many who are not at all given to taking poetical views in such matters, who hold with Goldsmith, that "Ill fares the land" in which such is the case; that, increasing revenue returns notwithstanding, it is "to hast'ning ills a prey." What we have been saying with regard to irregularity of employment, applies only to the artisan class and the unskilled assistants *directly* associated with them. The remaining portions of the working classes are in a still worse position, both as regards the rate of payment when in work, and the frequency with which they are out of work. The general result of this is that the condition of the working classes, as a body, is of a most unsatisfactory and, rightly considered, alarming character, and shows an appalling amount of misery—misery going down through all its bitter degrees, to the last and bitterest of all; for, despite all our physical means and appliances, our nineteenth-century enlightenment, our Christianity, and our nominal law that no man shall perish from want—despite all this, men still "pitifully die from hunger and cold.' According to a recent parliamentary return, one hundred and forty verdicts of death by starvation, or death accelerated by privation, were recorded by coroners' juries in the Metropolitan district alone, in the course of the years 1868, 1869, and 1870 ; while during the first two months of 1871, twenty-one more such verdicts were given in the " eastern district of Middlesex." This would be bad enough, even if we could in some measure console ourselves by thinking that it showed the worst, and comprehended the whole of this part of the case. But any person having the least know-ledge of how the poor among us live and die, will know that the instances that form the subject of coroners' inquests are a mere fraction of the deaths that are actually, though perhaps not technically, the result of starvation. The real total of such deaths cannot be known, but some idea of it may be formed from the circumstance that in presenting the returns of mortality for 1868, the Registrar-General, in language that left no room for doubt as to the popular meaning of the professional phraseology, drew attention to the fact that in that year there " perished in London, of atrophy and debility, 3,794 persons." The Registrar-General's return, large as it was, probably missed many who had died this death, and it must be borne in mind that his figures referred only to the metropolis. Occasionally it happens that one who has come to die thus "pitifully" has fallen from some comparatively high estate ; but for all practical purposes of judging of social condi-tions, it may be safely concluded that the victims belong to the labouring classes, for certain it is that neither the criminal nor professional pauper class will starve. But even such grim facts as these, and the "graphic" descriptions we sometimes get of such poor quarters as Bethnal Green, or the almost ceaseless labours for starvation earnings of some particular kind of unfortunate workers, fail to convey an adequate idea of the mass and variety of misery existing among the working classes, or the extent to which it penetrates upwards towards the least miserable portion of them.

The home life of a vast number of the working classes is something simply horrible—" a thing to shudder at, not to see." It is a life that puts decency, morality, and religion, as well as physical health and comfort, out of the question ; and so degrades and brutalises those condemned to it that they live as well as die like the beasts that perish. Indeed, as a literal fact, the poorer members of the working classes often fare worse than the beasts of the field. In every requisite of health their dwellings are inferior to most stables ; we have seen piggeries in comparison with which the same might be said of them ; and any master of fox-hounds would be indignant if he were asked to kennel his hounds in such foul dens for a single night ; while any master of hounds or owner of horses who fed his animals as scantily as some of the poor are fed would be in danger of prosecution by the Society for the Prevention of Cruelty to Animals. In a dozen parts of London, and in some one or more "low" quarter of all our large manufacturing towns, there are hundreds of houses in which—

> " Packed in one reeking chamber, man,
> Maid, mother and little ones lie ; "

each apartment being tenanted by a family—a family not unfrequently consisting of as many as nine children. Nor is this state of things—in the Metropolis, at any rate— confined to what are usually classed as the "low" districts. Misery has increased until it has overflowed its ancient receptacles. There are numbers of comparatively roomy, respectable, and cleanly-looking streets—many of them quite new streets—in which the same overcrowding pre- vails, though any person unacquainted with the outward signs and tokens characteristic of over-inhabited dwellings might pass through them without at all suspecting that such was the case. Those who occupy the houses in these streets, in preference to residing in courts and slums in which poverty has the doubtful advantage of not being at the trouble of attempting to veil itself in any way, are those who still fight against their poverty and strive to make the best of it. In many instances they have within the working-class range seen better days, and carry the habits of those days with them into the lower grades of poverty. Though they may be without a chair to sit upon, and their bedding may consist of a pile of rags, they will have a curtain for their window, they will keep their ragged

children out of sight as much as possible, and they will
endure the direst hardship rather than seek aid from the
hand of charity. Having nothing else to be thankful
for, they will thank the Lord that in all their distress they
have never troubled the parish. They feel that the bread
of charity would be bitter, and they pay for their moral
sensitiveness in physical suffering. Except in so far as
their sense of independence may be a compensation to
them, they are a degree worse off than the more reckless,
more shameless, more pauper-spirited poor ; to distinguish
them from whom we may, for want of a better term, style
them the respectable poor. It is mostly members of this
division of the working-class poor that " perish of atrophy
and debility," and furnish the cases of " death by starvation " and " death accelerated by starvation." In the
day-time a person might, as we have just said, pass
through a street inhabited by the respectable poor without
gathering from exterior appearances that he was in the
midst of poverty as great as that to be found in courts
and alleys, in which everything that meets the eye tells
of the want and squalor reigning among the inhabitants.
It is at night that the signs of the overcrowding of dwellings that indicate the extremer degrees of poverty, show
themselves. The lights in every window, and the numerous
shadows that may be seen flitting about, tell of each room
having its family ; and in the hot summer time the wide-
open doors and windows reveal the scantiness of furniture,

while the little crowd seated round each doorway, or lying about on the pavement in front of the houses, give some idea of the number crowded into a single dwelling. Many of the inhabitants will be found thus camping out, as it were, until well on in the small hours of the morning, to avoid as long as possible the stifling atmosphere and plague of vermin in their rooms.

This unhealthy and demoralising overcrowding does not always stop even at a room per family. We know parts in London where not only houses, but even single rooms are sublet, so that when families fall out—as under such circumstances very often happens—they tell each other to keep, not their own room, but their own corner. Decency and cleanliness cannot be maintained among the respectable poor ; among the reckless poor there is no attempt to maintain them. When in the summer evenings the latter class lounge and loaf about outside their vermin-infested dwellings, " chaff " of the most ribald and blasphemous character is freely bawled out, regardless of the presence of the ragged children who are playing about, and who are picking up the language of their elders, often as their first instruction in the art of speech. The bringing up of the children is perhaps the most horrible feature of all in this matter. The sexes mingle together promiscuously; and as not only are they not taught anything of morality, but immorality both in word and deed is openly practised before them, the result is that many, very many of them are physically as well as morally corrupted while yet mere children. Of the slop-shop seamstresses, and other women working for their own hand, in such quarters as we are now speaking of, those only are considered really *unfortunate* whom age or personal appearance prevents from adding to their scanty earnings by means of prostitution; while parents are pleased to profit by—and provided they *do* profit by, will willingly connive at, or if need be actively encourage — what higher grades of society rightly hold to be "a daughter's shame." If a girl has got on in the world of prostitution, and can visit the parental slum dressed in gaudy finery and with money in her pocket, she will be received with pride by her relatives, flattered by the neighbours gene-rally, and envied by the girls of about her own age, who, without fear of rebuke, will openly express their wish that they could go and do likewise. In such neighbour-hoods disease and death are rife, and it need scarcely be said that there is very little in the shape of religion to be found in them. So far as religious belief or creed exists among not only the extremely poor, but the working classes generally, it may be summed up in two ideas: First, that it *ought* to be hard for a rich man to enter the kingdom of heaven. That verily the rich do have their good things in this life, and the poor evil things, and that therefore as a principle of justice the poor ought to be considered first in the distribution of the life to come.

Secondly, that if there is any truth in the doctrine of eternal damnation, then it would have been well for the poor had they never been born, the life of many of them being even in this existence little better than a hell upon earth.

The poverty among the working classes is spreading rather than abating. Among the better-off sections of them the increasing uncertainty as to regularity of employment, and the difficulty, yearly becoming greater, of "placing" children as they reach the age for going to work, is deepening the feeling of anxiety and discontent. Numbers of artisans who, so far as they are individually concerned, are well placed, who have saved money and are in constant and well-paid employment, are emigrating on account of their families, for whom they can see no opening here. In this way we lose many of the best of our artisans—the skilfullest workers and thriftiest, most thoughtful men. Others of this stamp are only kept from emigration by a belief that they are too old to start afresh in a new country; but though they remain, the burden of their song to those of their male children who have reached or are approaching manhood is:—Get away from this old country as soon as you can; there is not room for you to make a decent living here. Whatever may be thought in other ranks of society, the working classes are certainly not of opinion that blessed is the man who has his quiver full of children. On the contrary, children are regarded as burdens, not blessings; and in families in which there are already one or two children, the discovery that the wife is "in a way to become a mother" is received with feelings the reverse of joyful, each succeeding child being regarded as an addition to a weight which tends to sink the family towards the lower depths of poverty. Resulting from this is one evil of which few are probably aware. While we send missionaries to "the heathen Chinee," we are approaching them on the point which more than all others is held to mark them as barbarians and degraded. We speak from personal knowledge in saying that abortion is practised to a considerable extent among the working classes, and is a growing evil—not among the extremely poor, who having no further fall to fear are reckless, but among those who, while still above the lowest depth, are yet so near to it that the expenses attending the birth and bringing up of a child may perhaps drive them into it, and will certainly drive them a step towards it. Of course in such a matter "things are managed quietly." Even in the circles in which the practice is resorted to, it is rather understood than talked about, and referred to—if at all—euphemistically; but opinion with regard to it is condonatory, not condemnatory. It is regarded as a hard necessity arising out of the fact that there is no longer "room enough for all;" not as a legal or moral crime, or at any rate not so far as the individuals are concerned, any blame there may be being held to lie with the time and society.

In touching upon this point we can only repeat that our knowledge on the subject fully justifies our assertion. The worst features of the condition of the working classes are unpleasant to have even to allude to ; and the minuter details of it cannot be entered into here ; but neither, we think, should they be slurred over without mention when the general subject is being discussed. To ignore them is worse than whitening a sepulchre; it is shutting the eyes to the signs that tell that a social volcano is seething in our midst—a volcano of which French communism, English working-class republicanism, and the Workmen's International Association, are open craters. Traced to their sources, they all mean one thing—that the condition of the masses is becoming unbearable, both in itself and by contrast with that of the rich ; and that it is making men desperate and devilish.

We have spoken of the false-fact system of dealing with the question of the condition of the working classes, with a view to making it appear that that condition is not so unsatisfactory as the class themselves allege to be the case ; and before concluding this article, we think it right to point out the falsity of one very specious and popular mode of it, which has the weight of respectable authority, and the arguments of which are used as a reproach against the working classes. It is said that those classes as a body are not poor, or that, if they are, their poverty is their own fault; the result of their dissipation and extravagance. When the members who in Parliament opposed the motion for voting a " provision " for Prince Arthur, urged, among other reasons for not further burdening the country, the great poverty existing in the working-class grades of society, Mr. Disraeli rose in his place, and exclaimed that it was an insult to the working classes to speak of them as though they were paupers (no one had spoken of them as though' they had been paupers) ; that the fact was they were the richest class of society, having the largest income, and their accumulations being counted by millions. Mr. Disraeli, we are informed, spoke with all appearance of seriousness, and even of virtuous indignation, upon behalf of the working classes; but being a " smart " man, he discreetly confined himself to generalities. A few weeks later, the *Christian World*, in an article entitled " Wealth of the Working Classes," was imprudent enough to go into figures. A comparison of these figures with the deductions made from them will conclusively show that the doctrine of the " Wealth of the Working Classes " is a false-fact one. " Much," says the *Christian World*, " has been written on the poverty of the multitude. But are the working classes really poor ? " it asks, " and are they unfortunately without the pecuniary means of providing for themselves ? " Answering its own question, it goes on, " We very much doubt it. A

careful investigation of the matter will reveal some noteworthy facts. The labourers connected with farming
operations and similar pursuits number 2,957,000. Those
who are in the second class of skilled workers number
4,009,000, and the highest order of artisans amount to
1,178,000. These figures apply only to England and
Wales. Now, what is the computed income of the men,
women, and children comprised in the statistics we have
given ? It amounts to two hundred and sixty-seven
millions a year ! " With such a yearly income as this,
the *Christian World* is of opinion, " John Bull's family,
however large and hungry, should not be a poor one.
They should build houses and plant vineyards, grow flowers
and recline on sofas, buy libraries and insure their lives,
live well and die happy." That the working classes do
not do this is but too notorious, and the *Christian World*
accounts for it on the ground that " to them sensuality
is life ; " that " a beefsteak, a flagon of porter, a pipe,
and a sporting newspaper, form their chief joys." Now,
two hundred and sixty-seven millions is a tremendous
yearly income—so tremendous as to be apt to dazzle the
imagination ; but let us analyse and apply the statistics
given, and see how matters really stand. Added together,
the three classes of workers make a total of 8,144,000,
and taking it that the degree of dependence upon the wage-
earners only doubled the number to be supported out of
the wages, that gives a divisor of 16,288,000 to the divi-

dend of £267,000,000, and shows a quotient of £16 7s. 10d.
per year per head for the working classes, taken through
and through ; or, to come to round numbers (and give
the *Christian World* theory the benefit of fractions), let us
say an income of fifty pounds a year to support a man,
wife, and child. If it came in uninterruptedly, and was
managed with judgment and economy, such an income
would support a family of three in a certain degree of
comfort and decency.

The total income of the working classes, however, is
not divided in this manner. Many of them have incomes
out of which they *do* build houses, and put by savings
that in the aggregate *do* amount to millions; but far
larger numbers, and notably those " connected with farm-
ing operations and similar pursuits," are condemned to
exist upon incomes much below what an average division
would give—incomes which, as we have already incidentally pointed out, are insufficient for the requirements of
ordinary decency and comfort, and in conjunction with
which the idea even of revelling on beefsteaks and porter,
let alone the building of houses, is a bitter mockery. The
mode of the computation by which the above total income
of the working classes is arrived at is not given in detail.
We take it, however, thàt it has been entered into with a
view to showing that the working classes are a wealthy
body, and in that case we do not think we shall be doing
the calculators an injustice in surmising that they have

made their total by taking the whole number of workers as being employed all the year round at the average rate of wages of their respective classes. If they *have* done this, then their figures are misleading—are an over-estimate of at least twenty per cent. Their figures, as they stand, however, enable us to make a comparison between the income of the working classes and that of the classes above them in point of income. In the same debate in which he spoke of the wealth of the working classes, Mr. Disraeli, referring to the fact that there were eight hundred traders paying income-tax on incomes of from ten to fifty thousand a year, significantly observed that returns to income-tax commissioners were certainly not exaggerated in amount. But, even according to these returns, the yearly income of the income-tax-paying class would appear to be three hundred and sixty millions, since the Chancellor of the Exchequer calculates a penny in the pound income-tax to yield a million and a half. A few of the best-off members of the working classes are fortunate enough to be liable for income-tax, but a deduction of three millions from the total working-class income will, we think, be a fair allowance on that score; so that the income-tax-paying classes, who cannot be more and who are probably not so much as a third of the number of the working classes, are in receipt of a total income of ninety millions more than the total income of the working classes, even supposing that the working class income is as great as it is computed to be by those whose purpose it is to show the body as a wealthy one, and the income of the others no greater than they state it to be to income-tax commissioners.

To working men it seems a ghastly joke to have to demonstrate that the working classes are not a wealthy body, but the demonstration cannot be deemed altogether unnecessary when we find the reverse openly asserted in the House of Commons by the acknowledged guide and authority of one of the great parties in that House—a man who has been, and again wants to be and may be, Prime Minister of England ; and when, moreover, we find " Christian " journals alleging (and Christian men accepting the allegation with unquestioning belief) that it is the fault of the working classes themselves that their condition is not something very much in the nature of an earthly paradise.

The causes of the present condition of the working classes, and the future prospects of those classes in relation to their social state, might well be discussed in connection with those parts of the general question with which we have been dealing, but a proper treatment of the subject would require more space than our present limits will allow. We have therefore stuck pretty closely to our text, the existing condition of the working classes. Of that condition we emphatically repeat that it is as bad and dangerous as it well can be. It is a condition which, if it cannot be amended, must be taken as telling of a nation not ripening, but rotting to a fall. It is bad for the working classes themselves, dangerous to society at large, threatening its peace and even its existence.

Those classes think that what they are asked to believe is, the science of government is, in fact, merely a game of party politics, the real meaning of which is a struggle for the possession of power and patronage, *not* the study and practice of the noble art of doing the greatest good for the greatest number. They think they see this plainly, despite all the subterfuges resorted to for concealing it; they suffer by it, and they will scarce stand by *quietly* and see it go on much longer.

THE PEOPLE IN RELATION TO POLITICAL POWER AND OPINION.

> " Patriots are grown too shrewd to be sincere,
> And we too wise to trust them. He that takes
> Deep in his soft credulity the stamp
> Designed by loud declaimers on the part
> Of liberty, themselves the slaves of lust,
> Incurs derision for his easy faith
> And lack of knowledge, and with cause enough."
>
> COWPER.

FROM the frequency, and still more from the *tone*, with which the name of "The People"—the phrase being used as a synonym for the working classes—is brought into the discussion of all kinds of political questions, it might readily be supposed that they are politically powerful; but those who know them best are aware that such is not the case. As they come before the rest of the world politically, they are chiefly represented by about a dozen men of the agitator species, and two or three associations professing political creeds that are generally held to be extreme, if not altogether impracticable or Utopian. These men, in their public speeches, and the societies in their resolutions, allege that they *do* represent the working classes, and by many who have no personal knowledge of those classes they are taken at their word. They speak with all the confidence of assured knowledge of the desires of "the great heart of the people," the measures for which and against which the voice of the people is cast, and the statesmen or political parties upon which its eyes are watchfully, approvingly, or threateningly fixed.

Now, that these men mean well to the people, that the opinions they expound are sometimes those held by the people, and at other times such as perhaps ought to be held by them, may be admitted ; but they are not, in any legitimate or reliable sense, the representatives of the people. They are not infallible indicators of the beatings of "the great heart of the people," are not the tongue of their voice, or the eyes of their vision. Some of them, and especially the associations, represent themselves alone, others themselves and a small personal following. They are not elected or accredited by those in whose name they profess to speak, and even if they were, could not represent their political power for the all-sufficient reason that, practically, there is no such power to be represented. The much-talked-of political power of the people, though not an absolute myth, is as yet in embryo, and at best must be counted in the category of desirable things, which ought to be, but are not.

The whole subject of the relation of the working classes to political power, or, to speak by the letter, the lack of political power, is scarcely less curious than important. That these classes labour under social disadvantages which an equitable system of politics, equitably administered, would remove, is a position which we think most people, even in other grades of society, will admit. That such is the case is, at any rate, the first and firmest article of their own political belief, and, as a consequence, the thinkers among them have always looked forward to the possession by their class of political power as a panacea for most of the social ills to which they found themselves heirs. After years of struggling, and hoping, and waiting, they at last appeared to grasp this long-coveted power. With the carrying of the Household Suffrage Bill, it seemingly passed into their hands in a proportion as preponderating as their numbers. And yet, what do we see? That though they are potentially the " new masters " of the political situation, the situation is practically master of them. That though notoriously the most clubbable section of society, having vital interests in common, and being supreme in numbers where numbers should be supreme, they are still politically powerless. What a picture! A giant, with all a giant's strength, and the will to use it like a giant, and yet impotent, defeated on all hands by comparative pigmies—a picture so strange as to seem unnatural, and yet a perfectly true one. In a general election under household suffrage, the working classes were unable to return a single special representative ; and unless their present attitude is speedily and materially altered, they will, in all probability, fail as utterly in the next election, and undoubtedly fail to make any appreciable modification in the present constitution of the House of Commons—a constitution in which theirs alone of all considerable special interests has not some more or less adequate representation. But whence, it may be asked, this difference between the possible, the desired and desirable, and the actual ? To account for it there are a variety of reasons, the chief of which are political ignorance, political inexperience, political apathy, and the want of a great political leader. A large percentage of the people are so utterly destitute of a knowledge of politics as to be unable to take any intelligent part in them. If they know that there is such a thing as political economy, that is the utmost they do know about it. They have no conception that it may be actually affecting their possession or want of employment, or the rate of wages they are receiving ; or that it is a science a general knowledge of which might be of material service to them. And such ignorance breeds an inertness that forms one of the several bars to the full development and effective application of the (potential) political power of the working classes.

Those of the people who have a knowledge of and respect for politics, and a belief that much may be done for the elevation of their class by political means, have, as a rule, little knowledge and less experience of the mechanism of politics—of getting up, supporting, and "inspiring" press organs; organizing a compact, disciplined party, and carrying out party movements and compromises. From a high standpoint such things may seem out of place in connection with the assertion of great principles; but certain it is that, in the existing condition of the political world, principles are not to be gained without both knowledge and practice of the tactics of political warfare—especially where the principles, though palpably just in themselves, are opposed to class interests, as is the case with those by which the people believe that the national policy should be governed.

The indifference of the politically apathetic section of the people, though leading to the same ultimate result as the inertia arising from ignorance, already spoken of, is distinct from it. It is found chiefly—and very largely— among the two extremes of the working classes, the *best* and *worst* off portions of them. The first are apathetic in a selfish kind of "rest and be thankful" spirit. They are the fortunates of their class. They have had constancy of health and employment, fare comfortably every day, have generally saved a little money, and in some instances are even men of property to the extent of a house or two got through building societies. They have done well themselves, and are given to "wonder" that others of their degree have not done the same : to wonder in a manner implying that the others might have done so, and that blame must lie with the individuals rather than with any fault in our political or social system. They are comfortable enough under the system, are not predisposed to see blots in it, and do not need to seek for them as a probable cause of personal hardships. They do not care to " bother themselves " about politics, and, indeed, many of them are imbued with an idea that to bother one's self about them is scarcely respectable. They may have heard in a general way that the labour market is greatly overstocked, and subject to violent fluctuations, but they do not trouble themselves about it sufficiently to bring the fact home to their " business and bosom ;" to understand from it that some *must* suffer. They do not see that in not being among those who do suffer, they may be rather specially fortunate than specially meritorious, and they decline to mix themselves up with matters in which, in their short-sighted selfishness, they believe they have no direct self-interest.

The other division of the apathetics is more to be pitied than condemned. It consists of those who are constantly doing battle with abject poverty, whose whole lives are a from hand-to-mouth struggle to live—a struggle that exhausts energy, breaks the spirits, and crushes even hope, causing men to say in bitterness of heart, that such things as politics are nothing to them; that no matter what party or minister is in power, there comes no gleam of light into their dark lives, no improvement in their miserable condition.

Seeing how many so-called "leaders of the people" there are before the public, it may seem to many outside the working classes, a somewhat startling thing to say that the people have no leader ; nevertheless those inside those classes will know that the assertion is strictly true. Let any person who has taken it for granted that the so-called leaders of the people have been really such, look at the matter questioningly. Let them remember what a vast aggregate the working classes form, and then ask themselves by whom, and when, and in what manner the political leadership of this great body was conferred by itself upon any man, or being assumed was ratified. Let them again, when, under the heading of the Working Classes and this or that political question, they read an account of some meeting, ask themselves how far the meeting *was* the Working Classes. Let them, if they are in a position to do so, attend a few of such meetings, and critically note their composition and proceedings. The so-called people's leaders are the speakers at them. A deal of what they say is true, sensible, and to the point, but a deal of it also consists of mere truisms, platitudes, bombastic oratory, and stock flatteries of the Working Man. Many of the audience are working men. Some of them are there from strong personal political convictions —convictions fully in accordance with the avowed object of the meeting, and generally arrived at after more or less of political study and individual suffering under existing social conditions. These are mostly to be seen on or near the platform, listening with a satisfied expression of face, and a general air of taking an active part in the proceedings. They *are* represented by the meeting, but then they do not in their turn represent the working classes at large, or even any considerable section of them. So far as they are a class, they are, though few in numbers, substantially the class itself. Their faces are as familiar at such meetings as are those of the leaders, and, in fact, they are a sort of *aides-de-camp* to the leaders, taking up their points and fugling the applause.

The other working men at these meetings—and they form the bulk of the working-class element in the audience—it is easy to see from their manner, attend simply from curiosity, or the hope of excitement or amusement. They are only roused to anything approaching sympathetic enthusiasm when the praise of the Working Man is sounded. They are greatly given to shouting, and appear best pleased and most interested when an opportunity arises for the display of their capabilities in that line, making a glory of howling down any person who seems disposed to dissent from anything that has been put forward upon the working-class side of the question.

These meetings do *not* represent the working classes.

They simply represent as many London workmen as attend them, and — with all due respect and good feeling be it spoken — considered in this connection, London workmen are not the best possible examples of the working classes. Locality has an influence in giving bent to the mind, and the surroundings of a London life tend to make working men superficial, excitable, easy to be pleased, and averse to the trouble of thought. High rentals drive them into squalid neighbourhoods, and cause them to be "cabin'd, cribb'd, confin'd" in the matter of actual house-room and of domestic comforts. This condition of home life has a material influence in causing them to largely avail themselves of the thousand and one amusements which London offers to all classes — amusements which, though perfectly unobjectionable in the abstract, have a tendency to make men thoughtless and mercurial when indulged in habitually. The London workman craves for and indulges in amusements to a greater extent than any other, and more than any other is a man to take part in a showy or exciting demonstration simply *as* a demonstration, and without being imbued with the feeling or understanding the doctrine of which the demonstration is supposed to be an outcome. But while this is the real state of the case, they have a self-complacent belief in the Gospel so often preached to them, that as dwellers in the great metropolis, they are as a matter of course in advance òf, and fitted to set an example to, their comparatively benighted provincial brethren. And so the few of them who attend political meetings style themselves The Working Classes, and assume .a We-the-People-of-England tone, though, as we have already said, they represent only themselves, and are not even good individual specimens of the politically inclined men of the working classes. The best political element among the people will be found principally in the provincial manufacturing towns, where workmen are more given than in London to spend their evenings at home, and read, and think, and brood. There is, of course, a proportion of this element in London, but those constituting it hold aloof from the demonstrative clique. They do not care about attending meetings which censure governments, and pass momentous resolutions with an amount of "tall talk" and assumption of authority which, when compared with their inability to give any practical effect to their words, make those in whose name they profess to speak appear ridiculous and contemptible in the eyes of outsiders.

Let the inquirer for fact in these matters examine also for himself the constitution of the various leagues and associations whose proceedings are occasionally chronicled as those of the working classes, and he will find that they consist of from a dozen to a score of members, who are much more bent upon the practice of flowery oratory than the acquisition of political knowledge, or the organization of the political power of the people.

Sometimes the views put forth by those whom it has become a fashion to speak of as leaders of the people, are really those held by the working classes as a body, but that is a matter of chance. Very often, indeed, it happens that not merely do they not express the true feelings of the working classes upon a question, but that the question itself concerning which they allege the mind of the people is chiefly exercised, is by the people—as their mind is to be gathered from their conversation in workshops, workshop dining and reading rooms, trade and benefit club rooms, wherever working men most do congregate and most freely speak their thoughts—regarded with what is mere indifference compared with the unanimity and passionate intensity of their feeling upon some other question. So far from serving the political cause of the working classes, these reputed leaders of the people do it a positive injury. Whenever they set up as working men's candidates, or are very active in advocating the candidature of others who adopt that " platform," they create a division among the class they express themselves wishful to serve. They may be all honourable men, and taking them broadly and as a body it would be ungenerous to question that they are both honourable and well-meaning. But there is an influential section of the working classes which does not think so. They are, on the contrary, of opinion

that they are self-seeking, place-seeking, wire-pulling
men, whose object is to promote their own interests—not
those of the working classes. A feeling of personal
jealousy or envy may have, and in some instances at least
most likely *has*, some share in creating such an opinion ;
but, however that may be, the opinion exists, and tells
against that unity which among other things is required
to make the political power of the working class a reality.
It is among the better-educated portion of the working
classes that this opinion principally prevails, and they
certainly give considerable ground for their mistrust.
They say that in professing to speak in the name of the
people, when they do not really represent them, these
supposed leaders show an intention to trade upon them
for ends of personal ambition. They further say that in
persistently " cracking up " the working man, and preaching what substantially amounts to the doctrine that a
working man must be a good man simply because he is a
working man, these men show either a spirit of bigotry
or toadyism that stamps them as unworthy to be entrusted
with any authoritative representation of the people's
power—a spirit which, even as matters stand, does injury
to the working classes, by tending to make the more
ignorant and prejudiced among them intolerant of any
suggestion that they too being men may have faults, and
may possibly be mistaken in their views upon a political
question. Of the men who entertain this adverse opinion

concerning the type of people's leader at present before the public, a little knot will be found in most large workshops, acting as the directing spirits in any movements in which their mates may be called upon to take part. They are in official positions in trade and benefit societies, yard sick-clubs, and co-operative associations. They draw up appeals or remonstrances to employers, the statements which head subscription lists, and other workshop documents of that kind. They preside at workshop meetings, and fellow-workmen seek their advice and look to them for initiatory action. In short, in political and social matters they have material influence with many of their shopmates, and this influence, for the reasons given above, they use against the so-called leaders of the people whenever a parliamentary election, or other practical issue, is to be dealt with. Very often these men are entire believers in the political creed professed by people's leaders, who are candidates for the people's votes; but they doubt the men. Another ground on which such candidates cause disunion among the working classes is that which arises from trade prides and jealousies. The majority of them, though they have risen out of the working classes, have only barely risen out of them, and are not in any other definite position—unless it be that of professional agitators. So far as social standing goes, they are still regarded as practically on a level with the artisan class, and are identified with the trade at which they have worked. This being the case, trade feeling steps in. At the election for the Metropolitan School Board, we were canvassing artisan voters for a working-class candidate. He was an active politician in the locality, and his views upon the education question were known to be those generally approved of by the working classes; but still many of those classes, while acknowledging that the views he pledged himself to advocate were more in accordance with their own than were those of any other candidate, refused to vote for him—because he was a baker. No, they said they were not going to vote for a fellow who carried home twopenny dinners. They were as good, nay better, men than him, and why should they put him in a position to think himself something grand, and to get in with a lot of big people, who would shove him into some snug berth? Such a feeling as this of course shows a discreditable narrow-mindedness ; and yet it may be a question whether, after all, it is not to some extent a natural one. At any rate, it is a feeling that largely exists among the artisan class, and that is likely to be found existing among them whenever they are asked to support, in the practical form of voting for, such people's leaders as we have been speaking of. The printer, the engineer, the carpenter, would in many instances be respectively of opinion that if their trades could not produce a man fit to represent working class interests, it was certain that no baker, shoemaker, or tailor could be fit ;

while many men of the latter trades would opine that it was "just like the conceit" of any man of the other trades who expected them to help to make him an M.P.

All this is no doubt very pretty, but it is a state of things that *does* prevail, and leads to politicians of the people's leader order working injury to the political cause of the working classes.

What the people need in the way of leadership is one really *great* leader, not a score of mediocrities. A leader great even to the point of genius—so exceptionally great that if originally of the working classes, the innate force of the genius within him *must* raise him to such a height above the rank and file of his class as would preclude the idea of their drawing self-comparisons between themselves and him, and secure him against being the object of petty cavillings and suspicions. A born statesman in the higher and not merely red-tape and routine sense of the term. A great organizer, a great debater, a great agitator and orator. One who, given a just cause, could raise a good battle and rallying cry, and preach such a political crusade as would really stir "the great heart of the people;" and a leader as fearless as great. A leader who would speak evil (when it was also truth) of dignities; nay, who, if the true interests of the people demanded it, would not even hesitate to "rail against the Lord's anointed," to break through "the divinity that doth hedge" royalty—and say to it in a voice of power,

Thus far and no further shalt thou go into the purse of the nation. One who would proclaim against a hereditary legislature, and point out that such a barbarism had no right to be in existence in the present age, and that since its living representatives would not practise what in their case would be the virtue of self-immolation towards the institution, it was the duty of the country on whose freedom its being was a blot to stamp it out. One, too, who would strenuously insist upon the abolition of all sinecurism at the public expense, and argue that " place " should be given only to the most capable workers, pension (under any form) only to those who had done the State some service. A man who, without fear or favour, would cry aloud in the high places in which his position as a veritable leader of the people would place him, that a professedly Christian Church, which puts its offices up to public auction, placed little - working and highly - paid bishops in its pulpits to preach on behalf of charities for the aid of hard-working curates, who are not paid sufficient for a decent maintenance, and did other like things, was a monstrosity that it was the duty of a State to blot out, not foster.

A leader fearless in such things as these, but equally fearless on the other side. Who would not hesitate to tell the working classes that they too have faults, that many among them are drunken, many improvident, many —very many—culpably negligent of the means of self-education fairly and abundantly within their reach ; the means of acquiring that knowledge that to them would be truly power. That, in short, of the various reforms required to elevate the working classes self-reform is one.

This is the kind of man that the people stand in need of for a leader—the only kind of man who would be to them what a leader should be. The only kind of man that they would as a body look up to, be proud of, trust, and stand reproof from. A real people's tribune—such a man as John Bright was in the strength of his early prime, and to the full as advanced in opinion for this day as John Bright was for that time.

If there are ever to be " working men's M.P.'s " in anything like adequate numbers, they will have to be of much the same stamp as such a leader. Men of assured position, dignified action, and proved intellectual ability. Men of thought and education and a tolerant spirit, who would only be working men's M.P.'s in the sense that on grounds of high principle they would fearlessly advocate broad measures of general and all-equal justice, by which the working classes, as those who suffer most from the want of such measures, would be the greatest gainers. Men in regard to whom there would be no room for even envious or jealous working men to say that they were not only no better than themselves, but, in the popular meaning of the phrase, no better than they should be. Men of the like of whom we have one example in Professor Fawcett. Men in the returning of whom to Parliament many of those who oppose the style of working-class candidate hitherto brought forward could join, feeling safe in the conviction that they would not be class representatives in a mere class sense, would not be likely to drive working-class "rights" up to a point at which they would become other class wrongs, or to yield to any clamour urging them to do so against their own better judgment.

In combination with such a leader and such representatives the people would require some of the more machine-like appliances for developing and concentrating political power. They stand in need of an "organ" in the shape of a leading daily paper—a paper that would bear comparison with other leading dailies, and would have *its* opinions quoted in the opinions of the press; that could be thoroughly "slashing" or "scathing" on fit occasion, but that would not, after the fashion of some weekly papers calling themselves working-class organs, descend to mere blatant abuse, or to the use of arguments or misstatements that show either that editor and writers are grossly ignorant in political matters, or that they desire to trade, and have an unquestioning belief in the possibility of trading, upon the ignorance of their readers.

Lastly, though anything but leastly, to make their own political power a practical fact instead of a legal fiction, the people need an electoral union constituted on the model of their great trades' unions. The political interests of the people at large are as much in common as are the trade interests of the men of any trade, and the machinery that correctly ascertains the feeling and gives effect to the decisions of the grand majority in the one case might be advantageously applied in the other. A trade union can obtain the opinion of " the trade" upon any given subject, can, where there is a difference of opinion, take an exact vote upon it, and can at all times be relied upon as an authoritative channel for the expression of the feeling of the trade. It can circulate all documents requiring general signature, and it is a standing and ever-ready means of combined action. All this an electoral union could do for the people in political matters, and such an union would be a very simple affair, and might be easily established. It would have a central office in London as the seat of government, and branches in every town; each branch, of course, electing its own officers. As its members would be numbered by millions, and branch meetings, at any rate, need not be frequent, the expenses of general management would be very trifling, probably not more than a penny a month per member, while for occasional " monster " demonstrations—and such a union could organize demonstrations that would really be "monster" ones—a very small levy per member would be sufficient. By means of such an union the working classes throughout the country could at election times arrange a general "platform," and draw up a sort of candidates' catechism that would serve as a test on great principles, and the leading questions of the time. Through it they could become aware of each other's intentions and position, and act unitedly. And while it would be an invaluable machine for the actively political to work with, it would give the least possible trouble to those who did not wish to be "bothered."

With such a leader, such parliamentary representatives, and such machinery, the political power of the people would become a great reality, would make them truly the "new masters" of the political situation. Without them, with only leaders who are no leaders, and lacking any means of united action, their political power will remain as it is, chaotic and useless: a thing frequently referred to with sound and fury, but signifying nothing.

THE VIEWS AND PROSPECTS OF THE WORKING CLASSES.

"If I believed that Mammonism with its adjuncts was to continue henceforth the one serious principle of our existence, I should reckon it idle to solicit remedial measures from any government, the disease being insusceptible of remedy. . . . . But it is my firm conviction that the 'Hell of England' will *cease* to be that of not making money, that we shall get a nobler hell, and a nobler heaven! I anticipate light *in* the human chaos, glimmering, shining more and more, under manifold true signals from without that light shall shine."—CARLYLE's "Past and Present."

THE subject of the Prospects of the Working Classes is a very large one; much too large and many-sided to be ranked—as it often is—as merely one of the many questions of the day. It is a great deal more than that, comprehending, as it does, within itself most of the questions of the day, however varied in themselves or remote from it those questions may at a first glance appear. Indeed, taken broadly—and it is worse than useless to approach a consideration of it in any but the broadest spirit—it is less a question of the day than the problem which the questions of the day seek to solve. It cannot be relegated to any one of the great spheres of thought or action under which questions of the day are usually classed. It enters into the domains of religion, morality, politics, physics, and psychology. They all bear upon it, while it belongs exclusively to none of them ; and, though politicians claim it as lying chiefly within their province, it is perhaps not too much to say that it belongs to no one of those spheres more than to another. Certain it is, at any rate, that no one of them, or all but one of them, could deal with it effectually while ignoring the influence and operation of the others, or other. It is as important as it is large and varied ; and it is, moreover, a subject the discussion of which should have an attraction for every one, even on the low ground—supposing no higher one prompted attention to it—of self-interest. The future of the working classes means more than a strictly literal interpretation of the phrase would indicate —means the future of *all* classes, the future of civilized society. Though they may not be—as they are so often told they are—the entire salt and savour of the earth, and the sole props and support of the social system ; though they may not be all this, they are, undoubtedly, the most important division of society, and their importance is daily waxing greater as it becomes more and more evident that they are realising the commanding extent of their potential strength, and moulding it into practical shapes. That there will always be distinctively working classes may, we think, be taken for granted—taken, that is, as a law of nature—but that they will remain in the same position relatively to other classes that they occupy now is highly improbable. So far as they can be taken as foreshadowing the future, the "signs of the times" all seem to indicate that there will be material changes in the condition of the working classes, and a moment's consideration must, we think, make it evident that this will involve changes in all other classes. And though the probabilities are in favour of the supposition that the coming changes will be for the better both for the working classes and society, that is not necessarily the case; therefore, as we have said, the subject of the prospects of the working classes concerns every one.

Before entering upon the direct consideration of these prospects, it is for the sake of clearness necessary that we should first glance at the existing condition of the working classes—the stand-point from whence the prospective outlook commences. There are some who hold that the present condition of the working classes is of a flourishing and satisfactory character, and that if it is not all that could be desired the fault lies with those classes them-selves—with their drunkenness, animal indulgences, im-providence, and (self-removable) ignorance. Those of this opinion, however, are few in number, are all outside the working classes, and, so far as our own experience enables us to speak, are either very simple people, or people who are *not* very simple; who have a case involving this view to make out, and who are greatly wronged if they are not capable of manipulating and dislocating facts to make them appear to suit their view. For all practical purposes of dealing with our subject, it may be taken as a substantial and demonstrable fact, that the condition of the working classes is—to them at any rate—of so hard and unsatisfactory a character as to, in a great measure, justify the bitter and, to a certain extent, dangerous discontent existing among them on the point. With nothing but their labour to depend upon, and the wages of labour so low as in a vast number of instances to make it a practical impossibility to do anything beyond provide in a coarse and limited fashion for the material necessities of the passing day—with things in this state working men cannot be sure of constant employment—cannot when in work be sure that it will last, or know when the evil day may be drawing nigh. Thus a carking care is laid upon them, and prevents them from fully enjoying even the passing good of the times when they are in employ. Their homes are often distressingly unhealthy and comfortless, and at best are very scantily supplied with the health and comfort-giving appliances which are things of course in the homes of even the moderately rich. Either from the early age at which they have to go to work, or from the neglect of parents too ignorant to be able to understand the value of education, a majority of the working classes are unable to enter upon those pleasures of the mind which education opens up to all, and which do so much to soften or make us for a moment forget the hardships of life ; while others again, though having the necessary education, and a natural inclination for such pleasures, feel themselves deadened towards them, by reason of the sordid cares of poverty dulling their finer feelings, and the labour-tired body so jading and enervating the mind as to unfit it for the exertion of even a pleasurable pursuit. Supposing they linger long upon the stage of the world, after their capacity for labour has been so deteriorated by age that they are no longer able to find sale for it in a market in which there is an excess supply of a younger quality of the article, the generality of the working classes have no better prospect before them than the workhouse, or some other more capricious, if less degrading, form of dependence.

This, broadly put, is the condition of the mass of the working classes, and to its material hardships is added a sense of injustice suffered, which rankles all the deeper from being blind and impotent. They are certainly born unto trouble. To labour with but scant reward, to endure with but little prospect of relief, is their lot from the cradle to the grave, and, to crown all, they are but too often told that their evil fate will go with them beyond the grave. While they read in The Book that it is the rich who will find it hard to enter the kingdom of heaven, they are assured by those who assume to speak with authority upon such matters that it is they, the poor, who are likely to be excluded from the heavenly paradise, as they have been from the earthly. At an annual meeting of the Scripture Readers' Society held at Sheffield a few years ago, the Archbishop of York stated that " out of a district with two thousand families, nine hundred and fourteen, or nearly one-half, entered themselves as going to no place of worship whatever." From which he drew this conclusion : " that one-half of them had been accustomed to live, and had settled down to live, in a state which professed no hope hereafter, and .confessed no God here." In the case of the Archbishop some allowance is probably due to the sermonesque rounding of a period, but his doctrine as to the meaning of non-attendance at places of worship is substantially the one that is preached to the working classes by Scripture readers and ,others—and it is a doctrine that does more than any other to keep the poor from places of worship. Uneducated though they may be, ignorant of theology as they mostly are, their common sense still tells them that to make church-going the be-all and end-all, as a test of religion, is to confound religion with the observance of one of its mere mechanical rites; to put a premium upon hypocrisy and cheap self-righteousness. In individual instances they see the strictest religion—in the church-going sense of the term—associated with an utter want of Christianity ; and, scoffing at the narrow-mindedness that puts so supreme a meaning upon so (comparatively) secondary a thing, they come to think but very lightly of church-going altogether. That it would in some respects be better for the working classes if they attended places of worship in the same degree that other classes do, may be freely conceded. But to say of them because they do not, they have no hope hereafter, or even that they have no real religion or true Christianity, is, upon the part of those indulging in such utterances, saying in periphrastic language that they know nothing whatever of the working classes. And there are members of those classes who do not hesitate to say that it is in the same way saying that such speakers themselves lack one of the grander essentials of Christianity—the charity that thinks no evil. Though there is much in their life that at times is almost enough to drive them to doubt the existence of a principle of eternal justice, they do firmly believe in it; believe that though it is often set aside here, it will be asserted hereafter. Such a belief is to them a hope. They *do* "profess hope hereafter"—the hope of a brighter, better, juster, more all-equal hereafter, by which they cannot but be gainers, as those who have not had their good things in this life will get them there. And it is well for society that the masses have this hope and belief. If they had not, if they *were* hopeless as regards the hereafter, were really persuaded that—

"Vain as the has-been is the great to-be,"

then would they not endure the present as patiently as they have done, and do. If they thought that all that they could know of good or evil was to be found in this world alone, can it be doubted that they would attempt to seize a larger share of the good things than now falls to their portion? and though they might be frustrated in such an endeavour, they would destroy others, even if they were themselves destroyed in the effort. Of those who speak of the working classes in relation to religion, as the Archbishop of York did on the occasion to which we have referred, it may be safely and charitably said, " They know not what they say;" they cannot have realised the terrible significance of the idea of those who have so little to hope for here having no hope hereafter. If ever such a state of things does come to pass, a time will have arrived when there will be no highly-paid and narrow-thoughted prelates to moralise about it. In the essentials of Christianity—the feelings of brotherly and neighbourly love and kindness, and the virtue of patience—the working classes are not lacking. Their non-attendance at places of worship has not the grave meaning that even many of the more charitably inclined in other classes attach to it, and the reasons for it are simple and not far to seek. To many of the poor and uneducated, as well as to many of the rich and educated, the actualities of public worship are repellent rather than attractive. To minds that do not regard public worship as an essential of religion, but only an optional accessory, formalised services, however fine in their conception, become ineffective and meaningless by constant and mechanical repetition. Then sermons are, as a rule—for there are many noble exceptions—dull, and exhibit a sameness and mechanicality that cannot but remind *attentive and intelligent* hearers that the manufacture of sermons is as distinctively and commercially a trade as is the manufacture of three-volume novels. They are often delivered either with an evident lack of all earnestness, or with an earnestness that it is as palpable is directed solely to clerical mannerisms and oratorical effects; and in tone they are more sectarian than broadly or charitably Christian.

These things constitute the ground upon which many of the more thoughtful of the working classes justify themselves for not attending places of worship. Another reason often assigned is, that Sunday being the only day the working classes have entirely to themselves, they require it for rest, fresh air, and certain phases of social intercourse that the limited leisure of other days does not admit of their carrying out. But the reason most frequently given to Scripture readers, district visitors, ministers, and others who put working men to the question concerning their non-attendance at places of worship is, that they—the working men—have not clothes good enough to go in. "What a paltry, contemptible reason!"

perhaps some reader exclaims. Indeed, what a no-reason, what an *excuse;* and with the ministers and Scripture readers they would doubtless make the obvious reply— " God does not look at clothes." But there is an equally obvious—to working men—answer to that : " Congregations and the guardians of the temples do." Nowhere do the " pomps and vanities of this wicked world " assert themselves more strongly than in " the house of God." Any moderately close observer who has given attention to the point must know that such is the case. Broadcloth and silk shrink from fustian and print in the church, as much or more than they do in the theatre. It is generally those who attend worship well dressed who are inclined to regard a working man's plea of want of good clothes as an evasive one, but they might easily see for themselves that the reason is a substantial one. Let them enter a strange place of worship dressed, as tens of thousands of working men would have to be, in a washed and worn suit of " working " moleskin, or cord, and note the result. Let them see whether any half-filled pew will be opened for them as it would be for a well-dressed stranger ; let them observe the different expression of the glance cast upon them and a well-dressed stranger, and notice how they will be avoided as the congregation streams out at the close of the service. Let them do this, and they will be convinced that want of good clothes alone may be *the* reason for working men not attending places of wor-

ship. It would be no reason for a high-souled Christian
omitting to fulfil what he conceived to be a duty. But,
as we have pointed out, the working classes generally do
not regard attendance at a place of worship as an essential ;
and it is not every m·n who *is* sufficiently high-souled to
brave even a petty social martyrdom.

To some it may appear that we have dwelt at an
unnecessary length upon this point of the existence of a
religious feeling among the working classes ; but though,
at a first glance, the question may seem distantly incidental, it has, in the connection in which we have been
considering it, a really important bearing upon our subject.
The statistics quoted by the Archbishop of York, though
gathered from a single district of a single town, are, as
regards the matter upon which they bear, largely representative of the condition of things among the working
classes generally. The Archbishop's deduction from the
figures is also largely representative, and showing, as it
does, that the working classes are very much misknown
upon a point that cannot but have a material influence
upon both their present and prospective ideas and actions,
it was necessary to combat it, to show that in this case
narrowness of view meant also falsity of view. If the
working classes had no comforting belief here, no hope
hereafter, the constitution of society would be very different
from what it is, and the attempt to estimate the prospects
of those classes would involve an altogether different set

of circumstances and probabilities from those that now offer themselves for consideration.

To come back, however, to their social position. It is, as we have pointed out, hard, unsatisfactory, and, as they themselves hold, unjust. So much we may take as certain, and the next question that arises is : what are the causes of its being so ? All parties—both those who suffer by it, and those who do not—seem to be agreed that it is not a necessary result of the natural order of things. All say that there is fault and blame in the matter, the differences of opinion being as to who and what are in fault or to blame. Political economy, which professes to deal with the subject without respect to persons, or to sentiment, as apart from, or trying to evade, the " inexorable logic " of facts, and which moreover claims to treat it scientifically, comprehensively, and *authoritatively*,—political economy says that it is the working classes themselves who are to blame. Though it has side issues, that in some slight degree modify its main conclusion, that conclusion is substantially that over-population is *the* cause of which the miserable condition of the working classes is the unavoidable effect; and that those classes being responsible for over-population, are the authors of their own degraded and suffering state. The gist of the case of political economy upon this point is very clearly summed up in a few sentences at the end of the tenth chapter of the first book of J. Stuart Mill's work (page 100, people's edition) where he says :—

"It is but rarely that improvements in the condition of the labouring classes do anything more than give a temporary margin, speedily filled up by an increase of their numbers; the use they commonly choose to make of any advantageous change in their circumstances, is to take it out in the form which, by augmenting the population, deprives the succeeding generation of the benefit. Unless, either by their general improvement in intellectual and moral culture, or at least by raising their habitual standard of comfortable living, they can be taught to make a better use of favourable circumstances, nothing permanent can be done for them; the most promising schemes end only in having a more numerous, but not a happier people."

A strong array of statistics, arguments, and cases in point is brought forward to prove and demonstrate this proposition, and the conclusion is generally accepted as an ascertained and incontrovertible fact by those outside the working classes, and by a few inside them. But the great majority of the people do not accept the doctrines of political economy as an explanation of their condition. They do not say that over-population would not be a means of bringing distress upon the masses, but they do argue that it cannot be truly held to be the cause of their condition at the present time; that, practically, there has been no over-population; that, in one or another fully accessible place there is room enough, and food enough, and work enough for all who are born, or likely to be born, for generations to come; that, with the abundant facilities for removing population that is surplus as regards one country to another which stands in need of, could support, and would contribute to, the general wealth of the world through the labour of imported population—

that, with things in this state, the responsibility for the crowded condition of old countries, and the evils resulting from it, lies upon those who withhold while they could grant the appliances for emigration from those of the too many who have the desire but cannot command the means to emigrate. The large section who differ from the conclusion of the political economists further say, that primary causes of the existing misery among the working classes are a constitution of society unfair to those classes, and the proceedings of governments, the members of which being taken exclusively from among " those who have," legislate in their spirit and on their behalf, to the neglect, and injury of " those who want."

To roundly assert that the truth in the matter lies between these views would be to show both ignorance and arrogance, but it may be safely said that there is truth on both sides. It is true that " the standard of condition " of the working classes does lie ultimately with themselves, and is chiefly a question of their numbers; true that, by recklessness upon this point, they may render nugatory the best possible legislation; true that *some of them* have been, and still are, reckless in the matter, taking out improvements in their condition in shapes that augment their numbers in a degree that tends to cause to be merely temporary improvements which might otherwise become permanent in themselves and the steppingstone to others.

And, more than all, it is most painfully true that this country *is* over-populated in the sense that large numbers of her working classes are suffering the dire ills that result from over-population. All this, the teaching of political economy, is true, but it is equally true that there is local as well as general, relative as well as absolute over-population; that while, where absolute and general over-population is undoubtedly an evil, it may be, if rightly used, a good, when only local and relative; and that the relative and local kinds may be the result of unwise or unfair government, and remediable by just and justifiable governmental action. So much we take to be as fully, effectively, and operatively true as any of the axioms of political economy, for it should be remembered that the latter science is not—whatever its more ardent disciples may claim it to be—an exact science. In its calculations it has to deal with so many unknown quantities, that its deductions, however closely reasoned, are, after all, more in the nature of problems than demonstrations. Leaving, however, these comparative certainties, and coming to points which we suppose must be taken as debatable, since they are much debated, we can only say that we *think* that those of the working classes are right in their view, who hold that the over-population of England is only relative and local, and more the fault of the legislature than of the people. That we manufacture much more, and employ a far greater number of hands now than we did twenty or five-and-twenty years ago, innumerable tables and returns conclusively testify; but, for all that, there can be no doubt in the mind of any unprejudiced person acquainted with the technicalities of the case (and this is, of course, to a great extent a technical matter), that our manufacturing operations have fallen off *relatively* during that time. It may be that neither France, Germany, Belgium, nor any of the other countries that now compete with us in supplying themselves and the world with manufactured goods, which a generation ago they and others obtained exclusively from England—it may be that none of our manufacturing rivals are singly our equal, but the sum of their operations must have materially altered proportions. Such gigantic establishments as those of Krupp of Essen, Govin of Paris, and the great iron-works at Creuzot, and those belonging to the Terre Noire Company, *must* tell a tale upon the markets. If England were now doing the same proportion of the whole manufacturing work of the world that she was twenty-five years ago, she would not with her present population be over-populated, or at any rate would not be over-populated in anything like the same degree that she now is. This should be remembered and taken into account in bringing the fact of the existing over-population to bear upon the subject of the recklessness of the poor in regard to it.

So far as any considerations upon this point influence

their actions with respect to their marriages—which of course involve the question of the regulation of the *rate* of their increase—the present extent of the working classes must be weighed in connection with such notions as the working classes could fairly be expected to have from twenty to thirty years ago. At that period "foreign competition" in our leading manufactures had not been heard of, and had it not intervened at a later date, England would, as we have said, been able to have fully and remuneratively employed her present working-class population. It may of course be said that if there had been more work and greater prosperity for them, they would have "taken it out" in the form that would have increased their numbers to such a degree as would still have led—though perhaps a little later—to as disastrous a state of over-population as now exists. A good deal might also be said in reply to this were it worth while to say it, but we do not see that any practical good is to be got by discussing "what might have been, but is not." As late as the Exhibition of All Nations in 1851, it was England first, the rest nowhere, in all the largest employment-giving branches of manufacture. Then she witched the world with noble workmanship—workmanship that was unapproached, and thought to be unapproachable. All the world admired, and the more energetic portions of it did something more—took to heart and profited by the lesson thus offered to them. From this point foreign competition began to be a reality, and gradually grew to be what it is, and to affect England as it has; to break down her position as a practical monopolist of the chief manufacturing industries. And from that time, too—and the importance and significance of this in the connection in which we speak of it should be well marked—the rate of increase of population in England began to come down, as may be seen by a comparison of the last with the preceding census. That during the years that have elapsed since that time the legislature have, in reducing taxes upon commodities, materially benefited the working classes, and rendered the existence of the principal sufferers by over-population—the ill-paid and irregularly-employed members of the working classes—less hard than it would otherwise have been, those of the working classes who take note of or think upon political matters readily acknowledge. But at the same time they, as has already been incidentally mentioned, hold the legislature responsible for the over-population, by reason of their having refused the means of emigration to those of the surplus and unemployed population who solicited it at their hands. They quite understand that a few ship-loads of unemployed workmen assisted to our colonies on the occasion which they take as their case in point* would not in

* The occasion on which a body of the workmen who had been thrown out of employment by the collapse of the Thames Shipbuilding trade, petitioned Government to assist them to emigrate.

itself have materially lessened the strain caused by over-
population; it is upon what they believed (whether their
belief is right or wrong need not be discussed here) to
have been the spirit and motive of the refusal that they
lay stress. They say, taking the tone of the parliamentary debate that took place upon the question as their
justification, that the refusal was not based upon any
doubt of the soundness of the principle, but upon the
circumstance that Parliament is composed exclusively of
those classes who have a material interest in perpetuating
any state of things that has the effect of making labour
cheap.

But whatever difference of opinion there may be as to
whether the working classes themselves, or the character
of our social and governmental constitution, is most to
blame in the matter, there can be no doubt as to the main
fact of the condition of the classes in question being of a
painfully unsatisfactory nature—being, in short, such as
we sketched it a little way back—such as imperatively
calls for amendment and reform. And now comes the
question of what are the prospects of the much-needed
amendment being brought about. The prospective outlook, as we have already said, is, we think, favourable, and
this is the general opinion among those who have given
the subject careful consideration; but still it should not
be too hastily or certainly concluded that this view will,
as a matter of course, be realised. It is an unpleasant

thing to contemplate, even in idea ; but there are some " signs of the times " that point to the possibility of a labour caste, whose position will be harder and more degraded than that of the present working classes. The wholesale importation of Coolie and Chinese labour going on in some parts abroad is a thing to " give pause " to the thoughtful among the working classes ; while at home there are things which, though at a first glance wholly favourable to the working classes, will be found, if closely observed, to have a reflex action that *may* help to create such a future labour caste as we have supposed. The aim of the great majority of the best members of the working classes—the cleverest, most energetic, and persevering men—is to raise themselves *out* of those classes. Numbers of them succeed in this aim, become in a greater or lesser degree capitalists, or get into positions in which their interests are identified with those of capital rather than those of labour. Still larger numbers—numbers so large that they form a considerable section of the working classes—though they do not rise out of their class, become, in their endeavour to do so, comparatively rich men—have money in banks, and shares in co-operative and building societies, and are as watchful against and strongly opposed to anything that it is alleged will tend to interfere with " the sacredness of private property " or lessen dividends, as are any of the great capitalists, who are usually the only persons associated with the interests of capital, as antagonistic to the interests of labour. There are tens of thousands of working men who as shareholders derive money from labour-created profits, and on that ground have a certain interest in some kinds of labour being kept cheap. What is usually called co-operation has undoubtedly been of great benefit to the working classes, and is in all likelihood destined to benefit them to a yet greater extent; but it has in it one of the elements of the possible danger of which we are speaking. It should be borne in mind that it is not in the true or best sense of the term co-operation, but only an extension of the joint-stock principle. There has been no attempt among the working classes at co-operation in production, upon any considerable scale, that even if started upon a purely co-operative basis, has not speedily become a mere joint-stock company of small shareholders, who, if they worked in the concern themselves, also employed labourers who had no interest in it, and the profits from whose labour came to them (the shareholders). And it is a well-understood and ascertained fact that a non-shareholding workman working alongside of shareholding ones, has, to say the very least of it, no better a time of it than one engaged in the ordinary class of workshop. Another well-known fàct in working-class circles is that no master is so hard as the working piece-master who has only day-workers under him; and in a general way it will be found that the lower down you go in the ranks of those who are above or partially above, and in authority over, labour, the greater is the disposition to grind the bones of labour to make their bread. Were there to arise a *general* dispute between labour and capital, it would be found that many of those who, to a superficial observer, would appear to be the natural vanguard of the army of labour, would be discovered forming a rank and file under the great captains of capital. The *tendency* of this state of affairs is obvious. That the worst result that could flow from it will ensue is not probable, but the possibility is so far substantial that it could not be and should not be overlooked in a dispassionate consideration of the general subject of the prospects of the working classes.

To come now to the favourable, the hopeful view of these prospects. The things needful to the improvement of the condition of the working classes are a general and higher education; a friendly, open, non-aggressive federation of the labouring classes throughout the civilized world; and Christianity. These are, in our opinion, the three grand essentials, comprehending within themselves the many minor ones necessary to the desired end. To speak of Christianity as one of the wants in a matter that is generally held to be wholly political is, we know, to lay ourselves open to a charge of Utopianism, idealism, and so forth; and as the charge of being unpracticable is the most damaging that can be brought against a writer dealing with such a question as our present one, we hasten to explain. In all civilized communities there always has been, and it may be taken for granted that there always will be, a stronger and weaker race of men, the stronger, though fewer in numbers, rising above and ruling their weaker brethren. The form and name of the relations between ruler and rulers may alter, but the relation has always existed, and with the same relative result—the earth and the fulness thereof falling to the lot of the strong, the hardest toil and bitterest suffering to that of the weak. And so substantially it will continue to be, if we have not Christianity to make the strong men merciful, to bring them to love their neighbours as themselves, and to cease to act upon such principles as that self is the first law of nature, and the weak must go to the wall. It may, of course, be said that we have Christianity, that we are a Christian country. But this is only nominally the case. Though we have undoubtedly many individual Christians among us, we are *not* a Christian nation—have not a general, living, fruitful Christianity. The Christianity which we speak of as being one of the things needful for the permanent and general improvement of the condition of the working classes is not that of mere creeds, rites, and Sunday church-going ; not the formal Christianity which is adopted as an element of respectability, but the Christianity of Christ, of the Sermon on the Mount, a Christianity under which brotherly love would abound, and the spirit of which would be visible in

the life of the week-day, work-day world, which would
lead the rich to consider the poor, employers to be kind
to and thoughtful for the employed, and the latter class
to be just and honest to employers, not the mere eye-
servants and time-servers that so many of them now
are. This is the sort of Christianity that we want,
and it is strictly practical to say that if we do not
get it, whatever else may or can be done for the benefit of the working classes, will be less efficient without such Christianity than it would be in conjunction
with it.

The hopefulness of the outlook in regard to the condition of the working classes lies, in our opinion, in the fact
that progress is already being made in two of the three
things that we have spoken of as needful, while there are
not wanting some slight signs and tokens favourable to
the idea of progression in the third—Christianity. The
anxiety, the warmth, and even the intolerance of feeling
that are being displayed in connection with the Christianity of creed-ism, Ritualism, vestment controversies,
and the like, may, we think, be taken as indicating a
tendency, a direction of mind, that may ultimately result
in a more extended development of that truer, nobler
Christianity of which, as we have said, there are many
individual instances among us—a Christianity that would
cause an unjust balance to be an abomination to the conscience of man as well as to the Lord, and the now pre-

vailing worship of mammon to be recognised as the ignoble idolatry it is.

The once favourite ideas about men being educated above their stations, and working people being made discontented with their lot by education, are now happily exploded. The necessity for universality of education has been admitted upon all hands, and the machinery for securing it set in motion. How much—taken in its full sense as meaning higher intelligence, wider knowledge, and greater refinement—it is capable of doing and likely to do, need scarcely be pointed out. It will serve as a common ground to bring the various sections of the working classes closer together, and give to the general body something of that coherence the lack of which is, at present, their greatest weakness. It will enable them to discern what are the functions of government, what those of individuals; and to wisely and effectively use the political power which is already legally and potentially in their hands, though it now remains a dead letter by reason of the want of a higher and more general education among them. Moreover, it will be a powerful means to the second great end—international federation. Internationalization is even now a great, though as yet but insufficiently recognised actuality. Steam, telegraphy, machinery, the spread of the mechanical arts, and general facility of intercommunication, have internationalized the productiveness of all civilized countries. The stronger

men, the governing and capital-possessing classes, are—
even when they are unconscious of the true meaning of
the matter—profiting by this, and the working classes
are beginning to see that if they, too, would share in the
good of the general material result of such a state of
things, there must be international federation among
them. The thinking men among them see this on two
chief grounds. Firstly, that unless there is, those of the
dealers in labour who hold it to be simply a marketable
commodity—and at present a very large number hold
that opinion—will play off the working classes of one
country against those of another. Secondly, that for the
working classes of any one country who happen to be at
present in a more advanced position than those of others,
to push on altogether regardless of any interests but their
own, will be to create a Nemesis for themselves. Without some friendly understanding among themselves—
without a knowledge upon the part of the ill-paid
labourers of one country that the better-paid labourers of
another sympathise with them, and are anxious to see
their condition brought up to the higher level—without
this there will always be the danger of the worst-paid
labourers being used as an instrument to drag down the
best-paid ones. These are the views that induce some of
the working classes to join the International, and many
others to regard at least its central idea with high favour.
It may be that the International is but a blind struggling

towards the desired thing—that the wire-pulling and wild political notions associated with it are reprehensible; but it at least shows that the thoughts of the working classes are falling in the direction of federation. It is true that the actual progress in the matter is but small, but that there has been progress let some of the proceedings in connection with the great Newcastle strike, which successfully inaugurated the nine hours' movement, bear witness. That the present want of unity among the English working classes themselves may be used as a sarcastic comment upon the idea of a working-class "federation of the world" we are well aware. But the idea has taken root, and is destined to be more or less fruitful in results, as education gradually eradicates the weeds of ignorance which now retards its growth.

Of our grounds for looking hopefully towards a development of the higher and truer Christianity, we have already spoken. The force of many noble examples is at work. The desire to be "written as one who loves his fellow-man"—to write it of one's self in the golden lettering of Christian deeds—is spreading. A wider development of the veritable Christian life seems to us to be among the coming events that are casting their shadows before, and from it, should it come, the working classes have more to hope from than from aught else. It, too, like education, and even more than education, will tend to effect the realisation of the grand idea of friendly international federation. It will bring us infinitely nearer than we now are to a state of things in which—

> " Man to man the world o'er
> Shall brothers be and a' that."

WORKING-CLASS EDUCATION AND MIS-EDUCATION.

"That there should one Man die ignorant who had capacity for knowledge, this I call a tragedy, were it to happen more than twenty times in the minute, as by some computations it does."—CARLYLE.

"Without entering into disputable points, it may be asserted without scruple that the aim of all intellectual training for the mass of the people should be to cultivate common sense; to qualify them for forming a sound practical judgment of the circumstances by which they are surrounded."—J. STUART MILL.

WE take it that it is rather matter of fact than of opinion that the three essential and comprehensive elements of social strength—and more especially of relative class strength—are numbers, necessariness to production, and knowledge. Of these, knowledge, though the least palpable, is, as practical results conclusively demonstrate, the greatest. In point of numbers the working classes are overwhelmingly, in necessariness to production preponderatingly strong, but a deficiency in knowledge as compared with other classes more than neutralise their advantages on the other two heads. By subdividing prime social problems into "questions of the day," and such like, it is of course easy to show that the weaknesses of the working classes are many, and variously acting.

They are so. But they are also converging, centring in, and growing from—*ignorance*. Not want of natural intelligence or receptive capacity for knowledge, be it understood, but ignorance in an educational sense—a lack of that education which as matters stand is the only stepping-stone to the knowledge which is power. Given a knowledge bringing and commanding education, and the working classes would be, as they ought, and in that case would be fit to be, the most powerful section of the community. The need for improvement in their education has been generally admitted for many years past, but to our mind the sincerity of the expressions of regret with which it was the custom to accompany the admission seems very doubtful, so far at least as regards the majority of those who had it in their power to have established and set in operation means for the accomplishment of the desired improvement. The loss of the working classes in the matter was the gain of other classes; and it is a very significant and suggestive fact that it was not until this position was altered, was in a certain sense reversed—not until, on the last extension of the franchise, the weakness of the working classes in respect to education became a danger to others—that statesmen gave any proof of their alleged regret being a verity. Then they did what it was in their power to have done at any time for a generation past : took practical action in favour of popular education ; passed an Education Act, which, though of course, like all new acts of parliament intended to have a wide application, showing the botchings and want of thoroughness that comes of party legislation — of thinking of the "Opposition" rather than of the general public—will yet have much of good in it when that public have by the pressure of their opinion enforced the necessary and practicable revisions and excisions in it.

The need for improvement in working-class education, long universally admitted, having at length been practically acted upon by the legislature, no more need be said on that head. The great question that remains to be discussed—and in saying that it remains to be discussed we do not forget that many regard this point as also settled —is, how is the improvement to be effected. The answer of Government and—with certain limitations which those taking an interest in the education question will understand without our expressing them—"the country " to this question is—the Education Act. It is not our present purpose to go into any criticism of the details of this Act. As we have just said, we believe that apart from faults of " parliamentarism," that will be amendable by reformers out of parliament, it has much that is good in it, and there can be no doubt that it was sincerely well intentioned. What we have to say concerning it refers not to its constructive details, but to its vital principle, its conceptional idea. It (the Act) is primarily founded upon the notion that the working classes are largely uneducated,

or we should rather say *unschooled;* and takes no cog-
nizance of, and indeed shows an unconsciousness of, the
existence of the fact that they are *mis*-educated. Now a
more fatal omission than this there could not be, for, as
we hope to be able to show before the conclusion of this
article, it is mis-education that is *the* educational weakness of the working classes—the thing which makes what
should be the stepping-stone to knowledge a stumbling-
block in the path to it. That among the lower and lowest
stratums of the working classes a large percentage of
children are never sent to school at all, and grow up in a
state of brutish ignorance in consequence, is most unhappily but too true. But this phase of the educational
weakness of the mass of the people is as nought compared
with that arising out of the mis-education of those of them
who *are* sent to school. The aim of the Education Act was to
make the existing system of schooling of universal application ; its first object ought to have been the organising
and substitution of a radically different and better system.
To us the fact that the present system has, after years of
trial, been found wanting seems so palpable, so obtrusively
self-evident, that we are at a loss to understand how it
could have been overlooked even by those who had only a
general knowledge of the working classes, who had at any
rate broad results to guide them to a judgment. Millions
of the working classes have had the fullest advantages of
the system, and a great majority of working-class children

are sent to school, and yet there is no really educated section of the working classes. Individual instances of well-educated working men are tolerably numerous, but compared with the vastness of the general body they are exceptional, are by the others regarded as exceptional, and not always as favourably exceptional. In some types of mind it is a phase of educational ignorance to contemn the education the value of which it is incapable of appreciating; in other types it leads to hatred, envy, and suspicion of the moral superiority which education gives, and to a mostly affected, but in some degree real contempt for educational advantages, on the ground that they are effeminate, and of no practical utility to their possessor. Those entertaining this last idea are much encouraged in it by their detecting the falsity in practice of a very common, very plausible, and—in its effects upon ignorant minds, as we are going to show —very pernicious platitude, which is constantly being uttered or written by all manner of men who set up as teachers or advisers of the people. Some little time back there appeared, first in *Reynolds's Newspaper*, and subsequently in the *Daily Telegraph*, a letter from "A Gardener at Kew," stating that his wages were only fifteen shillings per week, and giving a detailed account of how that amount was expended in the support of himself and a wife and child. Upon this letter the *Telegraph* had a leader, which, after criticising the mode of expenditure given as not being so judicious as it might have been, waived that part of the subject as of secondary importance, and wound up by significantly asking, " But what can a man who writes such a letter as that of our correspondent's have been doing all his life to be working at fifteen shillings a week?" This was an example of the most popular method of putting the platitude of which we speak. When those outside the working classes discover that an individual low down in the ranks of those classes is tolerably educated, they exclaim, " What can such a man have been doing that with his education he should be a gardener, or hodman, or dock labourer, or be found starving, and unable to obtain any employment whatever?" What can he have been doing, they ask in a manner that implies that no working man who is capable of making a clear statement or writing a fairly composed and not misspelled letter, need be in any very subordinate or distressful position. This, when it is put into doctrine, instead of implied in a question, is what is preached to the working classes. They are told in effect that they have only to be educated to be sure to rise in the world. This saying is akin to those that there is a marshal's *bâton* in every (French) soldier's knapsack, and a thrice-Lord-Mayor-of-London career open to every shop-boy. Such sayings are well sounding, and are spoken with the intention of being incentives to worthy and beneficial action; but those to whom they are addressed know that they are not generally

or effectively true. In regard to this especial theory of
the educated working man necessarily rising above the uneducated one, the working classes see that it is practically
false, and from this many of the more bigotedly and lazily
ignorant among them deduce that it is a bait thrown out
to them to induce them to tackle the dry and—as they
think—profitless task of educating themselves. One of
the lessons of the experience of their daily life is to teach
them that this theory does not hold as a rule, while the
exceptions in which education alone—we are speaking
now of general, not technical education—leads to a man
obtaining employment, or being promoted in it, are very
rare; so rare that a man might spend a lifetime in workshops without witnessing an instance of it. The really
educated men among the working classes are not, as we
have already said, sufficiently numerous to be ranked as a
distinctive section of the body, nor do they belong exclusively to either of the two great distinctive sections—the
skilled and unskilled. Their being educated is not the
result of the system under which working men are educated, and is therefore in itself no evidence of their having
belonged to the better-off section of their body—the section
that is in a position to avail itself, and as a rule does avail
itself, most largely of that system. It is the result rather
of some individual taste or chance that may as readily fall
to the lot of one who is a gardener at fifteen shillings per
week as to that of a mechanic with two guineas a week;

that very often does fall to the lot of the unskilled labourer, and *not* to that of the artisan who is in immediate authority over him, earns double his wages by lighter and cleanlier work, and regards himself as belonging to a superior grade of society. For a labourer to be a better-educated man than the skilled workman whose assistant he is, is a common phase of workshop life, and it is a still more common thing for a foreman to be a less well-educated man than numbers of both the skilled and unskilled workmen who are under him. Indeed, it is by no means an unknown thing for the qualifications of an uneducated, rather than of an educated man—loud-voicedness in swearing, and a general capacity for bullying (in workshop phrase, "horsing") men over their work—to be found the recommendation to a foremanship in the eyes of some employers. If an educated labourer complaining of the inadequacy of his pay to decency and comfort of living were asked, " How comes it that you who are evidently an educated man are nothing better than a common labourer, and are under men of inferior education ?" he could soon place the matter in its right light. He would probably answer that his father before him had also been an unskilled and poorly-paid labourer, and had consequently not had the pecuniary means of apprenticing his son to any skilled craft. That to " pick up " an education was, for one with a natural taste for it, or who had been fortunate enough to be put on the right path for acquiring it,

infinitely more easy than for any outsider, however desirous
or persevering, to pick up a trade. That it was acquired
mechanical ability, not general educational knowledge, that
gave the higher standing and pay. That to read Mill,
appreciate Carlyle, and be acquainted with and able to
enjoy the literature of your country was one thing; to be
able to chip level and file true, another. That when he
had turned his thoughts to callings in which educational
capabilities were more directly available, he had found that
clerking, store-keeping, time-keeping, and the like were
overstocked, that employment in them was precarious,
men who had been at them all their lives being often out
of work, and that, moreover, entry into them by an outsider—and more especially an outsider who lacked what
is generally styled "respectable attire"—is scarcely less
difficult than entry into a trade-union guarded, mechanical
craft. That, in short, he had been made and been kept
an unskilled and ill-paid labourer by circumstances which
it was beyond his power to control—which it was not
within the direct action of education to alter.

　　If all men were educated there would still have to be
gardeners and unskilled labourers, and other chances
beside that of the exact degree of general education would
still decide a man's being in this or that grade of working-
class life. It may be a "healthy tone" of talk, but, followed to its legitimate conclusion, this doctrine of education directly elevating the individual workman, as a

workman, is—nonsense. Working men, even ignorant
working men, see that it is nonsense, and the fact that
they do see it in this light makes it most pernicious nonsense. When it is preached to them, they sneeringly
point to some living contradiction of it, and hug themselves in their ignorance. "Look at Bill What's-his-
name and Jack So-and-so," they will say; "they're
educated men, a lot better educated, at any rate, than the
general run of working men. They've got any quantity
of book learning; if we don't understand anything we
hear or meet with in the newspaper, they can explain it to
us off-hand; they can talk like a schoolmaster on almost
any subject that turns up, and if you'll only give them a
rough idea of what you want, they'll write you a letter
that shall read like print. And yet what has their education done for them; what are they? Common labourers,
at the beck and call of every mechanic in the shop,
whether he be an educated and gentlemanly man, or a
bullying ignoramus who can scarcely tell a big B from a
barn door." This is how workmen comment in the workshop upon much of the "healthy" talk anent the immediate material benefit of education to them individually,
addressed to or *at* them out of the workshop. They resent
it as an attempt to treat them as children, and, if those
"friends of education," or of "the people," who indulge
in it only knew the injury they were doing, they would
abjure their doctrine. It is something very like the

contrary of this healthy sounding, but to ignorant minds —the only minds to which there can be any need to address it—injuriously misleading sentiment, that will have to be told to the working classes in putting the point of the material advantages to them of improved education. What should be taught them on this head is, that though they may now see educated men in their own ranks in a worse position in life than uneducated ones; that though education was no royal road to wealth or ease, and might never be of special individual benefit to any particular working man; that though it could not banish hard and disagreeable employments, or insure such employments falling only to the lot of the least educated; that though all this might be, education was still, even from a material point of view, and as an individual concern, a great thing. That it meant knowledge, and power, and progress; that though its materially beneficial action might be hard to define, and was necessarily of a broad and aggregate character, it could, and if general among the working classes would, benefit the individual through the class. That were the working classes generally as well educated as the best educated individuals among them now are, they would acquire such a knowledge of *all* the leading facts and opinions constituting the social problems of the day as, combined with the strength which their numbers and potential political power gives them, would enable them to deal with those problems in a manner beneficial to themselves—so greatly beneficial, perhaps, as to bring about a state of things in which even the worst paid callings would yield a sufficiency of the common necessaries and decencies of life to those following them. And this, in conjunction with those higher pleasures of the mind which education opens to all, would leave little more to be desired.

This is the candid and practical way of putting the strictly utilitarian incentive to education before the working classes—the only way likely to be effective with them. It is the line of argument resorted to by the educated few among them, and it cannot be gainsaid, as can the sort of talk we were condemning just now by those who think, or affect to think, that it is folly to be wise. It is only with men, however, that argument or exposition as to the utility and power of education has to be used; it is with children that the *work* of education has primarily to deal; and that brings us back to the more direct line of our discourse—the existing system of working-class education and its defects. We have already intimated that the result of the system is mis-education, and we have now to add that the fault of the system is, that it is based upon a false view of the true circumstances of the case; a radically wrong interpretation of the lesson of the fact which is the key-note to the whole position. A working man's child can at the utmost attend school only from five to fourteen years of age, and the idea upon which the

system has been constituted—in consonance with which
it, at any rate, actually works—is, that the education
must be completed, the child made a *scholar* within those
years. This too—most unfortunately—is the view of the
case taken by the bulk of the working classes themselves.
They believe, and act upon the belief, that the work of
education *is* completed in those years; that when a boy
leaves school he is, as a matter of course, done with
education, and in this belief the boy, generally speaking,
is—from reasons that will be presently adverted to—but
too happy to acquiesce. To our thinking, however—and
we will give grounds for our opinion—the proper and
practical deduction from the fact is obviously, that during
the youthful and limited period named, only the foundation of an education can be laid, or should be attempted to
be laid. It should be regarded as only a preparatory
period or stage, and its purport should be to qualify and
incline pupils to carry on the work of self-education during
later periods. Its actual effect is to produce a directly
opposite result. It is emphatically, and in the worst
sense, a *cramming* system, and as such implants not a
taste for, but a detestation of, anything in the shape of
study, or educative reading. It may vary in details in
different schools; but the central fault, that of attempting
too much, is common to them all, and worst in those that
are considered the best—because they are the highest
priced—schools. There is nothing that is sought to be

taught under the system that should not be learned, or lacking a general knowledge of which a *man* could be considered as educated. But O, the manner of the teaching! Its unutterable and exacerbating dryness—its stolid, self-defeating persistence in treating the boy as the man, not the father of the man! The idea that the children *must* be educated within the school period seems to have altogether precluded any idea of *interesting* them in their studies, of making learning pleasant to them, or giving rise to a spontaneous desire for knowledge. An examination of the lesson-books used in working-class schools is enough to give a shudder to any thoughtful friend to popular education, and more than enough to account for the distaste to education which working-class boys evince when they have left school. The disastrous idea of its being necessary to complete the education during the period of school-boyhood leads to the condensing of all subjects to their merest dry technicalities. Grammars are reduced to little more than a collection of rules, geographies to lists of rivers, mountains, capitals, and so forth, and histories to chronological tables. Even these are taught parrot-fashion, and test or develop only the *memory* of the children, leaving other and higher faculties dormant. They are committed to memory as task work, and are for the most part forgotten as soon as repeated, or, if remembered at all, remembered only as disjointed names or disconnected figures. There is thus nothing to

make study alluring, no creation in the mind of the pupil
of an interest that repays his trouble, nothing to make
the ways of learning ways of pleasantness, or to induce a
love of education for its own sake, or an appreciation of
its value as a means to an end—the acquirement of
pleasing, profitable, and elevating knowledge. In many
working-class schools there is an "upper" class in which
French is attempted to be taught in the same dry cramming way of which we are speaking; while in very many
instances the better-off grades of the artisan class will
send their sons for a year or two to what they call a
finishing school; that is, some private school of the semi-
genteel order, at which the fee is a guinea a quarter, and
the "list of studies" long and high-sounding, including
French, mathematics, and "the sciences." Boys who
have been to these latter schools, or through an upper
class of an ordinary national school, are regarded among
the working classes themselves as having had the best
chances of education, and being the best educated. And
really such a boy leaving school at fourteen years of age,
to be apprenticed, can be made to appear quite a marvel
of education to parents and others who are themselves
uneducated, or but little educated. At the show examinations of his school he will shine, will deftly go through
the few stock and much-rehearsed gymnastic tricks of
education which schoolmasters parade, and the friends of
pupils accept as proofs of a genuine education. He is put

forth as a grand (educational) combination—a calculating boy, a Lindley Murray, a gazetteer, a dictionary of dates, all rolled into one. Before the question is fairly out of mouth, he will tell how much twenty dozens of socks at a shilling and elevenpence three farthings per pair come to. He will glibly parse a sentence, will unhesitatingly spell long and formidable-looking words, name the highest mountain and longest river in the world, and repeat the catechism and whole chapters of the Bible "off book." He will reel off a list of the Roman emperors and English kings, and give the dates of, and parties opposed in, the great battles of the world. Finally, and as the crowning glories, numbers of those who have been to "finishing" schóols will demonstrate a problem in Euclid, and speak more or less of "the French not spoken in France." Wonderful enough seems all this to the working-class parents who have only some far-off touch of education to know they are not educated, who respect education, have a general appreciation of its value, are desirous that their children should have its advantages, and willing to make all reasonable sacrifice to that end. Wonderful enough, and, alas! satisfactory enough to them, seems this *mis*-education of show-examination questions, repellantly dry lesson books, repetitions " off book," and " night lessons," that are esteemed the more efficacious the more they are seen to be vanity and vexation of spirit to the student. But let any really educated man take these boys, even the prize pupils among them, and, lifting them out of the groove of show examinations, test them for genuine education, for knowledge, or any true desire for knowledge, or acquaintance with the best sources of it; let him see whether any solid foundation of education has been laid, whether the so-readily-given answers to show-examination questions are anything more than a mere mechanical acrobatical exercise of memory; whether the knowledge of principles or contextal facts which, to be evidence of true education, such answers should involve, is there; let any thoughtful, impartial, competent man test the boys to this purpose, and in nine cases out of ten there will ensue the sorrowfulest result, worse almost than no education, as we have said—mis-education. Detestation of education, too; desire to get to work as a means of getting rid of its thraldom (as they have experienced it), and determination to be done with it at the earliest possible date. This is no mere matter of opinion or assertion; it is but too painfully demonstrable matter of fact. Even when such a mode of testing as we suggest is tried upon the simplest scale, and with those engaged in the administration of the existing system of education forewarned and forearmed against it, and bringing up to the test only pre-tested and selected boys; even in this mild case we get a result that in itself, and still more in its suggestiveness, is as sad as it well can be. During the year ending August 31, 1870, there were visited, for examination to determine the proportion to each of its annual grant from Government, 6,382 State-aided Church of England schools, having an aggregate of 1,040,837 pupils. For examination in all the standards, there were presented a total of 551,531 pupils, of whom 344,841 were under, and 206,692 over, ten years of age. Standard VI., however, is the only one that needs to be dealt with here, as it is the highest, and shows the ultimate results of the system of education prevailing in our working-class schools. The Standard in question, which certainly does not err on the side of severity, is constituted as follows :—

" IN READING—A short ordinary paragraph in a newspaper or other modern narrative.

" IN WRITING—Another short ordinary paragraph in a newspaper, slowly dictated once by a few words at a time.

" IN ARITHMETIC—A sum in Practice or Bills of Parcels."

For examination in this Standard there were presented only 24,019, the whole of whom, it may be safely and justly presumed, belonged to the " over ten year " division. Of these there passed—

In Reading	22,316
In Writing	20,112
In Arithmetic	16,287

Thus broadly, out of upwards of 6,000 schools and 1,000,000 pupils, of whom more than 200,000 were the pick of the elder children, we have only 16,000 who can pass in all the simple requirements of Standard VI. Not three pupils per school, not two per cent. of the total number of pupils—only two-thirds of the twenty-four thousand who, after all manner of sifting and pre-testing, masters finally presented to stand the ordeal. If these figures, weighed in conjunction with the simplicity of the Standard, do not point their own moral, no words of ours will do it. So far as it goes, the testing of the Government examiner is genuine. He takes the pupils for a moment out of the lesson-book groove, selects his own newspaper paragraphs, gives his own test sums; with what results let the Reports of the Committee of Council of Education, from whose last issued blue-book the above figures are quoted, bear witness. And yet thousands of pupils who failed to pass this Standard, and hundreds of thousands whose masters would not risk submitting to it, would under a show examination have been made to appear—to the thoughtless and uneducated—as prodigies of educational attainments. Those who could not work a sum in practice given " out of the head" of a Government examiner would answer the problem of the nails in the horse-shoe and other puzzle questions in arithmetic with suspicious alacrity; while thousands who could not be trusted to read a newspaper paragraph correctly or write it from dictation, would have been shown as unshakable in the pronunciation of "Scripture proper names," in reciting the pedigrees of the patriarchs, and the list of the kings of Israel who " did evil in the sight of the Lord," as faultless in the repeating chapters and collects

" off book," and telling what were the three things that their godfathers and godmothers did promise and vow in their name. In the private " finishing " schools of which we have spoken the examinations are, generally speaking, only of the show order; and though by means of such examinations boys are made to *sound* like scholars, there is but too sufficient grounds for believing that Standard VI. would have much the same " flooring " effect upon them that it has upon the pupils of the rate-aided schools. But apart from any question of school examinations or stand-ards, there is proof positive of the most conclusive kind, and upon the largest scale, that the system of education applied to the very large proportion of the working classes who are sent to school is not an educating one— does not produce educated men, or an educated class. If even only those boys who had the fullest advantages of the present system, those who are kept at school until they are fourteen, were to become an educated section of the working classes, the general body of those classes would be in a much better position than they are in now. There would be then, what there is not now, a sufficiency of education to leaven the mass. There would be an educated phalanx to act as natural leaders to the body, to stand between it and those who now take advantage of its ignorance, and to give a *tone* to it that would lead to education being more rapidly extended to all other sec-tions of it. But these boys, going into the workshop in

all the glories of their show education, and with the reputation of being " fine scholars," will ten or twenty years
later be found as men—in the great majority of instances,
that is—ignorant, bigoted, ill-informed, guiltless of their
country's literature, knowing little or nothing of the
great social problems in which the welfare of their class
is involved, and very often utterly indifferent to them.
That this is a true statement of the case, that there really
is no educated class among the working classes, those best
acquainted with them will the most readily admit, and
none more readily (or sorrowfully) than the exceptional
few among themselves who *are* educated.   There can be
no disputing the fact ; the only question is how comes such
a state of things to be ? and this question we have, according to our lights, already answered by anticipation.   The
uneducated condition of the working classes arises from
the system of their schools being a wrong one, a funda-
mentally mistaken one—a dry, repellant, cramming, over-
reaching, self-defeating one—one that in striving to be a
whole chain fails to be even a link, fails to lay even the
foundation of an education, and creates an antipathy to all
work of self-education.   If the working classes are ever to
be a generally and beneficially educated body, we must
alter all this.   We must bring their teachers, and still
more themselves, to understand that education is *not* to
be completed between the ages of five and twelve, or at
the most fourteen—that show-examination education, the

answering of horseshoe-nail questions, and repeating of lists of names and dates by rote, is not in any best or veritable sense education at all. They must be brought to see that the school-day's period is only a preliminary one, that in such manner as the circumstances of the case admits of the *direct* work of education should be continued till manhood, and that education in its higher sense could and should go on through life.

Speaking broadly, the converging aim of the school education of working-class children should be to implant and direct a taste for sound and educative reading. Therein, rightly considered, lies the true path to knowledge, to power. "In Books," says Carlyle, "lie the *soul* of the whole Past Time; the articulate audible voice of the Past when the body and material substance of it has altogether vanished like a dream. Mighty fleets and armies, harbours and arsenals, vast cities, high-domed, many-engined—they are precious, great : but what do they become ? Agamemnon, the many Agamemnons, Pericleses, and their Greece; all is gone now to some ruined fragments, dumb mournful wrecks and blocks : but the Books of Greece ! There Greece to every thinker still very literally lives; can be called up again into life. No magic *Rune* is stranger than a Book. All that Mankind has done, thought, gained, or been : it is lying as in magic preservation in the pages of Books." And so it is— books, reading rightly applied, are *the* means of education, and to the working classes more largely and emphatically so than to any others, since the greater and better part of their education must be self-education—must be an education of common sense and general knowledge rather than of exact sciences or specific accomplishments. This kind of education books are specially fitted to give to working men ; and therefore, as we have said, the ultimate object of working-class education ought to be to create a taste for reading, to send pupils to books of their own free accord, and with a fair knowledge of what books and authors can be advantageously consulted for any desired kind of general information. The thing, we believe, could be done—should at any rate as a matter of duty and necessity be attempted. At the present time we have a committee of scholars engaged in a consultatory revision of the Bible, but, speaking with all due reverence, we think that not only was a committee for the revision of school books more needed, but that, well done, its work would be of greater service to both God and man. We want much less of lesson book, task work teaching, much more of teachers' teaching, and the latter might be had in conjunction with a system of school " readers " that were calculated to interest where the more dry lesson books now disgust pupils. An historical " reader," consisting of extracts— with explanatory head-notes—from the more dramatic and picturesque portions of the historical works of Macaulay, Froude, Freeman, Walter Scott, Motley, Prescott, and others, would do more to create an interest in and lead to the subsequent acquirement of a more extensive knowledge of history than any quantity of repeating " off book " of lists of kings, lengths of reigns, and dates of battles. In the same way, under a good teacher, a teacher with " knack," and having maps and globes at command, geography could be infinitely better taught in association with a geographical " reader" made up of interesting selections from books of voyages and travels, than by means of the cut-and-dried " Geographies " now in vogue. Grammar, too, might be taught in a less mechanical and more effective manner, and altogether the general intellect of the children—not their mere power of memory alone—might be more highly and profitably cultivated, might be cultivated to a point that would, generally speaking, make further self-culture a pleasure, that would make mental food scarcely less a necessity of life than food for the body. If this *were* done, and surely by a laying of heads together upon the subject means to do it could be devised, then we should get an educated working class, should get rid of the ignorance that makes the so large possession by the working classes of social and political power a possible danger both to themselves and others. The *means* of self-education and culture are now within the reach of almost every working man, and the capability of applying the means—such degree of receptivity of mind, clearness of comprehension, strength of memory and power of application, as go to make up a general susceptibility of being fairly educated —is common to the class. The only thing that stands in the way of self-education among the working classes is the system of schooling applied to the children of the class, or rather the results of that system—the distaste to learning that comes of cramming, the feeling that in the path of education all is barren, the idea that education is completed within the school period; that a boy who has "been through" an "arithmetic," a grammar, a geography, and who (while yet fresh from school) can repeat you the list of his country's kings, and stand cross-examination in the genealogies of the patriarchs, is a scholar of mark, can need nothing more in the way of education. These are the feelings and ideas that stand in the way of sound national education; that prevent the growth of an educated working class within the working classes; that *must* be amended before there *can* be an educated working class. An improved system of primary school education would lead to a considerable degree of subsequent self-education, though, so far as we can see, there is no reason why an efficient system of evening schools could not be established to continue in a direct line the general education of boys who had gone to work, and also to give them an opportunity of acquiring that technical education for the lack of which our artisan classes are placed at a disadvantage as compared with many Continental workmen.

As matters stand, the fruitful time between boyhood and manhood is left a waste period as regards education, and any new system to be efficient would have to provide some means of educationally bridging over that period. If we want educated working men we must educate our working boys.

The Government Education Act, as we have said, shows upon its face that its framers were unconscious of the greatest educational weakness of the working classes—the mis-educating effect of the system of education applied to them. Still, that Act was a great point gained. It was an emphatic and practical recognition of the importance of and necessity for national education. Many of those elected as members of school boards under it are not only friends to education, but are also shrewd, clear-sighted men, who, as the operations of the Act brings facts to light, will probably be able to deduce from those facts wherein lies the real weakness of the case of national education, and be led to take steps for the remedy of that weakness. Should it prove otherwise—should those entrusted with the carrying out of the national Education Act fail to discover what is the one thing most needful to the giving of a substantial operative education to the great mass of the people, or, having discovered it, should they by factional or interested opposition be prevented from taking remedial action on the point—should this prove the case, then all else that the Act can do will be of comparatively little avail. If it is confined to enforcing the present system, leaving that system what it is, it will take "gutter children" from the gutter and place them in schools, and give a larger number of working men who have been through schools, and on that ground call themselves educated, but whose educational attainments if tested would be found not to go beyond a capability of signing their names, reckoning up their week's wages, and laboriously and not very understandingly reading the class of prints that take advantage of the ignorance and pander to the prejudices of their class. This it will do, and even in this will be doing some slight good. But it will not give us a really educated people. It will still leave the working classes as weak as ever in the most essential element of social strength—knowledge.

The "denominational question" that has arisen in connection with the subject of national education, though so contemptible in itself, and a *religious* squabble, not an *educational* matter, can scarcely be left altogether unnoticed in dealing with the general subject; and since it must be mentioned, it will perhaps be best worth while to briefly state the views expressed by really intelligent working men when discussing the point among themselves. In the first place, they distinctly recognise the fact that it is a religious, a sectarian wrangle, and, rightly or wrongly, they believe that either of the parties to it would sacrifice educational prospects to sectarian gains—to the pleasure of " spiting" each other. But since the question has been raised and blocks the way, since it stands as a bone of contention over which there is likely to be constant snarling, they would have it removed. They would have religious and secular education entirely separated, not only as a means of getting rid of the denominational question, but in the belief that both kinds of education would be benefited by the separation—especially the secular. They believe that clerical influence being strong in the schools in which the two educations are combined, the interests of the secular are sacrificed to those of the religious : they think that Scripture, collects, and catechisms might be very efficiently and sufficiently learned in Sunday-schools, and the considerable proportion of school-time now devoted to them in day-schools advantageously applied, to the better grounding of pupils in their secular studies : they say, too, with sneering significance and a certain grim satisfaction, that the " Church party " need not be so anxious for continuing to combine religious— *their* religious—with secular education ; that for the millions of working-class children they have had through their schools they can scarcely show units of working men church-goers ; that such church-goers are almost as rare and costly a production as a converted Jew. Those whom it may concern may at any rate be assured of this, that the denominational question is doing injury to the cause of religion as well as of education. It increases and embitters the feeling of contempt for the creeds, already so largely existing in the minds of the working classes, and intensifies their dislike to and suspicion of "the parsons."

In conclusion, we can but most earnestly repeat that the great educational weakness of the mass of the people lies, not in the number of them who are not sent to school at all, but in the mis-education of those of them who are sent; that this important truth does not appear to have been realised by those into whose hands have fallen the power of practically dealing with the question of national education, and that unless it is realised by them and acted upon we shall never get a really educated people.

ON THE GRIEVANCE IDEAS OF THE WORKING CLASSES.

"Neither let any prince or state be secure concerning discontentments because they have been often or have been long, and yet no peril hath ensued; for as it is true that every vapour or fume doth not turn into a storm, so it is nevertheless true that storms, though they blow over divers times, yet may fall at last, and as the Spanish proverb noteth well, 'The cord breaketh at the last by the weakest pull.'" —BACON.

WHETHER the working classes are the much and in many ways aggrieved, and wronged, and unjustly dealt-with and dealt-against body which they conceive themselves to be; or whether, on the other hand, they are the morbidly dissatisfied, unreasonable, grievance-mongering, self-tormenting class which many impatiently allege them to be—whether this or that is the correct view, or nearest to which of them, seeing that they are the extreme views, the mean of truth may lie, is a subject well worthy of examination and consideration. The bearings of the question are most important. Right or wrong, well or ill-founded, the belief of the working classes in their view of the case is most sincere—is bitterly, impassionately earnest. To their minds it is an unquestionable, deeply pervading, powerfully operative fact that they *are* aggrieved, that they are a wilfully sinned against class of society, a class upon which every other class either preys or is desirous of preying; and this belief has no small degree of influence in forming their distinctive characteristics and creating " class feeling "—that is to say, a feeling of class antagonism—among them. It is their weakest point, and fully accounts for much seeming inconsistency in their nature—for their being at once the most approachable and most unapproachable class, the most easily gullible and the most jealously suspicious. It invites the flattery by which the class have—though unconsciously—suffered so much, and leads to their being one of the strongest examples that could possibly be adduced of the truth of the saying of Edmund Burke, that " adulation is not of more service to the people than to kings." Few kings have been more largely, persistently, and fulsomely adulated than the working classes of this country have been, or more puffed up to their injury by the adulation. Flattery hath been the spoil of them. They have been beflattered to an extent that has created a morbid appetite for flattery, that has dulled their moral sense, and made them intolerant of truths that are not flattering, or that are contradictory of the adulation poured upon them. And hence it comes that while the applauding voices of large numbers of them can be gained by all manner of petty agitators who choose to tickle their ears with fine phrases, and pander to the extremest forms of their grievance ideas, they are as a body and as a rule inaccessible to and suspicious of any from other grades of society who not being agitators, or self-dubbed " leaders of the people," seek to approach them in a friendly but not a flattering way. Many do so seek to approach them with a view to understanding, as a means to serving them, and find, as we have just said, that they are inaccessible and suspicious. Such approaches are doubtless sometimes ill-judged, but being well intentioned and, generally speaking, disinterested, or even self-sacrificial, those making them are often even more surprised than pained at the fruitlessness of their endeavours to " make friends " with the working classes, at the coldness and distrustfulness with which their advances have been received by those classes. But the fact of the matter upon this point is— we put it in the broadest manner at present, as we shall be dealing with it in a more detailed fashion further on —that the attempts of " outsiders " to gain their confi- dence is one of the specific grievances of the working classes. The list of their specific grievances is tolerably numerous, and, in order to arrive at a clear understanding of the grievance position as it exists in their minds, it will be necessary to deal at large with several of the more important and characteristic of them, otherwise they might all be summed up in one generic one : to wit, that there is something radically wrong in the constitution of society ;

that the times are out of joint; or rather, to speak by the letter, that the immense amount of physical suffering and social injustice resulting from the "something wrong" falls exclusively and most undeservedly upon them. Whether or not, as they cannot with anything like united-ness of voice say wherein the something wrong consists, to whom, if to anybody, it is attributable, or how it is to be set right—whether or not they are under these cir-cumstances justified in considering themselves, more than merely unfortunate, *aggrieved*, may be a disputable point, but we think there can be no two opinions about their having the fullest and bitterest justification for believing and asserting that the most and worst of the suffering resulting from the present imperfect constitution of society *does* fall upon them. If this is steadily borne in mind, their chronic discontent, and the exaggerated form and threatening tone in which they put their specific grievances, cannot surely be wondered at, even though they may be grumbled at. Their general position as they *feel* it, both as regards themselves and *against* society, is put by Car-lyle in words as bitter and burning as their thoughts :—

"I will venture to believe," he says in the chapter on Democracy in "Past and Present," "that in no time since the beginnings of society was the lot of those same dumb millions of toilers so entirely unbearable as it is even in the days now passing over us. It is not to die, or even to die of hunger, that makes a man wretched ; many men

have died ; all men must die—the last exit of us all is a
Fire Chariot of Pain. But it is to live miserable, we
know not why ; to work sore, and yet gain nothing ; to
be heart-worn, weary, yet isolated, unrelated, girt-in with
a cold universal Laizzez-faire : it is to die slowly all our
life long, imprisoned in a deaf, dead, infinite injustice, as
in the accursed belly of a Phalaris' Bull! This is and
remains for ever intolerable to all men whom God has
made. Do we wonder at French Revolutions, Chartisms,
Revolts of Three Days? The times, if we will consider
them, are really unexampled."

This is the direful position—the position of "infinite
injustice"—in which the millions of toilers feel themselves
as a body to be. The lot of a considerable proportion of
them is literally to "live miserable and die slowly all
their life long," while the others know that they are
barely above such a lot ; that a very slight turn of fortune's wheel—a new invention, a commercial crisis, a
passing failure of health and strength, or anything in the
exigencies of a chronically overstocked labour market—
may at any time reduce them to it. It is, therefore, not
to be wondered at that they should account themselves an aggrieved, a "down-trodden" class, that in
almost every important point of the present constitution
of society they should see some especial wrong to them.
All things considered, the wonder should rather be that,
strong as their language undoubtedly is upon occasion,

their only violence nowadays in connection with their grievances is violence of language. But while their vehemence of expression may be easily understood and excused, it is nevertheless a thing to be deeply regretted. It stands in the way of fair and friendly discussion with society; it discovers a strong feeling of class antagonism, and, in doing so, excites similar feelings in others. It leads to the grievances being stated in exaggerated forms, which are suggestive of impracticability and unreasonableness upon the part of those putting them forward, and affords an opportunity of pooh-poohing them, and denying at least their literal truthfulness.

Taken apart, however, from verbal exaggeration—and the separation, as a rule, can be easily made—and dispassionately examined, we think that the general conclusion that would be arrived at in regard to the grievance ideas of the working classes is, that " there is something in them." Something of a real grievance, in even those of them that at a first glance, or in the particular form in which they are stated, seem most unfounded; a good deal in several of the most harped upon of them. As an example of there being something in even the least tenable of their alleged grievances, let us examine the idea of the introduction of labour-saving machinery into a trade being an injury to the working classes. It may at once be answered that it is an absurd, oft-exploded idea—an idea in direct contradiction to the demonstrated facts, and unvarying experience of the position. So it is, and many, perhaps a majority, of the working classes clearly understand that such is the case—*broadly*. But as put, and when put by working men, the idea that "new-fangled" machinery is an injury to the interests of labour has something in it. They *feel* that they have a grievance, though they cannot very well express it; but here again a great man has recognised it, and expressed it for them. No one has answered the objection to machinery more conclusively than Stuart Mill, or shown more distinctly that the *ultimate* result of progressive mechanical invention must be beneficial to the labouring classes *in the aggregate*. But no one also more plainly sees, or readily acknowledges, that the immediate results of an introduction of hand-labour superseding machinery, may be—and frequently is—a most disastrous and distressful thing for large bodies of workmen; and that unless workmen who are injured by inventions which benefit the community at large, receive some special consideration at the hands of the Government as representing the community, they *have* a grievance against Society in the matter. Having shown that the tendency of improvements in production is ultimately to increase the gross produce, and thereby benefit all, he goes on to say— " But this does not discharge governments from the obligation of alleviating, and if possible preventing, the evils of which this source of ultimate benefit is or may be productive to an existing generation. . . . Since improvements which do not diminish employment on the whole, almost always throw some particular class of labourers out of it, there cannot be a more legitimate object of the legislator's care than the interests of those who are thus sacrificed to the gains of their fellow-citizens and of posterity." This is exactly how the working classes see the matter: they too think that "there cannot be a more legitimate object of the legislator's care" than the one Mill puts, as quoted above; and their grievance is that legislators not only do not care for "the interests of those who are thus sacrificed for the gain of their fellow-citizens," but repudiate the idea of their being in any way called upon to care for them. If an invention that cheapens some article of produce to consumers happens to extinguish the employment of some class of labourers, and so reduces them and their families to starvation, legislators are willing enough to admit that the latter circumstance is one to be regretted. As individuals they are very sorry for the sufferers, but as legislators—for this is what it comes to in practice—it is no concern of theirs; they cannot interfere with the chances of trade and the times, and—they *don't* interfere. So superseded artisans who are too old to acquire other mechanical trades —even supposing there was room in any trade for any considerable addition to the number of the "hands" engaged in it—sink down into old job-men or paupers, and "fall like Lucifer, never to rise again." It is men who have been cast down in this manner, who have, on the first introduction of some new invention, been made trade-less, or had their wages greatly reduced—it is men who have suffered thus, that occasionally revive the old cry of machinery being the curse of the country, the ruin of the working man. It is of course a foolish cry, though, when we consider the sufferings of those giving vent to it, we can scarcely be surprised at their uttering it.

And, after all, as we have said, there *is* something in it. Its foolishness consists in the form of words in which it is put; in its laying the blame for the degree of evil to individuals associated with the benefit to the community, upon the invention, instead of upon the something-wrong in society, and social legislation which leads to the repu-diation of the idea of its being in any way the duty of the legislature to care for " the interests of those who are thus sacrificed to the gains of their fellow-citizens and of posterity." But if the feelings of those who from time to time revive the old outcry against machinery were analysed, and traced to their springs, it would be found that it was really the social something-wrong of which they complained. Uneducated and ill-informed though they be, they have yet such a modicum of common-sense as would enable them to see that whatever increased pro-duction would be an unqualified blessing, if individual interests to which a passing injury was done in order that permanent, general good might come, were considered in a broad spirit of social justice and brotherliness. But where the working classes are concerned such interests are *not* considered—are held, according to the practical doctrine of Society, as shown in the action of the legislature, to have no claim to be considered. And hence the feeling among working men, which the more ignorant of the class sometimes put into the shape of an outcry against labour-saving machinery, but which really means an idea to the effect that it were better that Society went without the *additional* wealth and luxury that new inventions bring, than that it should be gained, so to speak, at the price of blood, the utter misery and ruin—the direst physical suffering, mental anguish, and social degradation —of hundreds, or perhaps thousands of men and their families. In a country so densely populated as England, and with the legislature acknowledging no obligation to care for the interests of working men under the particular circumstances of which we are speaking, the invention which takes away his trade from a man dependent upon that trade for his daily bread, *is*, as regards him individually, an evil thing, not from any natural necessity of the case, but by reason of the attitude of Society in the matter. As against Society such a man has a real grievance. He might say to it with but too sorrowful truthfulness—

> "You do take my house, when you do take the prop
> That doth sustain my house : you take my life
> When you do take the means whereby I live."

That rough uneducated men, from whom have been taken the means whereby they live, should not in the bitterness of their sufferings be able to draw fine distinctions is by no means strange. But though their cry of "No new-fangled machinery" is, in its immediate meaning, a proof of suicidal short-sightedness, it has in their mind a more than literal and immediate signification. They quite understand that it is the action (or rather the inaction) of Society in the matter, that leads to machinery being the evil that it undoubtedly is to working men, whom it directly supersedes. That under the foolishness of the stock phrases in which they are given vent to, the objections of working men to the introduction of labour-saving inventions into the industrial arts have "something in them," we trust we have conclusively shown, but the *sting* of the grievance idea upon this point has yet to be mentioned. It is this : that it is only where working men are concerned that the legislature repudiates the idea of its being their legitimate duty to take care of the interests of those " who are sacrificed to the gains of their fellow-citizens and of posterity." If some advance in public opinion or improvement in organization comes to affect any body of upper or middle class workers, in the same way in which an important invention sometimes affects the operatives in a mechanical trade, there is never the slightest hesitation upon the part of Government to liberally consider the interests of those prejudicially affected. When

clergymen, officers, or civil servants are in question, the
State can recognise its duty to citizens fast enough. When
the Irish branch of the Church was to be disestablished,
the cry was full compensation to every interest either
extinguished or injured. The cry was still the same when
purchase in the Army was abolished ; and when there took
place a readjustment in the Civil Service, involving a
reduction in the number of servants, retiring allowances to
men in the prime of life, and even upon the under side of
it, were the order of the day ; and that, too, upon a scale
that the general public were inclined to think more than
liberal—extravagant. But when the same kind of State
policy that led to abolition of purchase and reconstruction
of the Civil Service, brought about the closing of the
Government dockyards, there was no talk—except to dis-
claim obligation in the matter—of compensating the dis-
banded artisans, who in a time of almost unparalleled
dulness of general trade were turned adrift in shoals, to
starve if they could do no better. Many of them, indeed,
did starve. And yet many of the discharged dockyard
" hands " had a far stronger moral right to compensation
from the country than had the army officers in respect to
the over-regulation prices. Until the coming event of
their closing was unmistakably casting its shadow before,
working men regarded the Government dockyards as a
permanent institution. With a view to being, in course
of time, placed upon the " establishment "—being assured

against discharge, and of a small pension in old age—
many men worked in the yards for years at rates of wages
considerably below what would have been paid to them
by private firms. But when the closing came no account
was taken of this, not a penny of compensation given for
the actual money sacrifice that the men had made in the
expectation—for which there was every justification—that
they would be recouped by being made "established
hands." As it happened, however, they had not become
"established," and they had therefore no legal claim upon
the Government, which, when appealed to fervently,
alleged themselves to be constitutionally unable to give
anything that it was not specifically nominated in the
bond they must give. But when a rich class, the army
officers, came to be dealt with, this same Government,
which stood on strictly legal rights, and flaunted its
watchwords of "retrenchment" and "economy" with
starving artisans, voted millions in payment of compensation of a claim which not only was not legal, but in
direct violation of an explicit written law, specially
bearing upon the matter. And when the dowering of
princes and princesses came in question, this—to working
men—strictly economical and letter-of-the-law-abiding
Government both preached and practised the doctrine that
an implied obligation was if anything more binding than
a written and legally complete one. With what feelings
working men looked on at and marked this contrasted

action may be easily imagined. Their recollection of it
has been added to their treasures of (political) memory,
and the remembrance is not a pleasant one or likely to
produce pleasant fruits.

Of course no sensible person would for a moment
attempt to argue that the case of artisans thrown out of
employment by new inventions in mechanics, was *fully*
parallel to that of men whose material interests were
prejudicially affected by disestablishment or reorganiza-
tion of State institutions which had been regarded as
permanent by those taking service under them. Working
men do not argue so; they merely hold the opinion
expressed by Stuart Mill in the passage we have quoted—
that it is the duty of the legislature to care for the interests
of the few who are sacrificed for the good of the many.
This duty, as we have said, the legislature repudiates where
working men are concerned, and herein lies the essence of
the grievance idea, the real meaning of the outcry against
"new-fangled machinery." Even where the case of working-
class men *is* fully parallel with that of men in other classes
of society affected by the suppression of State establishments—even when this is the case, as in the instance of
the discharged dockyard hands, we see the same *special*
disregard to working-class claims to consideration.
Through all the legal technicalities, or plausible generalities, by which the action (or inaction) of the legislature,
as representing society, may be justified in any given case,

the working classes see* and grasp the broad truth that their interests are considered in a different—a less favourable, a less just—spirit than are the interests of other classes of society.

Their firm conviction that such is the case is what is rankling in the depths of their mind under all their grievances, no matter how absurd may be the " cry " in which any particular grievance is expressed. And this brings us to the greatest of the grievance ideas of the working classes, the one that may almost be described as all-inclusive—the idea that there is one law for the rich and another for the poor. In the minds of the poor the phrase is axiomatic, and has a signification far wider and deeper than the one literally attaching to it, though it is usually in connection with some instance of its more literal application that the "cry" is raised. There are many even in " society " who are willing to admit that there is " something " in this cry, but a far larger number profess to regard it as pernicious nonsense, a figment of a dissatisfied, self-tormenting imagination. The latter class can of course point out that there is but one code of laws written in our statute-book, and that it stands applicable to all, without respect to persons or caste ; and they speak of the security of trial by jury, the stainless character of our judges, the folly of impeaching justice, and so forth— but all commonplaces to the contrary notwithstanding, it is substantially true that in practice there *is* one law for

the rich and another—and harder—for the poor. Innumerable cases in point might be adduced to show that
such is the case, but a few instances will be sufficient by
way of illustration here. Let us take, for example, the
action of the law in regard to the matter of Sunday
trading. A year or two back, a society for the suppression
of Sunday trading raked up an unrepealed statute of that
godly monarch Charles the Second, according to which it
was an offence at law for any man to ply his ordinary
avocation on a Sunday. Under this statute they, through
their agent, instituted proceedings against sundry costermongers, and itinerant vendors of water-cresses, peri-
winkles, and other cheap "relishes" much in favour with
the poor. These culprits did not deny the charge; they
merely pleaded that to prevent them from trading on
Sunday would lessen their already scanty incomes to an
extent that would make paupers of them. The truth of
their plea was not questioned, the hardship of their case
was admitted, but they were convicted and fined; the
magistrates saying that the law left them no option but
to inflict penalties. There were working men, however,
who presumed to doubt this. Judging by the general
tenor of legal and legislative action in respect to "the
Sunday question," they were very strongly of opinion that
if this particular law was brought to bear upon the
pleasures of the rich instead of the "relishes" of the
poor, a very different result would be witnessed. To put

the thing to a test, they followed the lead of the society who had prosecuted the costermongers. They took out summonses against the coachmen of the Lord Mayor and the Marquis of Lorne, for following *their* ordinary avocations on Sunday—and lo! the result fully justified the view they had taken. The magistrates *then* discovered that they were *not* bound to convict. They did not convict, and the statute, which was rigorously enforced when it only ruined the poor, was quietly allowed to fall into disuse again when it was shown that it could be made to annoy the rich.

It is usually in connection with some such case as this that the cry of one law for the rich and another for the poor is raised; but it is the principle and its broader generalities that constitute the essence of the grievance idea and make it a standing one. The things that sting and rankle, that perpetuate and intensify class jealousy and hatred, are such as the invention of kleptomania for the benefit of the well-to-do pilferer; the manner in which " mad doctor " theories are allowed to stand between the gallows and well-to-do murderers; the abolishing imprisonment in bankruptcy cases, and *not* in the cases of county-court debtors; the " raiding " upon small betting-houses, while Tattersall's remains untouched; and the attempt to close public-houses on Sundays, while leaving the clubs—the public-houses of the rich—unmolested. Such things as these, and the general costliness and tardi-

ness of law procedure, which often stands between a poor
man and justice, are the groundwork of the cry that
there is one law for the rich and another for the poor;
and while such things can be pointed to as existing facts,
it will be very hard indeed to persuade the poor that
there is not one law for them and another for the rich.
Furthermore, the poor are firmly of opinion that there
being one law for the rich and another for the poor is
intentional—is the result of the rich having the "upper
hand," and being practically the lawmakers. This is
the crowning sting of the grievance—the point that
maddens. This is what makes this particular grievance
idea a dangerous one—especially dangerous in such times
as those now passing. It may prove to be wholly and
only a dream, but the poor certainly do look forward to a
good time coming, when *they* will have "the upper hand,"
and be the lawmakers; and their lawmaking would
be *against* the rich—would not have in view justice, but
retaliation.

Nor is it merely in the more literal sense that they
believe there is one law for the rich and another for the
poor. To their thinking, the principle permeates the
whole constitution and action of society, and it is upon
the ground of such principle underlying them that they
regard the endeavours of outsiders to gain their confidence as a grievance. They are willing enough to
believe in the good intentions of the individual parsons,

scripture-readers, district-visitors, and self-commissioned amateurs of philanthropy, who aim at the spiritual and moral elevation, or regeneration, of "the masses," and who so largely be-visit, be-lecture, be-tract, and be-*question* the members of the masses. The poor are quite willing to take for granted that these people mean well. What makes them cold or resentful to their approaches is the belief that they never "tackle" rich sinners. That they come to the cottage in a manner in which they would never dream of approaching the mansion, and "take liberties" with the poor man that they would themselves *see as liberties*, did they think of applying them to the rich. Another thing that hardens the poor against the approach of outsiders, is the exceeding quantity and infinite variety of visitation and inquisition to which they are subjected. Few but the poor themselves can have an adequate conception of this point. Were this fully realised by the general public, the feeling of being *badgered* that the poor undoubtedly have, would, we think, be considered natural, and the snappishness that comes of that feeling understood and allowed for.

In conclusion, we repeat that, generally speaking, the grievance ideas of the working classes have more of substantial justification in them than is usually supposed to be the case. They constitute a political and social problem which, if one of the most difficult, is also one of the most important that statesmen can have to deal

with.   As a matter of policy, as well as a matter of
justice, they demand attention ; for if left unredressed,
to ferment in the popular mind, they can but breed evil
in the State.

Part II

ENGLISH REPUBLICANISM.[*]

"For the transgressions of a land many *are* the princes thereof."—PROVERBS xxviii. 2.

"As the average of matters goes, we account him legislator and wise, who can so much as tell when a symbol has grown old, and gently remove it."—CARLYLE.

"Concerning the materials of seditions, it is a thing well to be considered; for the surest way to prevent seditions (if the times do bear it) is to take away the matter of them; for if there be fuel prepared, it is hard to tell whence the spark shall come, that shall set it on fire."—BACON.

ON March 24, 1871, Mr. Gladstone was asked, in his place in the House of Commons, whether his attention had been called to the report of a meeting at which

---

[*] On the first appearance of this article in *Fraser's Magazine* for June, 1871, a special significance was attached to the circumstance—particularly by American journals—of its appearing in a magazine "edited by no less a person than Froude the Historian." We therefore think it right to state that the article was not "edited" to the extent of a single word; and to call attention to the fact that it appeared with the following editorial head-note: "Half the world is said to know nothing of the feelings and thoughts of the other half. We insert this article as an assistance towards removing so peculiar and dangerous a form of ignorance.—ED. *F. M.*" What Mr. Froude's individual opinions in respect to Republicanism may be we do not know. All that we do know—and we think it is as much as any one has a *right* to infer from his allowing such an article to appear in the pages of "Fraser"—is, that he is a liberal and unprejudiced Editor, and takes a strong interest in *all* that concerns the welfare of the Working Classes.

a resolution, declaring that "a Republican form of government was the only one capable of developing the great resources of the country, and worthy of the confidence and support of all true democrats, was reported to have been carried by acclamation; whether, if the report was correct, it was his intention to ascertain whether, in the opinion of the law officers of the Crown, such language was of a treasonable or seditious character; and whether, in the event of such being the opinion of the law officers, the Government was prepared to take any steps for dealing by law with those who held this language."

Mr. Gladstone replied that his knowledge of the subject was confined to the matter of the resolution as quoted by the member asking the question; that, whether the report was correct or not, it was not the intention of Government to take any steps whatever in the matter; that such opinions as those embodied in the resolution were "wrong and foolish," and needed but to be left unnoticed to sink into "that oblivion which was their destined and their proper portion."

As during the portion of the session that had elapsed up to that date Mr. Gladstone had evinced a decided inclination to verbal quibbling, it is, perhaps, not going too far to suggest that possibly he took advantage of the word "only" in the resolution referred to. To assert that only under *any* one form of government can the resources of this country be fully developed is an assumption of final knowledge in politics not only presumptuous, but wrong and foolish, and it must have been to that view of the case, we take it, that Mr. Gladstone applied those epithets. At any rate, it is scarcely possible to conceive that anyone, with even a tithe of his claims to be considered a statesman, would stigmatise as wrong and foolish the abstract proposition that a Republic is the best of the known forms of government. That surely is a fairly debatable question, as it is undoubtedly one on the affirmative side of which weighty arguments can be adduced.

That in its theory and possibilities a republic is a better form of government for the working population of a country than either a monarchical or autocratic one may be taken as an admitted truism ; and as a natural consequence there has, in England, always been a considerable degree of instinctive Republican feeling among the working classes, and a certain measure of philosophical Republicanism among scholarly and speculative politicians untrammelled by the exigencies of practical statesmanship. The latter phase of this feeling was, however, regarded as nothing more than a political dillettanteism, while with the working classes the feeling was known to be merely latent under ordinary circumstances, and blind, passionate, and self-harmful whenever, under the prompting of political or social excitement, it attempted to assert itself. The possibility of a Repub-

lican party in English politics having practical power to
enforce concessions to their views would have been regarded as an absurdity.   These are still pretty much the
ideas entertained in upper and middle class circles with
regard to Republicanism in this country, and until very
recently they were substantially correct.   At the present
time, however, such views are a dangerous mistake.   Republicanism has reached a new, an advanced and advancing stage—has become an important though a little
recognised or understood actuality of practical politics.
For years past Republicanism has been spreading among
the working classes *doctrinally* to such a degree that now
it may be safely said that it is—in some more or less
modified form—the political creed of ninety-nine working
men in a hundred, having any political feeling or belief
at all.   The last extension of the franchise made the
practical assertion of this creed a possibility, and the tone
of recent legislation has given a start to the one thing
needful for the realisation of that possibility—organization.

The fact of such a meeting having been held as that at
which the resolution already quoted was passed, need not
itself have been taken as material evidence of a Republican feeling among the working classes at large.   Any
petty, notoriety-seeking agitator can get up a meeting to
pass resolutions upon almost any conceivable subject, and
newspapers making an unthinking use of a stock heading

will report it as a meeting of the working classes, though more frequently than not it has about as much title to be so described as a gathering of a dozen discontented soldiers would have to be cited as a meeting of the British army. Though, however, the particular meeting referred to was in no way an authorised representation of the general body of the working classes, the resolution carried at it was, *as it happened,* in full accord with the prevailing opinion of those classes. The few avowedly Republican meetings held in the metropolis of which notices have got into the papers are not the only or the most important ones that have taken place. There have been many such, and a considerable number of Republican associations have been formed, and are increasing in extent. More significant still, similar meetings have been held and societies formed in the large manufacturing towns of the provinces, where such things when they do occur have a graver meaning, and indicate a more deep-rooted conviction, and greater firmness and tenacity of purpose, than they do among the (comparatively) mercurial Londoners. These clubs make only a small fraction of the numerical strength of the working classes, but they embrace a large percentage of the *actively* political, while the latent sympathies of the bulk are with them. In short, whether right or wrong, foolish or wise, English Republicanism has grown to be a great political fact—a thing that will not only not sink into oblivion by being left unnoticed, but will be increased in extent and embittered in quality by any high-toned affectation of ignoring its existence. It is a thing for statesmen to grapple with, and certainly a thing the causes, character, aims, and alleged justification of which are worth being looked into.

Republicanism as it now exists in England is founded less on pure admiration of its own professed principles than upon hatred and contempt for royalty and its concomitants. It has been selected as a creed rather as the broad antithesis to monarchy than from any immediate reference to or detailed knowledge of its working. "Take away the baubles" is a cry that sums up the political aspirations of the working classes; that would have summed them up at any time for many years past; and in their opinion our royalty is not only a bauble in itself, but the prime cause and support of the great amount of injurious baubleism that characterises the government of the country throughout—of an hereditary legislature, a State church, an unfairly privileged aristocracy, and a gross system of sinecurism. They regard the royal office as worse than useless, believing that its formalities impede the work of legislation, that its costliness tends to impoverish the nation, and its very existence to degrade true self-respect by making "loyalty" consist—in language at least—in fulsome adulation. To their thinking the Sovereign is the mere cipher of an unnecessary function, or at the best an ornamental official whose services, judged on the most liberal scale, would be amply paid by the salary of a master of the ceremonies.

These views and the feelings arising out of them were entertained by the present generation of working men with respect to royalty when it had to be considered in the person of the Sovereign only ; but as demand after demand came to be made upon the public purse on behalf of the royal family, the ill feeling was more and more intensified, until at last over the question of the dowry to the Princess Louise it broke out in bitter protest and reviling, and assumed the shape of an organized and formidable opposition. For though the formal opposition to it in parliament, appeared a fiasco, the opposition in the country *was* formidable. Though neither those who had to combat and overcome this opposition, nor any save those inside the working classes, could be fully aware of the extent and intensity of the feeling of which it was the outcome, it is tolerably evident that they knew the matter to be much more serious than they cared to admit. When, in asking parliament to vote the dowry, the Prime Minister spoke of the opponents to it in the country as " rare exceptions," he was rather arrogant than ignorant ; he would not have adopted the defensive and explanatory tone he did, had he really believed that the anti-dowry party had been rare exceptions. The attitude of the leading newspapers upon the question was in close keeping with that of the First Minister. They, too, affected to believe that the objectors to the dowry were a singular few; but side by side with rhapsodical leaders setting forth the overflowing and unanimous delight that the nation would feel in granting the dowry, were notices of anti-dowry meetings, and of members of parliament having been put to the question on the subject by their constituents. These papers must have known from details in the provincial journals that the meetings to protest against the dowry were of a more important character than would fairly be gathered from their brief intimations that such meetings had been held; and while they eagerly seized upon the slightest opportunity for making the opposition appear weak or divided, they persistently declined to insert letters explaining or defending its views. This mode of procedure upon the part of the monarchical portion of the press has, however, been chiefly detrimental to the cause of monarchy.

It is these papers that have been mainly instrumental in giving rise to the existing Republican movement. They stung latent feeling into passionate activity, furnished Republican journals and speakers with the best " points " they could possibly have for purposes of agitation; and by the diversity of their justifications of the dowry, made palpable the weakness of the case for the defence. Some of them based their support of the dowry simply on sentimental grounds: the Princess was young, amiable,

pretty, and was making a love match ; therefore to
grumble at her being dowered by the country was un-
chivalrous. Others pleaded precedent : her sisters had
received dowries, then why should she be refused one ?
To object in her case would look like a desire to punish
her for marrying the man of her heart. Others, again,
taking a bolder tone, said that to object to the dowry was
nothing more or less than dishonest, since its payment
would only be the stipulated fulfilment of the terms of a
contract between the country and the Crown. This being
to many people an astonishing statement, inquiries
naturally began to be made as to where the writings of
the contract were to be seen. Such inquiries were doubtless considered "too blessed particular," but they had to
be answered in some fashion ; and so these papers, modi-
fying their tone, said : " Well, the writings were not to
be seen at all ; the contract was not a written one, but an
implied one "—though the alleged implication was certainly not self-evident. The straits to which the defending journals were driven by the inherent weakness of
their case are perhaps, however, most strikingly exemplified
by a statement in the *Pall Mall Gazette* for December 10,
1870. All the other papers taking the same side on the
dowry question were at one with each other and the anti-
dowerists in taking it for granted that the £30,000
wedding portion and £6,000 a year asked for were regarded as a substantial matter by all parties concerned ;

that the income was to be granted *as an income,* on the understanding that it was required for the usual purpose of an. income—the support of those drawing it. But according to the *Pall Mall Gazette* this was not only a mistaken and unworthy view of the case, but the working classes in particular were aware that it was so. Speaking of a resolution of the Land and Labour League, the *Pall Mall* observed that "the working classes know that the dowry to a royal Princess on her marriage is neither given nor accepted on account of its money's worth, but rather as a tribute of respect and affection to the family of the Sovereign." To point out that this is sheer nonsense would be a work of supererogation. That any person writing in a high-class journal like the *Pall Mall Gazette* could have really entertained such a belief is not for a moment to be credited. Many assertions and arguments of this kind were palpably aimed at the working classes, and in some cases, as for instance that just cited, "fathered" upon them; and it should therefore be no matter for wonder that the fact of their finding themselves considered to be so easily gullible by self-evident nonsense should have aroused in them a strong feeling of antagonism.

The simulated ecstasy, slavish tone, and meaningless, unmanly drivelling in the daily papers in reporting the Lorne marriage, upon which the *Saturday Review* commented with such contemptuous scorn at the time, need not be dwelt upon here; but it may be mentioned that these "gushing" articles were especially effective in intensifying the ill-feeling towards royalty. "To-day," said the *Times* on the morning of the wedding, "a ray of sunshine will gladden every habitation in this island, and force its way even where uninvited. A daughter of the people in the truest sense of the word is to be married to one of ourselves. The mother is ours, and the daughter is ours. We honour and obey the Queen; we crown her and do her homage, we pray for her, and work for her, and fight for her; we accept her as the dispenser of blessings and favours, dignity and honours; we share her joys and are cheered by her consolations." Now, the assumption of the universality of such a tone of feeling as that embodied in the above "loyal" outburst was not justifiable by even the most liberal interpretation of literary licence. The assertions were untrue not only in the letter, but in the spirit. In hundreds of thousands of "habitations in this island" the marriage was regarded as a gloomy, not a sunshiny matter, so far as it concerned the dwellers in the habitations—a thing which saddled the country with a further large payment to the idle rich, though millions of the industrious poor were in a state of semi-starvation. By the working-class section of "the people," the Princess was not held to be in any sense their daughter, but rather a daughter of the horse-leech, of whom they had chiefly heard in association with a cry

of " Give, give," and they certainly looked upon her husband more in the light of a vampire fastened upon them
than as one of themselves. Being unused to making fine
distinctions, they connect the office-holder with the
office ; and speaking in this sense they do not honour and
do not pray for the Queen ; and though they do work for
her and hers, they are very decidedly of opinion that it is
more the pity that they should have to do so. And however unorthodox the belief may be, their idea is that not
she, but a higher, is the " Dispenser of blessings."

These were the real feelings of the working classes
with regard to the marriage and royalty generally. By
means of meetings, protests, and such press organs as
would make known their views, they gave expression to those feelings ; and that after this they should
find themselves represented as going into ecstasies of joy
over the event naturally enraged them. To them such
misrepresentation seemed a scornful challenge ; and the
answer to it has been the organization of a Republican
movement, which, however much pooh-pooh'd in its
earlier stages, will ultimately make itself felt. Taking
the dowry question in the light of a political contest, the
technical victory of the monarchical party was one of the
kind that are more disastrous than defeat. If, when it
became evident that there was a strong feeling in the
country against granting the dowry, the demand for it
had been withdrawn, that, combined with the fact that

the marriage was one in which natural affection had been allowed to override the unnatural Royal Marriage Act, would have made royalty more popular with the working classes than it had been for many years; now it is infinitely more unpopular than it has ever been before with the present generation. Those immediately concerned in the dowry business were not well served. Had they been allowed to know the extent of even the public opposition, it is only fair to them to take it for granted that they would themselves have insisted upon the withdrawal of the claim made upon their behalf; while, could they have known how they were talked about in thousands of workshops and by tens of thousands of firesides, they would have shrunk from touching a penny of the money as though it had been the price of blood. Curses both loud and deep were heaped upon them as callous despoilers of the poor. " The rattle of the royal begging-box," " Out-door relief," Able-bodied paupers," " Royal leeches," " Royal spongers," were the mildest terms of contempt employed in speaking of the subject. It became a stock workshop joke to speak of setting up the Marquis of Lorne as a greengrocer, or teaching him this or that handicraft to enable him to earn an honest living for himself and wife without coming upon the public. Men—decent, steady artisans, and not at all the fearsome kind of creatures whom it pleased " loyal " caricaturists to depict as the only objectors to the dowry—speaking amid applauding circles of shopmates, wished that "the whole tribe of royalty were under the sod;" while women, mothers themselves, prayed that its women might be made unfruitful, so that the race of royal paupers might not be increased. All this may seem both very trivial and very coarse, but it is both broadly and literally true; and though the task of telling it is an ungrateful one, we think it is a state of things which should be made known and faced, not slurred over. The spirit that prompts such ill wishes may be an evil one, but, bad or good, it is the one that is abroad among the working classes. With them, at any rate, the name and fame of the country's royalty has become a thing of scorn. Nor does the feeling end at that point. In connection with the subject of the dowry the question passed from mouth to mouth, "Why should we, who can scarcely find bread for ourselves, be forced to contribute, in however small a degree, to the sumptuous maintenance of others whom we have never seen, and who are not doing and have never done us or the State any service?" As might have been expected, such questioning, once started, soon went beyond the point out of which it had immediately arisen. "Why," working men went on to ask themselves and each other, "should they be forced to contribute to the support of royalty at all? What use was it? what return did it make to the country for the money it drew from it? It was admitted upon all hands that it performed no part whatever in the *practical* work of government, and for what else should the nation be called upon to pay it an annual sum far exceeding in amount the aggregate salaries of the entire executive ? The story of its life from day to day and year to year was to be found in the columns of the *Court Circular,* and to a common understanding it was hard to see how anything recorded of it there could be construed as being of service to the community at large. To men looking at it in this utilitarian spirit the whole thing appeared an all too costly fetish, the extinguishment of which would be a blessing.

Even in the overwhelming numerical defeat of the parliamentary opposition to the dowry the Republicans hold that there was a comparative moral victory for them. They point to Mr. Gladstone's laboured justification of the demand, and to the noticeably large number of liberal M.P.'s who were conspicuous by their absence on the night of division, with the purpose, it is reasonable to conclude (from the evasive answers given by some of them when questioned by their constituents as to how they would vote over the dowry), of being able to say that they did not vote *for* the dowry ; though that plea will avail them but little when the time for another election arrives.

In discussing the anti-dowry agitation, the *Saturday Review*—which, though strongly monarchical, did not descend to the pitiful twaddling of the other papers on the same side—observed that there was no room in England for a semi-royal caste. This was a remark that went very much to the heart of the business. In the existing state of public opinion there is no room for such a caste, and the working classes have instinctively seen this all along. To persevere in forcing that caste upon them beyond the point at which they showed their patience was exhausted, was a mistake—in the interests of royalty. Monarchy centred in the Sovereign alone and guided by a policy of non-intrusion might have passed without serious challenge for many years to come; but royalty becoming a caste, and constantly asking for money on behalf of its members, was a thing which the "responsible advisers" of the Crown might have known would lead to the whole institution being brought into question, and critically examined in regard to the proportion between its cost and its utility to the country. That it could successfully bear examination on that ground its most enthusiastic admirers would not, we suppose, attempt to maintain; and its advisers are therefore responsible for thrusting it into a false and dangerous position. It is on this ground that the working classes *have* weighed it, and they believe they have found it utterly wanting. Their unanimous verdict is that its cost to the nation is very great, its usefulness *nil*. Further, they are of opinion that it is worse than merely negatively useless. As they read certain facts, it seems to them that the nominal constitution and policy of the State are prostituted to give still more of the public money to royalty than is avowedly voted to it. In the House of Commons the Minister for War gravely defends the maintenance of sinecure colonelcies on the ground that they are reserved as prizes and rewards for specially meritorious and distinguished officers ; and yet they are bestowed upon the Prince of Wales, the Duke of Cambridge, and other more or less close connections of royalty simply because they are such connections, since it would puzzle even a courtly minister to point out their special merits or distinguished services as soldiers. Again, a government calling itself liberal, and taking office with retrenchment and economy as their watchwords, answers unemployed and starving workmen who apply for aid to emigrate, that they have no money for such a purpose, while at the same time they give thousands to fit up royal yachts and pay the travelling expenses of royalty's relations.

In proof of the argumentative strength of their case, the Republicans refer to the manner in which those who profess to answer them evade the point really at issue. The advocates of monarchy do not say that royalty *is* useful, or is *not* costly. What they say is, that practically we have the best Republic in the world ; that, even with the expense of our royalty, the total cost of our government is probably less than that of America, since, under the system of the latter, every member of the legislature is paid ; and that, even if the cost of royalty was abolished to-morrow, it would not relieve the taxation of the country to any appreciable extent. Or else they ask, " Would you, by attempting to subvert monarchy, bring about such a state of affairs as we have lately seen in France ?" To this the Republicans reply, that though, as compared with other monarchical governments, ours may be considered as of a Republican character—that though the sinecurism which is fostered by it may perhaps be less costly and injurious to the country than the extensive jobbery perpetrated by political wire-pullers in America, and though under it there is as great liberty of the subject as in any country—that though all this may be, it is altogether beside the question if brought forward as a justification for continuing to burden the country with the expense of a royalty whose part in the work of government is a legal fiction. If the fact of our members of parliament serving for nothing brings the entire cost of our government within that of the great Transatlantic Republic, the English Republicans reply, that it is only to money being paid to non-workers that they object. If our present scale of expenditure, or even a greater, were necessary to secure efficient Prime Ministers, Chancellors, &c., they would not have a word to say against it. As to the non-payment of our members, many of the Republicans are of opinion that it would perhaps be better for the nation if we did pay them. Some of our present class of members treat their office as an honorary one, valuing it only as giving them a handle to their name; while it is quite an understood thing that others use their position to promote some sectional "interest," rather than—and if need be at the cost of—the interests of the nation. And for such neglect and dereliction of duty a conscience-salving excuse is, that members are not paid. That the remission of the money-cost of royalty would not afford any sensible relief to the individual tax-payer is, say the Republicans, no answer to the economical argument for its suppression. That plea, if admitted, would put an end to all attempts at economy in State management. Because you cannot cut down expenditure by millions at a stroke, that is no reason why you should not retrench upon a smaller scale if there is an opening for doing so. Besides, the Republicans further argue on this point: if the money now paid to royalty were applied to organize State assisted emigration, or some other scheme of that kind, thousands of the poor might be immediately, sensibly, and permanently benefited; our colonies or waste lands made more valuable; and tax-payers *ultimately* relieved to an extent that would be worth considering individually.

To the question, "Do you want to bring about a revolution in this country?" the Republicans generally would reply: "Only a political revolution, led up to and carried through by political pressure and agitation." This would

in substance be the answer of the grand majority, but
there are some within the body who would probably give
a more extreme reply.   Here and there among the working classes will be found men whose political ideas are
summed up in the exclamation, that a " thundering good
revolution is what is wanted in this country," and that if
" there was one to-morrow they would throw down their
tools and join it."   But these are simply ignorant, self-
willed, violent-tempered men, who would talk in the
same fashion on any other subject on which they happened
to feel strongly.   Though they talk explosively, it is
exceedingly doubtful whether, if it came to a practical
question, they would be found to have even the will to
make a revolution ; and it is abundantly certain that in
any case they have neither the knowledge nor the power
necessary for doing so.   They have not the slightest idea
of warlike organization ; they are too hot-tempered and
open-mouthed to be members of secret societies ; and as
they generally manage to exhibit their violent and intolerant character in connection with workshop or trade
or benefit club affairs, their class know them too well to
let them become leaders.

Then there are the stagey, fanfaronnading Republicans
who hoist red flags, address each other as " Citizen," and
indulge in high-sounding revolutionary talk.   Taking
advantage of the spread of Republicanism among the working classes, this melodramatic clique has of late obtruded

itself before the public rather conspicuously, and by many
has been taken to be the whole instead of a very small
part of the Republican movement. If asked whether *they*
aimed at a revolution, these theatric Republicans would
likely enough answer that they did, but their doing so
would be of no material consequence. If they really have
any revolutionary aspirations, they are impotent to carry
them out. They are few in number, uninfluential, have
no man of mark among them, and, so far as any idea of
revolution is concerned, stand alone and out of sympathy.

The Republicanism existing among the general body of
the working classes—and it is only that we have had in
view in all we have been saying—is *not* of a revolutionary
character in the warlike sense of the term. It is not of
an ultra order even politically. Indeed Republicanism is
scarcely the proper name for it. Utilitarianism would be
more accurately expressive of its meaning. The best informed among the working-class Republicans, those best
qualified to form a judgment, and whose opinion and
example will have the greatest weight in influencing the
action of their fellows, are not inclined to cavil about a
word. They know that in many respects our constitution
is as beneficial to the country as any Republic could be,
and they would not care what the government was called
provided it was purged of the (costly) fictional and hereditary elements. That, however, if by any exertion or
pressure upon their part the thing can be effected, those

elements shall be eradicated, they are firmly resolved. Until they see some fair prospect of their removal they will be thoroughly dissatisfied, and their discontent will be increased, and their Republicanism made less and less moderate in tone, by delay. Before the dowry agitation many of those who are now labouring to establish Republican organizations among their fellow-workmen took no personal interest in politics, while the few who were actively political had no notion of being anything stronger than Radicals. The conduct of Ministers and the press over the Princess Louise dowry brought a wide-spread Republicanism to life as if by magic ; and should monarchical Ministers insist upon quartering the semi-royal caste upon the public purse to the bitter end, it would be hard to say to what it might not lead. This matter of semi-royalty is the sorest point of all with the Republicans. It alarms as well as irritates them. They see how prolific are the children of the Sovereign ; they know that their offspring stand in closer relation to the throne than some who are pensioned solely on the ground of such relationship ; and they ask themselves, Will it not be an intolerable burden upon the country to be forced to provide incomes for such a number ? And, to judge by late proceedings, they argue that only by completely disestablishing royalty can the nation hope to escape from being saddled with such a weight. At present the more moderate Republicans would be quite agreeable to disestablishment being coupled with equitable pecuniary compensation, but under another turn or two of the dowry screw they would probably incline to some more high-handed mode of procedure.

Though English Republicanism exists chiefly among the working classes, and is only openly avowed within those classes, traces of it are to be found in the middle classes, and the direction of the spread of its doctrine is upward. That some of the ablest writers and thinkers of the day are essentially Republicans is well known. In short, all the elements of a great Republican party lie ready; and were a Von Moltke in political organization to arise among the Republicans, he could make them the most powerful section in the State. Even without the aid of a supreme directing genius there is every probability of their speedily becoming a political party that will enforce consideration from others, if only on account of its strength. Stung by the tone of their opponents upon the dowry question, the Republicans spoke out with what many of their number now consider an unwise bluntness. "Let us," say these, "have some of the wisdom of the serpent in our proceedings. Let us not talk of a Republic, though we aim at the thing. Let us, if we can, make royalty as an old man of the sea around the neck of Ministers. Let us chop, and lop, and pare at its branches, and so weaken even if we cannot cut down the stem. Let us strain every nerve to return to Parliament a clique

sufficiently numerous to form a 'balance of power' between the two parties who now make a see-saw of government, and therefore also sufficiently strong to wring concessions from either of them by threatening to join the
others on any closely-fought party question. Let us do in
a political Rome as political Romans do. Let us be trim-
mers and intriguers. Let us aid the Liberals of the period
so far as their ultimatum is a step in our direction; let us
join with the Radicals as far as they will go with us, and
carry ourselves as much farther as we can force a way
single-handed." This is the counsel that is being given.
As, under existing circumstances, it is the most practical,
the line of action indicated in it will, in all probability,
be adopted in substance. Whether, however, such a comparatively "mild" policy will be adhered to for any considerable length of time is another question, since, so far
as may be judged from "precedent," Ministers will soon
be making further requisitions upon behalf of royalty.

That among those whose political cry is now Republicanism there are some who have wrong and foolish ideas
upon the subject—who think that under a Republic all
things are necessarily pure, and every man sure of constant work and a comfortable living—that there are
English Republicans holding such ideas as these, no
candid person having a knowledge of the opinions existing
among the working classes will for a moment attempt to
deny. Nor would one with such a knowledge deny, either,

that others, though calling themselves Republicans, are really levellers—men who, if they had their own way, would not be content with merely stopping the granting of State pensions to non-workers, but would likewise try to annex portions of self-earned incomes; who profess to be at a loss to understand *why* any other man should have more than them, and to consider it a perversion of the laws of nature that other men do have more than them. It is equally true, too, that the weekly newspaper which is the chief " organ " of Republicanism is often blatant and scurrilous, and habitually shows even a greater disregard than newspapers generally for the courtesy that should characterise honest political discussion. In short, English Republicanism, while having its good points, has also its blots, of which these are the chief. But they are only its blots : they do not, as many people suppose, constitute the thing itself. Among the working classes Republicanism has superseded Radicalism. Those who form the bulk of the Republicans do not expect impossibilities from a Republic, and are not so foolish as to hold levelling doctrines; while the better educated among them, even when agreeing with the arguments of the newspaper referred to, deplore and condemn its bad taste—not only *as* bad taste, but also as being an injury to the cause of Republicanism, since there can be little doubt that the coarse personality, violent invective, and bombastic tone of Republican journals and orators hitherto, have been instrumental in causing the higher class of Republican writers and thinkers to hold aloof from any movement for practical organization.

Even with all its present imperfections on its head, however, English.Republicanism is not a thing to be contemptuously "daft aside." On the contrary, anyone acquainted with the real facts of the case, and at all skilled in reading the signs of the times, will understand that it is a thing that will be dangerous to treat with either real or affected contempt. In so far as Republicanism means utilitarianism in government, the spirit of the age in this country tends towards it. In time it *must* become the predominating opinion practically, even if not nominally. Any danger to the State that there may be in it would lie in its being goaded into premature attempts to assert its supremacy. It has great thinkers in its ranks, and hosts willing to serve its principles disinterestedly ; but as yet it has not statesmen capable of carrying on the practical work of government, and until it has them it would be a disaster for it as well as for the nation at large if by any *coup* or fluke it was able to seize the reins of power. Acting statesmen are bound in the interests of all concerned to resist the too rapid advance of Republicanism, but they are equally bound not to oppose it in a manner that is calculated to urge it to extreme courses. The rate and manner of its progress is in a great measure in their hands. The Republicans do not expect any great or sudden concessions. They have no notion of anything in the shape of dethronement. They do not aim at taking away or reducing the present payment to royalty. What they seek—looking at matters practically, and having regard to the spirit of compromise that so largely enters into English politics—is to prevent the cost of monarchy being *increased;* to keep it strictly within its openly and directly avowed limits; and generally to pave the way to such a state of affairs and opinion that when another than the now reigning Sovereign came to be dealt with, a materially different arrangement—possibly an amicably settled abdication—could be effected. If they find themselves making reasonable advances in this direction, all will be well. If they find that they are defied, and their views set at nought, there will be a repetition of such work as there was before the repeal of the Corn-laws—perhaps worse.

In conclusion, we repeat that to believe that the anti-royalists in England are " rare exceptions " is a dangerous error. Republicanism is now practically the universal political creed of the working classes—the classes who, when they had not a tithe of the political power they have now, forced free trade and reform from the obstructives who stood in the way of those measures as long as they dared.

*   *   *   *   *

So the article stood in *Fraser's Magazine* for June, 1871 ; and though since that time the " cry " of Republicanism

has been comparatively silent, the Republican spirit has
been spreading and increasing in strength, as witness the
fact that while only three members of Parliament ventured to vote against the Louise dowry, eleven voted
against the "provision" for Prince Arthur, and a still
greater number for a substantial reduction in the amount
of that provision.

Even those who have been most willing to shut their
eyes to the fact, or most ready, from motives of interest
or policy, to pooh-pooh its significance, must, we think,
by this time be pretty well convinced that it is now an all
but universal opinion among the political section of the
working classes, that the Republican is better than the
Monarchical form of government; that it would be materially beneficial to the people at large were a Republic
substituted for the existing Monarchy in this country;
and that to work towards the carrying out of such a substitution is not only a permissible, but a highly laudable
and patriotic thing. That such is the case no observant
person, having a practical acquaintance with the working
classes, can fail to see, or, if candid, will attempt to deny;
and whatever may be thought of the opinion or those
holding it, we take it that it will be agreed upon all
hands that, seeing how prevalent it is, and that it might
possibly become a groundwork of social disturbance, it is
highly desirable that there should be as little misconception as possible as to the ideas upon which the opinion is

founded. The debate (?) upon Sir Charles Dilke's motion relating to the Civil List showed that a good deal of misconception does exist upon the point. Some of the speeches upon that occasion made it apparent that there is a tendency to a dangerously contemptuous over-estimation of the *degree* of mere class prejudice, and ignorance of the facts of the case, involved in the notions upon which the working classes base their belief that it would be greatly to their advantage to have the Monarchy disestablished and disendowed, and a Republican form of government put in its place. It is, therefore, worth while in the present connection to make a few observations upon the parts of the debate in question which more particularly bear upon the point of the Republicanism of the working classes. As a preliminary, let us repeat that, in speaking of the opinion of the working classes, we do not refer to the speeches of professional agitators or self-dubbed "leaders of the people," or the proceedings of peddling mutual admiration societies, who frame resolutions with a We-the-People-of-England air, and contrive to get them into the newspapers. When we speak of working-class opinion, we have in view the spontaneously expressed opinion of the rank and file of the working classes. With this understood, we come to the debate. Mr. Fawcett, referring to Sir Charles Dilke's Newcastle speech, observed that he felt that it " had done harm to the Republican movement, by misleading the working classes into the opinion that their poverty was due to what might be called a certain amount of extravagance about the Court." Now, in this instance it was Mr. Fawcett's feelings that misled *him.* Neither Sir Charles Dilke's speech nor anything else has led the working classes into holding such an opinion. They do not hold it. Little educated as they are, limited as is their range of knowledge, wrong-headed and unjust as are many of their political notions, they have still a sufficient common-sense acquaintance with primary social causes to be perfectly aware that the poverty so largely existing among the class is not, could not be, due to such a comparatively insignificant thing as the cost of royalty. They know that if the money cost of the monarchy were remitted to the nation to-morrow, the individual tax-payer would not, from a mere money point of view, be appreciably bene-fited, and they are not so prejudiced against royalty as to suppose that it tends in any way or degree to impoverish the nation, except by taking money from it. They do not attribute to it any specially baneful influence upon, or interference with, the law of population, or think that it stands in the way of invention or enterprise. The only manner in which they associate the idea of their poverty with Court extravagance is in arguing that, as the expenditure upon monarchy is for the most part upon a now meaningless pageant, it is all the more wasteful, sinful, and indefensible in a country in which there is so much and such extreme poverty as there is in England. While they would attack monarchy upon its money side, believing that to be its most vulnerable point, the only substantial point now left to it, and for which alone it struggles to live on: while they would make it their point of attack, their fundamental objections to the continuance of the monarchical form of government go far deeper than a mere question of the amount of money involved. They object to it that whatever of practical utility there may once have been in it has now gone from it. That though it may have gathered *momentum* enough from the old times to still keep it going after a fashion, it has no longer any *motive power*, has no really natural or healthy vitality, though still admitting of being occasionally galvanised into a sort of puppet life. That it impedes and unnecessarily formalises the actual work of government, and is the cause of what ought to be one of the noblest features of a national constitution being basely prostituted—the object to which it *is* prostituted. For, as has already been pointed out, offices and emoluments, that it is a breach of the spirit of the constitution to bestow upon any but those who have specially distinguished themselves in doing the State some service, are openly bestowed upon men who it is not even pretended have served the State, and whose only claim to distinction lies in the accident of their being members or connections of the royal family. These are the really important grounds on which the working classes desire to see the monarchical system effaced in England, and it is only in connection with these that they regard its costliness as a grievance. If they believed that the monarchical form of government so called was really any "form of government," took any effective part in, or was in any degree necessary to, the practical work of governing the country, they would not consider it dear at the price. But to sum up their opinion of the monarchy of this country in one word, they believe it to be a *sham*—a nationally injurious, degrading, and costly sham—and it is in that belief that they seek to displace it.

In the course of his speech in the debate of which we are speaking, Mr. Mundella paradoxically defended monarchy, on the ground that our government is "more republican in essence than that of any other country in the world." Well, the working classes fully admit this, but their deduction from it is directly opposed to Mr. Mundella's. They regard it as one of the strongest points of their case against monarchy. They say in effect —We *are* practically a republic; even the supporters of royalty admit that. As regards the actual and responsible work of government, the introduction of the Sovereign's name is a mere legal fiction. Whatever stronger or more practical proof than this could there be that monarchy's day has gone by in this country! And seeing that it is shelved and set aside as regards *doing*, why should it still be continued in *having?* Why should we still be burdened with its cost, and outraged by the malappropriation, for its benefit, of State appointments that are intended to reward merit, not "the accident of an accident?"

Speaking of the recognition by the working classes of the fact that the government of the country is in essence a republican one, leads up to Mr. Gladstone's speech in the Civil List debate. In the course of that speech he observed that the first duty of anyone descanting upon the Civil List before a miscellaneous audience was "to produce on the minds of his hearers the recollection that, with respect to the arrangements of the Civil List, there is no responsibility whatever, and there can be no discredit whatever attaching to the Sovereign. The Government and Parliament alone are responsible for it." Now, if Mr. Gladstone supposes that the working classes are not aware of this, or have not realised to what an extent *he* was responsible for the late addition of £21,000 a year to the income of the royal family, he is seriously mistaken. They *do* believe that the members of the royal family are personally greedy of money, but they know that a Prime Minister who had been so minded could have stood between them and the gratification of their greed. They know that Mr. Gladstone did not so stand between them, and one of their chief grievances against him is, that since he has been Prime Minister he has—

" Sir Pandarus of Troy become "

to the money lusts of the reigning family. They think,
too, that they know the value and *meaning* of his shuffle
in refusing to give the desired information concerning the
Civil List on the ground that it was asked for by Sir
Charles Dilke, and they believe that the whole disgraceful
conduct of the House of Commons upon the occasion of
the debate—the cock-crowing, yelling, and persistent
howling down of the speakers upon Sir Charles Dilke's
side—was designedly based upon the principle of abusing
the plaintiff, because there was no answer to his case. It
was all very well for Mr. Gladstone to try to make a little
capital by a comparison between the cost of royalty at
this day and in the days of the Georges; but he should
have remembered that the present is a time in which, as
Burke put it, "men will not suffer bad things because
their ancestors have suffered worse."

What has been said here of English Republicanism is
no mere expression of personal opinion. It is a *statement*
of the views generally prevailing among working men,
and seeing the importance of the subject upon which
those views bear, and the misunderstanding that exists
among other classes of society respecting them, we believe
that many even of those who are most strongly opposed
to them will agree with us in thinking that, right or
wrong, they ought to be plainly made known.

THE ENGLISH WORKING CLASSES AND
THE PARIS COMMUNE.

"Alas! of fearful things
'Tis the most fearful when the people's eye
Abuse hath cleared from vain imaginings;
And taught the general voice to prophesy
Of Justice armed, and Pride to be laid low."
                                    WORDSWORTH.

TO those opposed to the idea of attempting to substitute any form of Republican for Monarchical government, in countries where the latter is already the established form, it seemed opportune that the cry of the working classes of this country for a republic—arising out of the opposition to the Louise-Lorne dowry—should be coincident in time with the Communist war in Paris. That war was a terrible thing—a thing that might very fitly be presented as a "horrid example" to the population of any Monarchical country in which there was known to be political dissatisfaction among the bulk of the people. As a horrid example, that war was held up to the working classes of England. They were asked with triumphant significance, whether tbis was what they

wanted, and told that "this" was what Republicanism
really meant; that such a state of things was a necessary
result of Republican ideas if carried to their legitimate
conclusion. This it must be admitted was a tolerably clever
piece of party sophistry, and it had considerable effect in
silencing the working classes; for as there was no practical question to be immediately decided, men did not
care about needlessly obtruding opinions upon others,
who either were, or affected to be, horrified by them, and
insisted upon confounding them with a desire for blood-
shed. That this cleverly made "point" raised a side
issue, and a misleading one, those making use of it were
doubtless aware. They were careful not to ask the working classes whether apart from the war—which was only
an incidental and, to a great extent, accidental phase of
the general question—they approved of the broad principles and aims of the Communists. That they did
approve of them was what was really feared, and there
was more ample justification for such fear than was
probably supposed. The working classes of this country
did sympathise with the Commune, though not upon
strictly Communistic grounds. In what feelings and
beliefs their sympathy was founded we will try to make
clear.

Average English workmen are not so political as
Continental, and especially French workmen are. Their
knowledge of governmental constitutions is limited to a

general idea of the differences between the monarchical and republican forms. Their capability of political feeling is dormant until roused by some incidents, or series of incidents, that at once raises their anger, and points to some person or persons against whom it can be directed. They have not the type of mind for which theoretical or philosophical politics have fascinations, or the habits of life which lead to the interchange of political ideas and the keeping alive and intensifying of political feeling. Of late they have come to know that among the ideas of regenerative social systems there is one of a *Commune,* having as its leading object that of placing the labouring classes in a relatively better position, not only towards the non-productive classes, but also towards capitalists, as sharers in the results of productive labour ; and that is about the extent of what they do know about it. Of such things as St. Simonism and Fourierism, they have, as a rule, never heard ; and in any case they have no knowledge of their principles. Their knowledge of the fundamental principles of general political economy is equally scanty, though in this last respect they are probably not more deficient than the majority of Continental workmen, whose minds are continually exercised with ideas of political panaceas for all the social ills of the working classes. Just at present their chief political wish is to unhorse monarchy in this country ; but in a general way their political thoughts and aspirations, though they scarcely recognise them as being strictly political, turn exclusively upon improving the position of labour in relation to capital. And this they seek to accomplish by direct action—as, for instance, by strikes and the strengthening of trades-unions—and not by the establishment of entirely new social systems.

Such men as these, it will be easily understood, could not be, so to speak, *en rapport* with the Paris Communists *as Communists*. This average portion of the working classes is the little educated one, below it is the uneducated, above it the better educated section of the general body. Those among them who take an interest in political matters do understand sufficient both of the principles and details of Communism to be able to form an opinion for themselves concerning its merits, and they are opposed to it as a technical system of society. They believe that, carried to its legitimate conclusion, it would make the skilful and thrifty workman suffer for those who are neither. There are thousands of well-to-do workmen, men who own houses, have shares in building societies, and money in banks; men also who, by reason of the " push " and energy which have, as a rule, enabled them to accumulate money or property, are among the most influential of their class and with their class, and these men are keenly opposed to anything that tends to trench upon the "sacredness" of individual property, or about which there is any savour of the levelling doctrine. Moreover they are of opinion that, though Communism may be a noble idea and a theoretic possibility, it is not practically workable on any considerable scale.

But while the working classes generally had no particular sympathy with the Paris Commune, simply as such, they entertained a warm and very decided sympathy with the Communists on the broader ground that they believed them to be thorough patriots and true republicans. They regarded them with admiration as being men having the courage of their opinions to the extent of fighting and dying for them, and with gratitude as being the soldiers of the general cause of the unprivileged against the privileged classes, and the boldest foes of the hereditary principle in government. The point, however, on which the English working classes were perhaps most unreservedly and emphatically in sympathy with the Paris Commune was that of the latter's avowed desire to extinguish international rivalries ; and their being so illustrates some of the characteristic differences between English and Continental workmen to which we have referred. In seeking to effect this object the foreign workmen have, among their other ideas on the subject, some sublime ones about universal brotherhood and the like ; but so have not the English workmen. Their motive in wishing to bring about a "federation of the world" is entirely a practical, some people would say a

sordid one.   Through the agency of the Workmen's
International Association the working classes of this
country generally, and the trade unionists in particular,
are striving to effect this extinguishment; but they took
up and are persevering in the object simply as a phase
of the question of Labour *versus* Capital.   They have
arrived at the conclusion—the soundness or unsoundness
of which need not be argued here—that only by friendly
relations and joint action with "the foreigners" can they
hope to make any permanently better terms with capital.
The capitalists, they reason, play off the foreigners against
them.   The mechanical schoolmaster has been abroad, the
mechanical arts have spread and are spreading.   Branches
of trade of which England had once practically a monopoly are now carried on extensively in various parts of
the Continent, where labour is cheaper than here.   Some
of the more thoughtful among English artisans have of
late years come to see that strikes, even when successful
for the time being, have proved ultimately detrimental to
the interests of labour in this country.   English manufacturers tendering for contracts, in the face of wages
forced from them by strikes, were cut out by foreigners;
and worse still, in some instances English capitalists, after
being engaged in contests with labour, have established
factories abroad, and employed foreign labour to produce
the same goods they had previously done at home.   It is
in connection with these matters that the English work-

men are so eager to extinguish international rivalries, so willing to do their part in sinking them. Knowing that to bring about a common good feeling, conjoint action, and a fusion of interests among the working classes throughout the world, was a chief object of the Commune; that some of the leaders of the Commune were also leading men in the Workmen's International Association; knowing this, they sympathised very heartily with them on that point, and wished for their success as a means to that end.

The general idea of the English working classes with regard to the Communist rising was, however, something like this: when the war with Germany was over, there was the royalty of Germany safe in person and covered with glory; while the ex-Emperor of the French, though defeated, was still in a position to live in luxurious ease, and still evincing a desire to thrust himself upon the French nation again. The people of that nation at large had borne the bulk of the bitter suffering of the war. One result of the war, however, they fondly believed, had been to purge the country of the imperialism that could create such wars for purposes of dynastic ambition; and this to them seemed almost sufficient compensation for what they had gone through. But simultaneously with the election of Thiers's Republic came rumours of Orleanist and Bonapartist intrigues, and signs of the Republican ministers having an inclination to the imperial system, and particularly to that part of it which enabled the government to use the ignorant priest-ridden peasantry as an instrument for overruling the—at any rate comparatively—intelligent town populations.

The Communists might have been wrong; but they *did* believe that, though names might be altered, the old accursed thing of a special governing and privileged class would be forced upon the people again, unless the people themselves could prevent it. To attempt to prevent it was the object of the Communists in taking up arms. They wanted a republic in fact as well as name; they believed they were well on the way to it, and that a determined attitude, and, if need be, a determined fight, at the point they had reached, would enable them to attain their desire.

This, in the opinion of English workmen, was substantially the motive and meaning of the rising; and, despite all that has been said against the Communists, they (the English workmen) hold that they fought bravely and disinterestedly, and that their battle was, as we have said, the general battle of the unprivileged against the privileged classes. When Paris was taken there was the most passionate indignation among the working classes of this country at the manner in which Communist prisoners were butchered by the mercenary soldiery, whom shame at the inglorious figure they made when opposed to the Germans should, if nothing else did, have made merciful to their countrymen, who, whatever may be thought of their cause, fought with a bravery that extorted the admiration even of the most bitterly opposed to their political creed. Though the working classes did not approve of the manner in which the Communists destroyed the public buildings, they objected to the proceeding rather as being bad policy than as being, as others argue, utterly unjustifiable and condemnable. They remembered that, in the minds of the Communists, the churches and palaces would be inseparably associated with the sacerdotal tyranny and monarchical selfishness from which the people have suffered so much and so long; and it was as monuments of these things that they were destroyed, not in a spirit of mere vandalism. The working classes bear in mind, too, that, if the Communists slew those they held as hostages, it was not until their own prisoners had been slaughtered like beasts. It would have been infinitely more noble on the part of the Communists to have left such an act undone, though no credit would have been allowed to them even in that case. It was a stern deed and a bloody one, but, according to the laws governing such evil things, it was a justifiable one. Had it been committed by the hired soldiery of a monarchy, its harshness might have been condemned, but their right to do it would not have been questioned.

The victims of the act were avowedly held as hostages, and were saved alive long after the strict rule of warlike reprisals would have justified their execution. The conduct of the Versailles soldiers in persisting in the wanton slaying of unarmed Communist prisoners was what really led to the death of the hostages. To stigmatise the shooting of the hostages as assassination and murder, while calling the wholesale butchering of Communist prisoners executions, shows partisanship ; and the working-class idea on this point is that partisanship and a desire to misrepresent are what the leading English papers have, in varying degrees, shown in dealing with the Commune. Any one taking the general tone of English public opinion from the " organs " which are popularly supposed to embody it would have been led to the conclusion that horror and reprobation were the universal feelings in regard to the Commune. But any one who could have penetrated into working-class circles, who, let us say, could have sat with the men round workshop breakfast stoves, or in workshop dining or reading rooms, who could have followed them into the lodges of their trade and benefit societies and to their own firesides ; any one who could have done this in the Metropolis, and such districts as the Black Country, the Tyne, Clyde, and the manufacturing towns of Lancashire, would have found from the talk of the men that newspaper public opinion was the opinion of a section only ; that, as we have been pointing out, the sympathy of the people was with the Communists. What is said here is no mere expression of individual opinion; it is the generalized opinion of working men as expressed among themselves in the places in which they most do congregate. The intention of the article is not to insist that the opinions are right or dispute that they are wrong, but to point out that they do exist, and are firmly believed to be right by those who hold them.

In the tone of the English newspapers upon the Communist rising, the working classes saw a special significance. As we have already said, they have but little knowledge of the technicalities of political systems, but they have a considerable degree of the useful quality called "rough common sense;" and this enabled them to see that, whatever the rising in Paris might be called, or whatever might be its theoretic details, it was essentially a battle between "the two parties who still divide the world—of those who want and those who have." Knowing this, they saw from the tone of the English newspapers that "those who have" were banding together throughout Europe to give their moral support to those who were fighting the Commune; and so, independently of the instinctive feeling leading them thereto, they argued that it also behoved the party of "those who want" to band together, and throw in their sympathy with the Communists. At the same time, theirs was not a mere blind party sympathy. What their idea of the meaning of the rising was we have stated, and the monarchist intriguing that has been going on since the fall of the Commune furnishes the most ample justification of the belief of the Communists that the old thing was to be thrust upon them again. What the Communists wanted—what if granted to them would have prevented their rising—was perfectly just. Simply put, the sum of their demands was only that those who had been elected as Republicans should show themselves to be really Republicans. The real traitors to France were not the Communists, but those who, after being chosen by the people as Republicans, lent a too willing ear to monarchist intrigues.

In connection with this matter of the sympathy of the English working classes with the Paris Commune, it is a significant fact that that the English workmen find satisfaction and consolation in the belief that the Communists, though beaten, have not failed. They hold that—

They never fail who die in a great cause.

And to their thinking the Communist rising was a great, even if not a faultless, cause. They believe that the rising, though defeated in its immediate aim, will yet be a material caution to, and restraint upon, the "right divine" school, not only in France but throughout Europe. If it is, so much the better for the peoples of Europe; if it is not, so much the worse for the party of right divine.

The spirit that in France took the name of Communism is stalking abroad, and it is an evil one—one that, if not exorcised, will mean social disturbance, and may come to mean social destruction. It has entered into the minds of the English working classes, and is sinking deeper, and becoming more dangerous as it sinks. The very concessions that it might have been thought would have laid this spirit, have only served to embitter it. Repealed corn laws, and extended franchise, and other things of that kind that they have fought for and won, under the firm persuasion that their condition would be materially improved by them, have in result left matters pretty much as they were—the rich growing richer and the poor poorer. It is not, of course, the fault of other sections of society that such measures have failed to realise the expectations of the working classes, but the disappointing experience has embittered them against the present constitution of society. They say now that these things may be very well in their way, but that it is apparent that they do not go to the root of things, that it is mere frittering to be struggling for Acts of Parliament, that what is wanted is a thorough change. If asked what was the change they desired, they would be unable to give any definite answer. They do not know, and, still worse, they scarcely care; their feeling is, that no change that would arise out of a disruption of the present state of society could be worse for then, while any such change might easily be better for them. In this frame of mind they are likely to grasp at any specious plan that promised to bring about revolutionary changes beneficial to them; and still more likely to be reckless as to the means whereby it was sought to carry out such plans. One fixed idea, however, they have, and that is, that the present constitution of society is unfair to them, and that the power of regulating that constitution is monopolized by those whose interest it is to make it continue unfair, and who persistently act for their own interests, yielding nothing until it is extorted from them by fear, and even then trying to give only the name, not the substance of the thing. They believe that, before they can rise, the class which is composed of the rich, the titled, and the privileged must be brought down, and the power of governing and law-making wrested from them. They have come to be of opinion that between that class and their own there is a natural and deadly antagonism. Further, they believe that the other class hold the same view, and act upon it. In justification of this latter belief they point to such facts as the hesitation of English ministers to say decisively whether or not Communists flying to England would be treated as criminals or refugees; the manner in which English newspapers spoke of the Communists as a handful of ruffians, bloodthirsty scoundrels, and so forth, and of the cold-blooded murdering of the Communist prisoners without any form of trial.

If the feeling of the working classes of Paris upon this latter point may be judged by that of the working classes of this country, it may be safely said that the deaths of those prisoners will never be either forgotten or forgiven until they are avenged. The soldiers of the Commune, it is held, showed practically that their view of duty was—

> Like men to fight,
> And hero-like to die ;

but instead of being treated as prisoners of war, their blood was shed as that of beasts ; and if ever an opportunity comes—and it will be closely watched for—the shedding of it will be repaid in kind. The " officers and gentlemen" who ordered or allowed this butcher's work have sown the seeds of a harvest that their class are, in all probability, destined to reap in blood. The Commune has only been scotched, not killed. Its essential elements are left alive, and they will breed and brood, and under that name, or some other, break forth again.

The existence among the working classes of such opinions as those we have been speaking of is a thing that should be heedfully noted by society. Mr. Gladstone has expressed his belief that such opinions had only to be left unnoticed to sink into "that oblivion which was their destined and their proper portion." Whether or not oblivion is their " proper portion " is a question that need not be discussed here ; but leaving them unnoticed will certainly not make it their destined portion, and, with the Communist war staring the world in the face, it is wonderful how a really great statesman could think that it would. No person, we suppose, will attempt to argue that the Communist rising was the result of any hasty plot or mere passing impulse. The spirit and opinion that made it possible must have been existing and intensifying for years. As they were shared by millions, they must have been known to those opposed to them; and it can therefore only be concluded that they had been left unnoticed in the hope that they would sink, and ultimately in the belief that they had sunk, into oblivion. Otherwise it is impossible to account for Jules Favre making the fatal condition that the National Guard should be left armed; or the fact of the Thiers' Government being so ill-prepared for the rising, so slow to comprehend its extent after it had taken place. The policy of leaving unnoticed is a dangerous as well as a mistaken one. Those who won't see in such matters become in time those who cannot see; and they mistake the sinking into lethargy of their own perceptions for the sinking into oblivion of the opinions to which they are opposed.

That the views both of the French Communists and the English working classes are to a considerable extent chimerical is, of course, obvious to those who possess a comprehensive knowledge of political economy; but, unfortunately for themselves, the working classes have not this knowledge. They do not see that a mere reconstruction of present society on grounds more favourable to the interests of labour is really in the same category with, though upon a larger scale than, those measures which have proved to them, in comparison with their anticipation, a sort of Dead-Sea fruit. They imagine that there could be a form of government by means of which the labouring classes could be raised to and maintained in a position of material comfort. They fail to see that *any* form of government can only be *part* of a scheme of social regeneration ; that to depend on that alone is to overlook fundamental principles not only of political economy, but of *nature ;* principles that would speedily override every temporary expedient in the way of changed forms of government. But even those who can see that the working classes make the disastrous mistake of imagining a part, a mere detail, to be the whole, must admit that there is much in their ideas that to little-educated people must appear plausible ; while at least some of these ideas are certainly founded on principles of justice. It is the plausible portions that catch the minds of the working classes. Though there is undoubtedly much that is wrong in their ideas, they do not see it, and consequently the ideas are in their minds practically operative as fully right and just, and in their being so regarded lies the chief point of the whole matter as it affects society. It is the one great reason why the opinions should be made known, and why they should *not* be left unnoticed. To ignore them is not the way to deal with them, or prevent their culminating in violence. Those who would consign them to oblivion should show themselves willing to concede the parts of them that are just, and seek to qualify those holding them to understand that the other parts are erroneous. It is the duty of those in power to so deal with them. If they neglect this duty, or wilfully shut their eyes to the fact that such opinions largely prevail and are still spreading among the working classes, the responsibility will in a great measure be upon our rulers if ever we see such wild work in England as there has lately been in France.

THE TWO SIDES OF THE SOCIAL
IMPROVEMENT QUESTION.

"In place there is licence to do good and evil; whereof the latter is a curse: for in evil the best condition is not to will, the second not to care. But power to do good is the true and lawful end of aspiring; for good thoughts, though God accept them, yet towards men are little better than good dreams, except they be put in act; and that cannot be without power and place as the vantage-ground."—BACON.

THOUGH there is not, and though it is strongly disputed that there ever had been, a gift of prophecy, in the absolute sense of the phrase, it can scarcely, we think, be considered superstitious, or even impracticable, to believe that there are a few great minds to which are given a clearness and depth of insight, and a faculty for reading the inner meaning and ultimate tendency of past and passing events, such as enables them to infer the future from the present with an accuracy and far-reachingness, that when realisation comes seems nothing short of prophetic to lesser minds.

In the second part of *Henry the Fourth*, Shakespere makes his Earl Warwick say,—

> "There is a history in all men's lives
> Figuring the nature of the times deceased,

The which observed, a man may prophesy,
With a near aim, of the main chance of things
As yet not come to life."

And it is this relative, this *natural* gift of prophecy—
the prophecy of observation and deduction—that we speak
of as being not merely a possibility but an actuality.   In
its highest degree it is a very rare gift, so rare that it is
not given to every generation to witness an embodiment
of it, but we in this present day have undoubtedly one of
these highest gifted men in our midst—Carlyle.   "Like
reading some old prophet!" is a summing up that we
have more than once heard concerning his works; and
though the remark was intended to apply to the grandeur
of the manner of his writings, it might without hyper-
bolical exaggeration have been applied literally to the
matter of them.   So much distinctly foreshadowed in
them, at times when the superficial probabilities, the
only probabilities visible to ordinary minds, seemed to
point contrarywise—so much thus foreshadowed has come
to be accomplished fact, that we feel sure that many of
the thoughtful of his readers must hold with us that
where his utterances are prospective they are also prophetic in the sense we speak of.

To those holding this view, and watching the signs
and tendencies of the times, from the position of middle
or upper class Englishmen, it will in all probability seem
that we are with greater or lesser rapidity, but with

undoubted certainty, approaching the final struggle between rich and poor which Carlyle prospectively pictured
thirty-seven years ago. The Dandies and Drudges he
styles the two great sects of civilised society, and speaking of them says, "To the eye of the political seer, their
mutual relation, pregnant with the elements of discord
and hostility, is far from consoling. These two principles
of dandiacal self-worship or demon-worship, and poor-
slavish or drudgical earth-worship, or whatever that same
drudgism may be, do as yet, indeed, manifest themselves
under distant and nowise considerable shapes : nevertheless in their roots and subterranean ramifications they
extend through the entire structure of society, and work
unweariedly in the secret depths of English national
existence; striving to separate and isolate it into two
contradictory, uncommunicating masses.

" In numbers, and even individual strength, the poor-
slaves or drudges, it would seem, are hourly increasing.
The dandiacal, again, is by nature no proselytising sect ;
but it boasts of great hereditary resources, and is strong
by union; whereas the drudges, split into parties, have
as yet no rallying point ; or, at best, only co-operate by
means of partial secret affiliations. If indeed there were
to arise a *Communion of Drudges*, as there is already a
Communion of Saints, what strangest effects would follow
therefrom ! Dandyism as yet affects to look down on
drudgism ; but the hour of trial, when it will be practi-

cally seen which ought to look down, and which up, is
not distant.

" To me it seems probable that the two sects will one
day part England between them; each recruiting itself
from the intermediate ranks, till there be none left to
enlist on either side.   Those Dandiacal Manicheans, with
the host of Dandyising Christians, will form one body; the
Drudges gathering round them whosoever is Drudgical,
be he Christian or Infidel Pagan, sweeping up likewise
all manner of Utilitarians, Radicals, refractory Pot-
wallopers, and so forth, into their general mass, will form
another.

*   *   *   *   *

" I might call them too boundless and, indeed, unexampled electric machines (turned by the 'machinery of
society') with batteries of opposite qualities; Drudgism
the Negative, Dandyism the Positive : one attracts hourly
towards it and appropriates all the Positive Electricity of
the nation (namely, the Money thereof) : the other is
equally busy with the negative (that is to say, the
Hunger), which is equally potent.   Hitherto you see
only partial transient sparkles and sputters; but wait a
little, till the entire nation is in an electric state; till
your whole vital Electricity, no longer healthfully Neutral,
is cut into two isolated portions of Positive and Negative
(of Money and of Hunger), and stands there bottled up in

two World-Batteries! The stirring of a child's finger brings the two together, and then—What then?"

Put into a word, his own answer to this "What then?" is, Chaos; and certain it is, that if the batteries are ever allowed to become so fully and all absorbently charged with their respective forces, as is here pictured, nothing can prevent the explosion from taking place, or the result from being anything less than social chaos. And with the divinity that *did* hedge a sovereign, made mock of and set at nought, with monarchy and those who would form a breakwater around it, called upon to show cause for its existence, or at the least why, in having and holding, it should be allowed to be more than the fictional thing it is in doing; with the rising water of the rude rough sea of opinion among the drudgical sect, threatening to sap its foundations, and sweep away that other bulwark of the dandiacal body, the House of Lords; with labour wresting hardly-fought-against concessions from capital, the embodiment *par excellence* of the positive force of the dandiacal sect; with the recent social explosion in France staring the world in the face, and the Paris Commune even now rather scotched than killed; with the International numbering its members by millions, and showing—as it incidentally did in connection with the Newcastle strike— that it is a veritable and increasing power; and with statesmen (?)—those who are, so to speak, entrusted with the management of the safety-valves of the social batteries

—affecting to ignore or make light of all such matters. With so many and such significant things unmistakably indicating the direction in which the social currents are setting, it might, as we have said, be readily and reasonably concluded that we are rapidly approaching the explosive condition, that we are at any rate ripening towards explosion, even if we are not already fully ripe for it, and only awaiting the metaphorical touch of a child's finger to produce the crash. There are ample grounds for such a conclusion. To the unprejudiced observer outside the drudgical sect, that is to say the working classes, it may seem that there is *every* ground ; but to candid observers inside the working classes, the danger will appear by no means so imminent. They will know, though others may not, that one of the chief elements premised as necessary to the realisation of the explosive condition is as yet wanting, namely, "a communion of drudges." There is often a something of good in things evil, and though the want of unity among the working classes is on the whole a great evil, it is perhaps well that in the present state of knowledge, and class-feeling among them, that they are not in full community. If they were, the chaos-producing shock would in all probability be inevitable. They are working towards community, but it is to be hoped —there are good grounds for hoping—that by the time they have attained to it, they will have come to be so much less a drudgical sect—

without having become in any objectionable sense a
dandiacal one—that their motive forces will have ceased
to be dangerously antagonistic to those of other great
social bodies. That explosion will ensue if the social
forces as they now exist are not neutralised before they
reach the fully charged state, no reasonable person
observant of such matters can we think doubt; and, in
our opinion, there can be as little doubt that the
neutralising power must be the improvement—the material
and general improvement—of the condition of the working
classes.

That there is much room and need for such improvement, and that despite the comparatively little progress
in the matter that has resulted from all attempts to effect
it hitherto, the thing is possible of accomplishment, is
agreed upon all hands. Expressions of willingness to
contribute to its accomplishment are also universal. The
great question is, how is it to be done ? This is *the*
problem of the age, involving that other one of whether
or not we shall have social crash and chaos. Could any
man, statesman or other, satisfactorily solve this problem,
he would indeed be a " benefactor to his race." But the
probabilities are that no one man will solve it, that it
admits of no one-ideaed elucidation ; that many men will
have to contribute their thoughts ; many things work
their results to its solution. And it is in the hope that,
from having a practical knowledge of some of the least

well-known phases of the problem, we may be able to
contribute in even the smallest degree to the store of data
from which the solution will have to be deduced, that
we venture to take up so grave and important a subject.

In dealing with the question of the improvement of the
working classes, one most necessary thing is candour—a
plentiful lack of which is, as matters stand, to be observed
in most of the discussions upon the subject.   Special
pleading, mere party argument, and all attempts to make
the worse appear the better reason in the matter, are—
putting it on the lowest ground—a mistake.   They may
appear to serve some immediate and subsidiary purpose,
but ultimately and broadly they do not good but evil,
obstruct progress, and give rise to feelings of distrust,
insincerity, and bitterness.   It is, therefore, in no spirit
of unkindness, but merely with a view to candour, that we
say that the chief obstacle to the improvement of the
condition of the working classes is—the working classes.
Their ignorance and the manifold evils that are the
secondaries of it stand in their light and block the path
of reform.   They fail to see that as regards them a very
large proportion of the needed reform must be self-reform,
self-wrought, and involving self-sacrifice.   They have a
perniciously misleading notion of the limits—or rather of
the limitlessness—of the functions and capacities of
governments, which causes them to overlook or neglect
substantial and obtainable things, while wasting their

energies, embittering their spirits, and weakening their position, in pursuit of political will-o'-the-wisps. Though by reason of what was considered the non-natural or un-natural selection of associates in connection with them, the, for a time, celebrated and much-talked-of "seven points" of the Council of Workmen and Peers, brought together by Mr. Scott Russell, put other things of that kind into the shade, they were not altogether a new thing under the sun. About a month before they were made known to the world, an association calling themselves the London Republicans put forth a programme of eight points. Like all such associations it assumed a very pretentious air, and as a matter of course spoke in the name of the working classes, though really only authoritatively representing its own limited number of members. Still its manifesto embodied ideas which are largely prevalent among those of the working classes who take any active interest in politics, and will serve as an illustration of the visionary—and as visionary, injurious, and progress-delaying—views with regard to the functions of government, and the possibilities of govern-mental power, of which we speak.

The object of the association was defined to be "the attainment of the highest standard of political and social rights for man, and the promotion of· the intellectual, moral, and material welfare of mankind." The means for carrying out this purpose were given as follows :—

"1. Application of the federation principle to all republican

States; 2. Abolition of aristocratic titles and privileges
3. Suppression of all monopolies; 4. Abolition of standing armies; 5. Compulsory, gratuitous, secular and industrial education; 6. Obligation of the State to provide
suitable employment for all citizens, and sustenance for
the incapacitated—none to live upon the labour of others;
7. Nationalisation of land; 8. Direct legislation by the
people." Among the means for gaining these points was
" The establishment of a high court of republican equity
under the name of the 'Republican Areopagus,' which
shall judge all violations of the laws of humanity, and the
rights of man, committed by crowned heads, statesmen,
parliaments, law courts, &c."

The Education Act had already become a thing of life
ere the programme of the eight points was issued. That
some of the other points may be ultimately realised, and
that they may be all highly desirable, may, not for the
sake of argument, but to avoid argument, be admitted.
Still, as it is scarcely necessary to point out, the programme as it stands is nothing more nor less than a piece
of bombastical nonsense whereby the issuers write themselves down asses, and bring upon their class (in regard to
political knowledge, and fitness for political power) the
contempt of all other classes. Nor is making them appear
ridiculous in the eyes of others the worst or most material
injury which such men inflict upon their class. Those
who draw the attention of the working classes to such

doubtful, distant, and vaguely general "points," draw it
from those more immediate, attainable, and definite points,
which must in any case form the stepping-stone to the
greater and remoter types of points, supposing the latter
ever *are* achieved. From points which, so far as they go,
would undoubtedly be beneficial to the working classes,
without being unfair to others, and the fairness and prac-
ticability of which could be shown clearly and in detail.
Points, finally, the consummation of which could be and
would be hastened if even such degree of political energy
as now exists among the working classes was concentrated
upon them, instead of being frittered away upon "programmes," "platforms," and "charters," which, judged
by all the operative circumstances of the case, are non-
sensical, however fondly and egotistically their framers,
or those who are led shadow-chasing by them, may
imagine them to be philosophical. The idea of being
themselves members of so tremendous a tribunal as the
proposed Republican Areopagus, would no doubt have
great charms for the glowing imaginations that could
conceive the thing; and there are minds for which any
opportunity of using fine words has irresistible attractions.
But with all due allowance made on these scores, the least
that can be said of those who put forward such things as
a "Republican Areopagus," as part of a present-day
political programme—and it is only in degree of foolishness that it differs from many of the ideas put forward in

programmes issued in the name of the working classes—
the least that can be said of such men, and of those who
put faith in them as guides, is that they show themselves
to be lacking in common-sense, utterly incapable of
dealing with the great social and political questions which
involve the problem of the improvement of the condition
of the working classes, ignorant of what constitutes the
essence of those questions, of what are or are not practical politics, and what does or does not come within their
domain. When working men, or men professing to speak
in their behalf, issue political (?) programmes, which
stamp them as men of this kind, what must a statesman
like Gladstone think? what must men like Bright,
Fawcett, and Hughes, and all other sincere well-wishers
of the working classes feel? The answer may easily be
imagined.

It may be said that the proceedings of such men are
mere harmless fooling, that their meddling and muddling
in matters they do not understand pleases them by grati-
fying their vanity, while it does not harm any one else.
This is a common view of the subject; but, as we have
already incidentally intimated, we think it is too light a
one. Such proceedings, in addition to diverting the
attention of the working classes from matters upon which
it could be advantageously bestowed, keep alive and
spread perniciously erroneous opinions. For instance, in
the programme we have cited, one of the demands is that

the State should provide suitable employment for all citizens; and that the State could do this is an article of political belief largely held among the uneducated and little educated sections of the working classes. That such a notion is preposterous, that not only from the constitution of modern society, but from the constitution of the human mind and character, it is a practical impossibility, need not be pointed out here. Those who hold this to be a function of the State have minds pleasantly above details. They ask for the thing without offering the slightest suggestion as to how it could be carried out; and are, for the most part, blissfully unconscious of such facts as that all who are qualified to give judgment on such matters pronounce the idea a dream, that no civilised country has ever attempted to do such a thing, and that America—the country to which such people as we speak of generally refer as *the* model for imitation—would be the first to laugh at, its people the first to resent, any attempt in that direction. The wish that the thing should be, is father to the belief that it could be.

Those entertaining the belief would put governments in the place of, or rather above, "natural laws." They have a vague general notion that but for the selfishness of statesmen, aristocrats, and capitalists, any government in the present day could practically realise the bombastic promises which Shakespere puts into the mouth of his Jack Cade when he tells his followers that "There shall

be in England seven halfpenny loaves sold for a penny:
. . . . and the realm shall be in common." They are
persuaded that men could be made happy by act of
parliament; that government could create a state of
things in which the working classes need take no heed
for the morrow, or of anything but to eat, drink, and be
merry; increase and multiply. That such notions are
largely held among the working classes, no *candid* observer inside those classes will deny, no *careful* observer
outside them but will know. How much they stand in
the way of the social and political advancement of the
working classes, how they embarrass statesmen who are
willing to work for that advancement, and what a handle
for scoff and scorn, and excuse for obstructiveness, they
afford to any who are really opposed to working-class
interests. To what an extent they draw upon the working classes the machinations of flattering, self-seeking
political adventurers, and how much it is the duty of
every disinterested " friend of the working man," and all
who would assist in the work of neutralising the antagonistic social forces, to point out, no matter at what risk of
resentment from feelings of bigotry or wounded vanity,
the foolish and mischievous nature of such notions—all
these points are, we think so obvious, that there is no
need to occupy space in demonstrating them here. In
whatever other respect Mr. Gladstone may or may not
have failed to realise the expectations of the people, he

has, at any rate, not been wanting in the fulfilment of his duty to them and himself in regard to the matter we are speaking of. In the course of his great speech at Greenwich he, addressing himself more especially to " those of the working community," distinctly pointed out that the functions of government were limited, that when all that legislation could do had been done, the question of the happiness of the people still lay chiefly with themselves, with the individuals. "While," he said, "I would impose upon the government and the legislature every burden that they are in their own nature capable of bearing, in my mind they are not your friends, but your enemies, who teach you to look to the legislature for the removal of the evils which afflict human life. It is the individual man, the individual conscience, and the individual character on which much of human happiness and human misery depends. The social problems that confront us are many and formidable. Let the government labour to its utmost, let the legislature spend days and nights in your service, but after the very most has been achieved, the question whether the English father is to be the father of a happy family and the centre of a united house is a question that must depend mainly upon himself." These utterances were, of course, mere truisms, but their expression was none the less necessary and wise on that account. They are truisms the truth of which large numbers of working men have yet to learn to recognise, the antagonising falsities to which have yet tò be rooted out of their minds. So long as English workmen are imbued with their present ideas concerning the office of the legislature and the potency of legislative enactments, so long will all legislative progress leave them still disappointed and dissatisfied. They will discover in regard to each successive measure—as they have discovered with respect to repealed corn-laws, free trade, and the extension of the franchise—that they are not the panaceas they have expected to find them—that they have been led to believe they would be. Under the influence of the bitter and angry feelings excited by such discoveries they will still aim at making impossible improvements in the constitution of government, while neglecting possible ones among themselves; will continue to be blind followers of blind, or worse than blind leaders—to put a misplaced faith in the teachings of those who, though claiming to be, and intending to be, their friends, are really, though unconsciously, their enemies; and to drift nearer and nearer to the explosive condition. The working classes have come to look, and are taught to look to legislation for the improvement of their condition. But while they have a perfect right to so look to it, and abundant justification for demanding from it much more than it has yet given to them, they should be made to understand that its powers in that respect are limited, and that even within its own limits it can only work effectively for the *general and permanent* improvement of the condition of the working classes by the aid of the active co-operation of those classes in regard to those points wherein the work of improvement lies with them, and without the legislature. Those who tell the working classes that great things are due to them from the government, and advise them to combine to force the granting of them, but who never tell them that all that government can do will be but of little avail unless there is self-reform and improvement in regard to the ignorance, bigotry, class-hatred, drunkenness, thrift-lessness, and recklessness in incurring the responsibilities of marriage, which are unhappily to be largely found among the working classes—those who act in this manner are not the friends, but the flatterers of the working classes. The education of the working classes in practical politics has yet to be begun, and it will have to commence in unlearning them; in clearing their minds of such ideas as that the State can "provide suitable employment for every citizen, regulate the prices of food," or, without conjoint and in certain respects self-sacrificial effort upon the part of working men, make a people happy and comfortable. Such a process of education would at first be unpalatable to those subjected to it, but we think it could be carried out successfully, the greatest difficulty in the matter being that those who set up as teachers of the working classes are themselves of those who require to be taught by being untaught. Some, at any rate, of the " Council of Workmen and Peers " were men to whom considerable numbers of working men look up as political leaders and teachers, and yet the seven points framed by them, though making up a much more sensible and reasonable programme than the eight points we have already quoted, were marred by the same would-be philosophical wideness of view, and ignorance or disregard of possibilities, to an extent that would enable Mr. Gladstone to fully justify himself, in strictness of interpretation, for having branded the originators of them as "political quacks," though to our thinking the term was an unnecessarily and unwisely harsh one, considering by whom and to whom it was applied.

A favourite political idea among the working classes is that of working-men M.P.'s. Taken barely, the idea is sound enough, but on coming to examine the question of fitness and qualification, it will be found that as held it is one of the most short-sighted and disastrous for their own interests that working men could entertain. After the fact that it is largely made up of members who represent and seek to promote special and sectional, rather than national, interests, the greatest vice of Parliament is its "parliamentarism"—its outpour of talk so large in proportion to the work done, so often poured out in wilful obstruction to the work done, or attempted to be done. None have suffered more by this than have the working

classes ; no measures have been more damaged or delayed
by it than have those favourable to the interests of the
working classes; and yet so great and blind is their
admiration for what, in slang phrase, is called the " gift
of the gab," that to the minds of the general body of
them this gift in a working man is the one thing necessary to qualify him to be an M.P. All who have been
or are in the mind's-eye of the working classes as " Working-men M.P.'s " are largely endowed with this gift.
" They can talk ! O Lord, how they can talk ! " in what
is known as the " talkee, talkee " style, and they please
most who talk most, and season highest their flattery of
" the working man," and abuse of other classes. To
audiences who applaud them to the very echo, and who
will not tolerate any attempt to argue with them, the
speeches of such talkers doubtless seem very fine. But
such auditors fail to imagine such speakers in the House
of Commons, and subject to its rules; they do not see
that about the worst thing that could happen to the
working classes, from a political party point of view, would
be for them to be able to return two or three voluble
working men to Parliament. There is probably nothing
that Mr. Gladstone or Mr. Disraeli would like better. In
such a case they would have good grounds for exclaiming
that their enemies had been delivered into their hands;
though they would have no occasion to further exclaim,
" O that mine enemy would make a speech." The

working-men M.P.'s would do that fast enough. Speech-making would be the end and aim of their parliamentary being. It would be alike a pleasure and a duty to them. They would be returned specially to make speeches; would be expected to "speechify" upon every possible occasion and subject. Considered as members of Parliament, they would have to speak or die. An accusation of being "dumb dogs" would be fatal to them with their constituents. Any working man who would have the least chance of being returned to Parliament as a working-men's M.P. would, in the existing state of political knowledge and feeling among the working classes, be one who took an exclusively working-class view of everything; who would treat all great political and social questions as though there could be no other view of them, no other class or classes concerned in or affected by them. How speeches embodying such short-sighted, impolitic, and injurious views could be knocked to pieces, and made to appear ridiculous, by clever statesmen and debaters understanding the many-sidedness of our social problems; what an opportunity they would afford for saying that the working classes were unjust and incapable of distinguishing between right and wrong, the practicable and the impracticable; and how they would embarrass men like Bright and Fawcett, and all others who had something of statesmanlike knowledge, as well as a desire to further the interests of the working classes—all these

and their evil consequences to the working classes are
things so obvious that there is no necessity to enforce
them by argument. That there are plenty of working
men of as good natural parts as the average M.P. there
can be no doubt, but that is saying very little for them.
To do credit to his class, indeed, not to do *dis*credit to
them, a working-man M.P. would have to be something
more than a colourless mediocrity. He could not be a
mere unit of the "following" of a party chief, voting as
he was told, and maintaining a discreet silence. If he
were not more than this he would be in very evil case, he
would labour under the necessity for speaking to which
we have alluded, and would lack the educational advantages that have generally fallen to the lot of the ordinary
M.P. Another difficulty of the working-man M.P.'s idea
is the question of the means of living. The working-
class notion of a working-man M.P. is certainly not that
of a man of independent means; a pecuniary provision
would have to be made for the member of this type. If
rich men assisted him, his independence would be sus-
pected, and he would on the slightest provocation, or
without any provocation at all, be accused of selling himself and his class. If the working classes subscribed to
afford him an income they would regard him as a servant,
with no claim to any such independence as would justify
him in differing in even the slightest degree from their
views, while, if he did venture to differ from them, they

would speedily remind him that they paid him, and threaten to stop his pay—perhaps carry out their threat. Unless it were arranged that the State should pay members who had no—or insufficient—means, it would be cruelty to a working man with anything of delicacy or sensibility of feeling to send him to Parliament as a working-man M.P.

In short, the idea of working-men M.P.'s is in its stricter forms a mistake, nor are such M.P.'s the necessity which some people assert them to be. It is greatly overstating the case to say that only working men can know, or make known, what are really the wants and wishes and views of the working classes. Any thoroughly liberal M.P. may easily ascertain for himself the substantial truth on these points. It is not in the nature of things as they stand that there should be working men qualified to be such members of Parliament as it is desirable for the credit of the working classes and the good of the country such special M.P.'s should be. Statesmanship is not a thing that comes by intuition, and politics, even in their higher and better sense, are an intricate subject, requiring time and study for their full and just comprehension, and working men have had neither the means nor leisure for mastering them. Moreover, those of the working classes who come nearest to being qualified to act as members of Parliament, who would in the first instance do least discredit, and soonest come to do credit to their class, would not be the men elected. It would be the talkers and partisan panderers to class feeling who would be returned to Parliament, if any working men were. In regard to these matters, the working classes generally can at present only be successfully appealed to through their ears and prejudices. There are men among them who read and study, observe and think, and who *as a consequence* do not give themselves up to the acquirement and practice of the art of stump oratory. But these men who recognise such facts as that the much-talked-of "rights of labour" have never been clearly defined, that generally speaking they have least of definite meaning to those who have the phrase most frequently in their mouths, and that in any case they are not the only "rights" in the world—the men of this stamp see that their class have prejudices, and are greatly swayed through them; and being disinclined to "knuckle down" to such prejudices, being, indeed, rather inclined to point out that they are prejudices, they would have no chance of being elected as working-men M.P.'s, even if they were desirous of it. Looking at the many instances of great native ability to be found among the working classes, the degree of attention they are giving to politics, the way in which they are gaining increased leisure for themselves, and the progress that is being made in the matter of education—considering these things, there is every reason to believe that the time will come when a working man qualified to sit in Parliament, and take an active and able part in legislating for his class and the country, will be by no means a rare personage—and when working men generally will understand that volubility alone does not make such a man. If there are at the present moment any such working men, they are little known beyond the circle of their personal acquaintance, and, as we have said, there is no chance that they would be the ones returned to Parliament as working-men M.P.'s. In conclusion, upon this point we repeat that the idea of working-men M.P.'s, as it now exists, is a mistake. There are men having as good natural qualifications as working men, and possessing those more or less accidental and incidental advantages which it is scarcely possible a working man could have, who would be as willing as any working man to further the just interests of the working classes, who could know as much about those classes as was necessary for all purposes of legislation, and who would be proud to enter the House of Commons as special representatives of working-class interests as against the special parliamentary representation of the interests of the landowning capitalist, and other classes which have hitherto had a practical monopoly of such special representation. There are examples of such men already in Parliament, and the object of the working classes should be to seek out more such men and return them to Parliament.

Before quitting the subject of the necessity among the working classes of self-reform in things political, we would just refer to one minor, but still not altogether unimportant point in which there is a good deal of room for such reform—to wit, the proceedings of many of the actively political among the working classes. It has become a fashion with them for a knot of them to form themselves into an association with a high-sounding title, pass resolutions, and issue addresses in a "We-the-People-of-England" tone, which brings deserved ridicule upon them and undeserved ridicule upon their class; and generally intimate to all taking leading parts in the political movements of the day that the association's eye is upon them, and that to be subjected to its watchful glance is no light matter. Worse than this, they frequently combine politics and drink, and lay themselves open to the reproach of being pot-house politicians. The social glass and friendly pipe may be very good things in their place, but they are out of place in association with the discussion of grave political problems. It is frequently asserted that working men having no social clubs must meet in public-houses. But this is *not* necessarily the case. Very often the number of members of a working-class political association that assume very grand airs is so few that they could comfortably meet at each other's houses; while if they are too numerous for that, or the plan is not convenient, the use of private assembly rooms could easily be hired at a price that would certainly not exceed in amount the money spent in drink " for the good of the house " when the meetings are held in a public-house. There are hundreds of chess clubs, whist clubs, singing classes, and the like, who hire rooms in mechanics' institutions and other public buildings, at rentals that are defrayed by an almost nominal subscription per member; and there is no good reason whatever why political associations should not do the same thing. In fact the real truth on this head is, that where a political caucus of working men hold their meetings in a public-house, it is because they like the drink and desire to have it. Upon this point, at any rate, all true friends of the working classes would say to them, " Reform it altogether."

The ideas of working men upon the subject of "the enemies of the working classes," is another matter in which self-amendment will be necessary before the best attainable condition of the working classes can be reached. The popular notion among working men upon this point is broadly that the upper and middle classes are the natural enemies of the lower or working class, preying upon them by living upon their labour, and trying to intercept all the good things of life before they can reach them, and as a matter of fact monopolising an unjust and undeserved share of those good things. The " bloated aristocrat " and the " bone-grinding, blood-sucking capitalist " are, by the bulk of the working classes, looked upon as "representative men" of the upper and middle, the landowning, and employing, and monied classes. Whether or how far this view is founded upon or justified by facts, are matters of opinion upon which it is not necessary for our present purpose to enter into argument. Our motive in touching upon the subject is to call attention to the points that whether or not other classes of society are the enemies of the working classes, the latter do not sufficiently recognise the fact, that some of their worst enemies are within their own body. There are tens of thousands of drunkards among them; and the general body do not see that they are among their most dangerous and damaging enemies, that they do more than any others to drag down the working classes and to give grounds for harsh thoughts, harsh conclusions, and harsh proceedings towards those classes. That is, they do not see this to such an extent as to induce them to seek to eradicate the evil, by adopting such a moral tone in respect to it as would tend to stamp it out. Let the tone of the workshop become earnestly and sternly condemnatory of drunkenness; let the drunkard be made *the* black sheep, and an habitual drunkard among working men will become a comparative rarity, and there will be no need of Permissive Bills to lessen the number of public-houses. Working men can do more in this way than legislative enactments, Good Templar Associations, and all other things of that kind put together. It is their *duty* to themselves to exert their power in the matter, and so long as that duty is ill or unfulfilled, all cannot be well with them. If a man work for under wages, or transgresses any other unwritten but understood trade law, he is sent to "Coventry" by his shopmates, is made to see and feel that he is despised by them and outcast from among them. This has a powerfully deterrent and reformatory effect in *all* cases, even in those wherein the justness of the proceeding is open to question. It would be equally powerful applied to the suppression of drunkenness, and in that case at any rate the application of the principle would be as justifiable as it would be salutary. The drunkards however are not dealt with in this manner; they are—generally speaking, for there are some of the more thoughtful among working men as sternly "down upon them" as they ought to be—treated with an unwise toleration. Their own frequent plea that they are nobody's enemy but their own, is too readily and lightly accepted. They are undoubtedly and very greatly the social and moral enemies of their class, and should be recognised and treated as such by their class. It is they who give employers cause and opportunity to say that workmen seem to have more money than they have time to spend or know how to spend wisely; who cause the necessity for harassing workshop regulations, and who being chronically "hard up," are the least independent of all working men and do most to lessen the general inde-

pendence of the body. When a drunkard coming to
work in the morning, showing the tokens of an over-night
"fuddle," is as much afraid and ashamed of being noticed
by his shopmates as he is by his employers; when the
first lesson of an apprentice or other working boy with
regard to drunkenness is, to look upon it as a degrading
and abhorrent thing—*not* to smuggle drink into the shop
for drunkards wanting the metaphorical hair of the dog
that has bitten them; when in workshops a youth would
as soon think of boasting of having been "tight" over
night, as he would of having committed a burglary;
when he is taught that it is *not* a manly thing to spend
his evenings loafing about street corners with a pipe
stuck in his mouth, that if he is really desirous of
"making a man of himself," he will rather spend his
evenings in improving his education, and acquainting
himself with the principles of those sciences bearing upon
his trade; when pot-house ribaldry in a workshop is
frowned down, *not* laughed at; when the moral tone of
workshop circles is such as to bring about these results,
then will the working classes be in an infinitely better
position with regard to enemies than they are at present.
They will have got rid of the enemies within their camp,
and be in a tenfold stronger position to fight any real
enemies without it. Let us be distinctly understood in
this matter; we are not advocating total abstinence, nor
confounding the use with the abuse of strong drink; nor

are we bringing a charge of intemperance against the working classes generally. It is because we know that an overwhelming majority of them are sober that we say that it lies in their power to, in a great measure at any rate, crush out the curse of drunkenness from among them. We speak only against drunkenness to point out that there is unfortunately a great deal of it among the working classes; that in members of those classes it is a crime against the general body; that drunken working men are the worst enemies of their class, and should by the class be treated as such.

But while so much, such important points, of that improvement of the working classes, the bringing about of which can alone be relied upon to prevent the coming about of social explosion and chaos—while so much of this improvement must be self-improvement, improvement wrought by the working classes among and upon themselves, a great deal is also due in the matter from government and the governing classes. Should the latter from selfishness, or class feeling, or any neglect to mark, or unwillingness to move with the spirit of the times, fail to do their part, the responsibility for any social explosion that might occur would lie with them. That in their ignorance of the principles of political economy and natural possibilities the working classes, and men professing to speak in their name, ask from governments things which it is not in their power to grant, which it is not desirable should be in their power to grant, we have freely admitted. We as freely admit that governments have a right to make a *legitimate* use of this fact as an argument for disregarding mere popular outcry, or a justification for holding the view that they know better than the people what is really for the good of the people, and acting upon that view. But at present there is a tendency to take an unfair advantage of that position, to make the demand by the working classes for impossible reforms a screen and shelter for denying or delaying reforms which in addition to being possible are just, necessary, and such as only a government could effectually carry out. The most palpable blot in the famous seven points, the most striking and damning instance of an utter ignorance or disregard of the circumstances that alter cases, was of course the demand for "something like the American homestead law," which for all practical purposes might as well have been a demand for the towing over to England a few million acres of the spare lands of America. On this the critics, scoffers, and "wonderers" at once seized, but to our thinking the most surprising part of the business was that men who had really mingled with the working classes should have been so ignorant of the feelings of working men as to suppose that they would desire "something like the American homestead law," even if physical possibilities admitted of it. English manufacturing operatives are nothing if not socially gregarious in their habits.

They would tell you, though not perhaps in Byron's exact words, that their "souls are social." They would have very decided objections to being "planted out in the open," would regard their being so rather as a grievance than an advantage. They like to "neighbour," and above all they like to live within sound of their workshop bells, and will willingly make sacrifices upon other points to gain that. But while it is easy to show that this point as put by its framers was impracticable, it is unfair to argue or imply from that, that Government cannot do, or ought not to be called upon to do, anything in the matter of giving the working classes generally improved dwellings. It was probably an unfortunate desire to show that they knew that there was such a thing as an American homestead law that betrayed the men of the seven points into using the phraseology they did. Apart from the phraseology, there was both matter and method in what many choose to consider their madness. What they really meant was that improved dwellings were one of the great things needful to the improvement of the condition of the working classes, and that Government could do much, and is bound to do all it can, to give them such dwellings. Taking this to have been substantially their meaning, they were right. Many of the essentials of comfortable or happy home-life are without the limits of legislative action. Managing wives are not to be made or mismanaging ones amended by Act of Parliament. Government cannot

plant the working classes " out in the open," cannot even
give them a detached cottage system of residence, nor, as
we have just been pointing out, would they be desired to
do so even if they could. Their attention will have to be
given to a contrary state of things. In the face of the
keenness of modern competition the tendency of the
manufacturing industries of the country is to gravitate to
the centres where the raw materials for them are to be
exclusively or most largely found, and everything points
to the conclusion that workmen's dwellings will be clus-
tered around such centres as closely as they can be built.
This, as it falls out, is a position of affairs in which what
legislation *can* do, and ought to do, and if it is wise *will*
do, can be most advantageously brought to bear. Government can pass and enforce measures of sanitary improvement, and it could if it would establish a standard of—if
we may use the word—"habitability" for dwelling-houses,
the minimum point of which standard would make *any*
house better than the grand majority of working-class
dwellings now are; would insure their being fitted with
at any rate the more important appliances necessary for
the maintenance of health, and the exercise of domestic economy. Semi-philanthropic associations may erect blocks
of improved working-class dwellings here and there, and
they deserve all honour for what they have done and are
doing in that direction, but it cannot be reasonably hoped
or expected that they alone will be able to overcome the

evil they grapple with to any largely appreciable extent. It is only Government, only sanitary legislation of imperial extent and authority, that can give the working classes generally improved dwellings. We quite understand that there would be difficulties in the way of Government acting effectively in this matter. Of course on the thing being attempted some " vested interest " or other would " rise with twenty mortal grievances upon its crown," and threaten to push the Government from their seats; to " vote against them at the next election." The representatives of the vested interest would probably resort to all the tricks of parliamentary obstruction, and more likely than not the section of the working classes most clamorous in demanding the reforms would also be the most clamorous in denouncing the taxation necessary for carrying them out. Such obstacles as these, however, are not insuperable, and should be lightly regarded when weighed against the satisfaction which *ought* to be felt in achieving so worthy a purpose as that of giving the working classes improved dwellings. In brave and unselfish hands the thing is as capable of accomplishment as it would be just and is necessary, and once accomplished it would be scarcely less beneficial to society in general than to the working classes; it would do much towards eliminating the antagonistic and explosive elements from the social forces.

As with the first of the seven points, so with most of

the demands for impossibilities made by or in the name of the working classes; it will be found upon examination that they are only impossibilities, in being exaggerations, distortions, or misexplanations of possibilities. Take again, for instance, the idea that the State is bound to "provide suitable employment for every citizen." *That* is an impossibility; but it does not follow that Government cannot do anything in regard to the employment of the people, cannot in any way interfere between employer and employed for the benefit of the latter. They can do much; and much is yet due from them in the way of reducing the danger of dangerous employments, and the unhealthiness of unhealthy ones to the lowest minimum which the resources of modern science and invention make practicable. And they can do more than they have yet done in the way of protecting the weaker portion of the working classes—the women and children—from being worked the killingly long hours that many of them still are.

Again, though Government cannot regulate the prices of provisions, cannot cause "retail quantities to be sold at wholesale prices," they could do much to suppress the crime of adulteration, by which the working classes—and especially the poorer and most helpless sections amongst them—are the greatest sufferers. In this matter the working classes can do little or nothing to help themselves. It is especially and distinctly the province of the legislature to deal with it; and not to deal with it, to leave it in the scandalous state in which it is, is to be lacking in the fulfilment of a bounden duty, and to withhold justice not only from the working classes, but from all who honestly pay for food and manufactured goods. If the hands of the legislature are clean in this matter, if they are not deterred from taking action in it by a large proportion of the body consisting of men who in some way profit by the permitted adulteration, the spirit of which is entering so largely into our commercial life—if this is not the case, then the course of the legislature is simple and clear. They have only to pass a law putting swindling by adulteration of goods, or the use of false weights and measures, in the same category as other modes of swindling; they have only to make it punishable by imprisonment and the confiscation of the adulterated wares; they have only to do this and adulteration will be knocked on the head. It would not be altogether extinguished; there would still be swindlers who would practise those lines of operation, as there are swindlers who practise others that are already dealt with as criminal offences, but as criminal offences the adulteration of commodities and the use of unjust weights and measures would become comparatively rare. To make a show of punishing a man by fining him a sum that is in all probability no more than a moderate percentage upon his gain by the fraud of which he is convicted, is something very like dividing the spoil with him It is at any rate a mockery of all substantial justice.

There are other matters in which the Government and governing classes are avowedly opposed to reforms demanded by the working classes, but in which they are nevertheless bound in justice, and in accordance with the progressive spirit of the age, to give reform if they would be held guiltless of the *crime* of wilfully keeping one of the great social forces in a state of chronic heat and agitation, conducing to the explosive condition. Let us take as our illustrative case, the most notable of its kind—the House of Lords. Its retention or abolition (as at present constituted) would have a less direct bearing upon the physical and material well-being of the working classes than any of the measures of reform that we have already spoken of as being due to those classes from the legislature; but still there is more ill-feeling, more disposition to *violence* among the working classes in regard to the House of Lords, than there is in regard to any or all of the other questions mentioned, or than there is in connection with almost any question within the range of politics. They do object to its obstructiveness—and it is generally in connection with that phase of it that they give voice to their indignation—but their great charge against it, the ground on which they found their demand for its abolition, is the hereditary principle of its composition. On this point at least their instinctive judgment is sound, and their demand involves no impossibility. They see what important principles are concerned in the matter, that the sense of abstract justice,

and the institution of representative government are outraged by the existence of a hereditary house of legislature.
They see and feel that an institution which makes it a
matter of chance whether those whom the people are
compelled to accept as legislators are able men, or mere
tenth transmitters of foolish faces, and which potentially
—and sometimes practically—makes a nullity of popular
representation; they see that an institution which does
this cannot but be a wrong and an injury to the people of
the nation upon which it is imposed, cannot be defended
on grounds of justice or even of expediency. A second,
an upper, chamber of legislature may be necessary, but its
composition should not be left to accident; it should be
brought together by some mode of election which would
admit of the application of the principle of selection.
This is so obvious, as a matter of common sense and of
right and wrong, that to us it seems nothing less than
wonderful to find so clear-sighted a man, and fearless a
politician, as Mr. Gladstone defending the maintenance of
the present hereditary basis of the House of Lords. That it
might be reformed in other matters, he was prepared to
admit, but its hereditaryism was a principle of composition to be let well alone; was not the evil and unjust
thing that many believed it to be. It was true that his
defence of it was more clever than candid, and more
roundabout and evasive than either, but that was a
necessity of the case, direct or straightforward justification

being impossible. The pleader had a weak case, and he knew it. Not being in a position to challenge the jury to an honest consideration of facts and principles, he attempted to amuse them and divert their attention from the point really at issue. He did not venture to assert that the hereditary principle was a good, or was not a bad thing. He carefully avoided really grappling with the point with which he was nominally dealing; he, so to speak, gave Hamlet, with Hamlet left out. A body should not be condemned for having occasionally done wrong. Though he had differed from the Duke of Wellington in some things, he had greatly admired him for the manner in which he had kept the House of Lords in hand; the majority of Englishmen had a sneaking kindness for a lord, and therefore he, Mr. Gladstone, "before he agreed and committed himself to expunging from the House of Lords what is called the hereditary principle, would think once, would think twice, nay, would even think thrice." It was perhaps only a part of the fitness, or unfitness, of things, that this most illogical of defences should have been made in the course of the same speech (the Black-heath one) in which he reminded the people that they were without the ballot, which their own representatives had decreed they should have, through the obstructive pro-ceedings of the House of Lords, concerning which he said:—"I am bound to say that though I believe there are some politicians bearing the name of Liberal who

approve of the proceedings of the House of Lords with
respect to the Ballot Bill at the close of the last session,
I must own that I deeply lament that proceeding." The
same speech also in which he took (deserved) credit to
himself and colleagues for having abolished purchase in
the army—another thing, by-the-bye, which he would not
have been able to have spoken of as done, only he had by
a little-thought-of technicality of the constitution been
able to thwart the obstructive will of the House of Lords.
We suppose he did not notice the analogy between purchase in the army and the hereditary principle in the
legislation, did not remember at the moment that the
same roundabout line of defence had been made for
purchase, that he made for hereditaryism, and had in the
House of Commons been sternly rejected as insufficient to
stay execution. The purchase officers, it was said, had
never been guilty of any very grave errors ; purchase
officers had led our armies in all our great campaigns,
and all really needful reform could be effected without
going the length of abolition. Well all that might be,
was substantially the answer; but the principle of purchase
was radically and perniciously bad, and must go if we
were to have our army on a sound footing. It prevented
the right men from being in the right places, stood in the
way of merit and fitness, and in many cases gave us
instead positive incapacity. On these grounds it was
abolished. That the hereditary principle does not act in

the same detrimental and unjust manner in the composition
of the legislation that purchase did in that of the army,
no sane person will, we suppose, deny; and yet Mr. Gladstone, who takes credit for condemning the one thing,
and likes to have credit for being logical and consistent,
defends the other. At one time the people did think that
they could rely upon him to assist them in "expunging
from the House of Lords what is called the hereditary
principle," but he had shown them that as regards the
Lords, "Ephraim is joined to his idols." The people,
however, are not likely to act upon the scriptural advice,
and "let him alone." If the House of Lords were a
harmless idol, the worship of which pleased its devotees
without injuring any one else, they might do so. But it
is an idol of the Juggernaut type. Some legislative
measures have to be sacrificed to it altogether, and others
mutilated by way of offering to it; and an idol of this
devouring type the people in their present mood are not
likely to tolerate quietly much longer. If Ephraim does
not cast it down, he may come to be dragged down by it;
he and it being thrust from the high seats of the temple
together.

These are some of the things and types of things in
which "those whom it may concern" will have to make
amendment if they would feel assured of being safe from
the danger of social explosion; if the condition of the
working classes is to be materially, generally, and per-

manently improved. We know that it is an unusual
thing for one speaking on the side of the working classes
to point out that self-improvement is needed among them.
As a rule, " the friend of the working man" is not a
candid friend. He will tell the working man that he is a
" brawny son of toil," and the only real creator of wealth ;
and that he is down-trodden by the tyranny of capital,
and of things in general, but he will not hint at such a
possibility as that of his having faults. Perhaps he thinks
that the latter is a task that should be left to the enemies
of the working man, and we know that very many working men do regard as enemies any who do venture to
suggest that the working classes are anything less than
perfect. This state of affairs, however, seems to us to be
one of the chief reasons for speaking out as we have done
concerning the working classes—for not being a party to
leaving those classes in the fools' paradise of imagining
that all improvement in their condition must or can come
from concessions wrung from the classes above them. We
have not referred to their faults, and the necessity for
self-amendment in respect to them, in any unkindly or
unbrotherly spirit ; have only done so at all under a sense
of duty ; and substantially we have said no more to working men than this—" To your own selves be true."

ON THE RELATIONS BETWEEN CAPITAL
AND LABOUR.

"Every man should eat and drink, and enjoy the good of all his labour; it is the gift of God."—ECCLESIASTES iii. 13.

"Above all things, good policy is to be used, that the treasure and moneys in a state be not gathered into a few hands, for otherwise a state may have a great stock and yet starve: for money is like muck, not good except it be spread."—BACON.

"All human interests, combined human endeavours, and social growths in this world, have, at a certain stage of their development, required organizing: and Work, the grandest of human interests, does now require it."—CARLYLE.

"DEPEND upon it, gentlemen, I do but speak the serious and solemn truth when I say that within and beneath the political questions that are to be found upon the surface, lie those deeper and more serious questions that enter into the breast, and strike home to the conscience and mind of every man, and it is upon the solution of these questions that the well-being of England must depend."

So spoke Mr. Gladstone in the peroration to his great speech at Greenwich, in the month of November, 1871; a speech which, it may be remembered, was delivered on Blackheath, and listened to and applauded by an audience variously estimated at from twenty to fifty thousand; and which formed a theme of discourse in all manner of circles for many weeks after its deliverance. In all his many speeches he never gave forth a truer or more statesman-like utterance. The questions that lie on the surface of politics, that are palpably and wholly political; such questions, for instance, as electoral districts, the severance of the connection between Church and State, or the respective merits of this or that form of government—such questions as these are really of secondary importance compared with some of a non- or only partially political character, from which they withdraw attention. Chiefest among these more important questions is, in our opinion, that of the Relations between Capital and Labour; and it is a question the difficulties of arriving at a solution of which are unfortunately greater than even its importance, while the need for solution is as urgent as the difficulty is great. It would be hard to overrate either the difficulty or importance of it, and these characteristics of it were perhaps never more expressively and forcibly put than we once saw them in the letter of a man who ranks among those whose views upon the problems of the day are a power in the land, and who, speaking of this question of the relations between capital and labour, said : " It is the modern sphinx ; society must answer it or be destroyed." It is a question which, carefully considered, will be found to go to the very roots of society, to materially affect every section of it, and to form an integral and ineradicable part of many questions with which, at a first glance, it may have nothing to do. It calls aloud for a settlement upon a substantially new basis—as regards the relative *results* to the two classes more immediately concerned—and, if it has to call in vain, social convulsion must ultimately ensue.

That labour and capital are alike indispensable to each other as agents of production, that in producing, their agency must be joint and mutual, and that indeed in this respect they are rather parts of a whole than separate things—this is a position upon which we take it there is no doubt or division among those who have given the general subject thoughtful consideration. That large numbers of working men dispute the proposition we know —and regret. They say in effect that capital is not a *necessary* agent of production, that labour—using the word in its narrower meaning—not merely could be, but *is* " the sole creator of wealth," and that not only the profits of capital, but capital itself, is an unjust tax upon labour. Speaking from a tolerably extensive acquaintance of the manner of men who hold this doctrine, we can conscientiously say that they are *not* men who have given the general subject thoughtful consideration, neither do they represent the best intelligence of the working classes. That capital and labour jointly produce an aggregate of wealth (wealth being taken in the sense in which it means all the materials of human subsistence and enjoyment) which could be so divided that while

many still had much more, even the humblest labourer
would obtain a sufficiency of the necessaries of civilised
life—that this is the case is, we think, another proposition
concerning which there is very little doubt. And, unfortunately, there can be no doubt whatever that the
material results of productive industry are not divided in
a manner to give this desirable effect ; no doubt that tens
of thousands of labourers do not obtain a sufficiency of the
necessaries of life. Taking these premises as substantially
indisputable, they establish the obvious conclusion that
the existing relations between capital and labour are not
the true ones, in the sense of being the best and justest
that the practical possibilities of the case admit of. The
specific conclusion, when standing alone, is, we know,
sometimes denied ; but it may be taken as generally
granted through the admission of its premises ; and this
negative, this deduction that the relations are not what
practically they could be and justly they ought to be, is
about the only point upon which, at present, there is anything like agreement or certainty. The Œdipus who
shall say what *are* the true relations between capital and
labour has yet to arise, supposing—what is extremely improbable—that it is ever given to a single individual to
rightly answer this modern sphinxal question. We are
hopeful that the problem will be solved, but in all likelihood the solution will be the work of many minds contributing to it in greater or lesser degrees ; and it is in

the hope that, from having seen a good deal of the effects upon the labouring classes of the relations in question as they at present stand, we may be able to aid the work of solution in even the slightest degree, that we—with a consciousness of a very limited understanding of the science that claims the question of the relations between capital and labour as its own, weighing upon us—venture to touch upon so important and intricate a subject.

The existing relations between capital and labour are said to be based upon and subject to the laws of supply and demand—laws under which labour is ruled to be simply a " commodity," neither more nor less. That, however, human labour is not a commodity in the same sense as are the inanimate commodities which it produces requires no demonstration. It is inextricably associated with human passion, and feeling, and life. When it is in demand, its reward is in many instances such as to barely enable the labourer to maintain the animal life to support which he sells his labour ; and when his particular labour is no longer in demand, this same life has still to be maintained in some fashion. It is therefore evident that the laws of supply and demand do not and cannot apply in their strictness and entirety to the so-called " commodity " of labour, which in its essential nature is no commodity, but an outcome, for the purposes of the material creation, of the faculties of God-created man. That the laws of supply and demand influence the re-

lations between capital and labour there can be no doubt,
but they are not, as is so often argued, synonymous with
them, do not in themselves constitute them. What things
do constitute them, and in what manner and relative
degrees they are operative, are points upon which scarcely
any two persons would wholly agree, and which we do not
profess to decide. But though it may be difficult to precisely define what are the existing relations between
capital and labour, there need still be no hesitation in
concluding that they are not the true ones. By their
fruits we may know them; know that they are unsound.
Their fruits are, capital feasting in palaces, labour
starving in hovels—starving Tantalus-like in the midst
of a plenty it has helped to create. The earth and the
fulness thereof falling to the lot of the rich and idle; all
the drudgery of the earth and but the husks of its fulness
—and scarcely a sufficiency even of them—to the lot of
labour. Capital, in its embodiment of money worshipped,
labour scorned, looked upon with greater contempt than
are many forms of roguery. In times of dull trade their
fruits are seen in the starvation and pauperisation of
thousands of "the unemployed." Such times are usually
held to show the worst of these fruits; but to our thinking
it is the briskest times of trade that show how bad they
are—that most conclusively demonstrate that bad is the
best of them. During the last two years most of our
manufacturing industries have been in an almost unex-

ampled state of briskness, and the largeness of our total manufacturing operations quite unparalleled. Work-shops have been full handed, and overtime the rule. Wages have been good (good, that is, according to present ideas of good wages, and relatively to the rates obtaining in periods of dull trade), and in some trades there has been an actual scarcity of *skilled* labour. The Revenue and Board of Trade returns have borne most satisfactory testimony to this being the state of affairs; and newspapers taking these returns as their texts came out with jubilant articles upon our national progress and prosperity, the elasticity of our revenue, the recuperative power of our industries, and so forth. And really there was a good deal—about as much as the present relations between labour and capital could give—to make up a bright picture of the national condition; but side by side with the brighter materials existed darker ones, which had they been used—as to make the picture a true one they ought to have been—would greatly have toned down the brightness. At this very time of exceptionally brisk trade and swelling revenue returns, we had still a million paupers in our midst, had still thousands of men unemployed, and tens of thousands working for wages so miserably small as to put anything like happiness, or even decency of life, out of the question. We had no appreciable amelioration of the hideous body-and-soul-destroying poverty characteristic of the poorest and

poorer neighbourhoods of our larger towns. A poverty
that either degrades those who suffer under it into a
state of savagery, or, if it leaves them anything of sensitiveness or thought, makes their life a continuous pur-
gatory; makes them so that "they rejoice exceedingly
and are glad when they can find the grave." It should
be remembered, too, that the time *was* exceptional, that it
was the flush season of our periodical trade fluctuation,
between such flush state and stagnation at the lowest
ebb. It had been preceded and, according to the lessons
of all experience, was bound to be followed by a general
slackness of trade. Many of those who were really
benefiting by it, inasmuch as that they were at work in
it when in a less busy time they would have been out of
work—many of these had to devote considerable portions
of their income to the defraying of debts incurred for
necessaries during the previous slack times when they
had been out of employment, while the general rates of
wages prevailing were not such as to enable even saving
men to make provision for tiding over a future slack
time—should the evils of it fall upon them individually—
without getting into debt. That capitalist manufacturers
should be making princely fortunes out of this flush
of trade, that the number of individual incomes, to be
counted by tens of thousands, should be increased and
the revenue returns wax great beyond expectation, are
undoubtedly indications of progress and prosperity, of

an increased production of wealth. But as the material and permanent result of this is, that only the rich grow richer, such progress cannot be considered of the most satisfactory character; and it is a very general opinion among the working classes that it is decidedly the reverse of satisfactory—that it is a positive evil, in that it adds a sense of injustice to the other bitternesses of poverty, and fosters and increases that spirit of "unbridled luxury" which is rotting into the heart of this Mammon-worshipping age. One great good—a good infinitely greater as a piece of true national progress than any of the statistics over which the newspapers were jubilant—labour by hard struggling did manage to win for itself, namely, the establishment of a nine hours' working day. But this gain, be it observed, and it has a significant bearing upon what we have been saying, was obtained sorely against the will of capital, and in the teeth of the fervently asseverated assertion that the acting condition of the laws of supply and demand—which of course include the operation of competition—forbade the idea of such a concession.

To conclude upon this point of what are the fruits of the present relations between capital and labour, as they are to be seen in social results, we can say nothing more forcible than that it is as true now as it was thirty years ago, when Carlyle wrote the words, that " Countries are rich, prosperous in all manner of increase beyond example. But the men of those countries are poor, needier than ever of all sustenance, outward and inward—of belief, of knowledge, of money, of food. The rule *sic vos non vobis*, never altogether to be got rid of in men's industry, now presses with such incubus weight that industry must shake it off, or utterly be strangled under it; and alas! can as yet but gasp and rave, and aimlessly struggle like one in the final deliration."

Statesmen and others often profess themselves anxious to know what really are the views of the working classes upon this or that social problem, and no doubt it frequently is a difficult matter to get such views in any clear and concise form—firstly, because there is generally considerable difference of opinion among the working classes; and secondly, because the vast majority of those classes lack either the capability or opportunity of expressing their views through channels that are likely to meet the eyes or ears of other classes. But, with regard to their views upon the subject of that material progress concerning which they hear so many songs of praise and thanksgiving, no person need be at a loss. In the few words of incisive and unmistakable meaning quoted above, Carlyle broadly and substantially sums up the working class idea. Working men freely admit that the increase and accumulation of material wealth going on around them is, in the abstract, a sign and element of national progress; is potentially a blessed thing. But they say, at the same time, that the increase of wealth goes only to the 'wealthy, serves to make only the rich richer, and the poor—of course, by contrast—poorer; and that by reason of this it becomes rather a curse than a blessing to the people at large. While, generally speaking, they admit that there is something, and may be a great deal, in all the talk that they hear about fair and customary returns upon capital—that is, such returns as it at present gets—being absolutely necessary to draw it into labour-giving and wages-paying uses; while they admit this, they plainly see, and bitterly feel, that the rule *sic vos non vobis* does press with incubus weight upon industry. They see that it is the drones and butterflies of society, not the working bees, who profit most by labour. Thousands and thousands who work not *do* eat, fare sumptuously every day, and are clothed in purple and fine linen; while tens and tens of thousands of those who work can obtain but a " crust of bread and rags." This is a condition of things which the working classes find largely prevailing, and they feel that in very deed " Industry must shake it off, or utterly be strangled under it." They are constantly striving to shake it off, and one chief reason why, in their endeavour to do so, they " can as yet but gasp and rave and aimlessly struggle," is that, to save themselves from being utterly strangled under it, they have, as it were, to be constantly fighting for dear life—are unable to gain breathing time, or opportunity for cool consideration. That the relations between capital and labour should be—as regards the sharing of the results of their joint labour—fighting ones, seems to us to be an unnatural thing. But it is the case ; and the army of labour, though infinitely the greater in point of numbers—that many consider it over-great, and its numbers its weakness, need here only be noted in passing— is, so to speak, an army without arms. It lacks, what in its battles as they are at present fought are more literally than in most others, the sinews of war. For generations it has maintained what it has conceived to be the good and necessary fight against the present position of capital, with but scant material improvement to its own condition. But still it is not discouraged, and indeed it holds that in a certain negative sense it has been victorious. If it has not conquered, neither has it been conquered. Some slight concessions—such as the nine hours' standard—it has wrested from its antagonist, and, in despite of strenuous opposition, it has considerably developed that important phase of its strength that lies in unity. And withal, they remain at this present time confident, deter- mined, and of good courage, believing that they have right on their side, and that theirs is a battle such as—

"Though baffled oft, is ever won."

That in their endeavours to reduce the *sic vos non vobis* principle to a minimum ; to bring about such changes in the relation between capital and labour as will lead to their conducing to the greatest good for the greatest number in a far greater degree than they do at present; that in their struggles for these desirable ends the working classes will have to seek aid from legislation, there can be little doubt; and it is therefore well to find that the foremost statesman and most influential legislator of the day distinctly recognises, and emphatically enunciates, the fact that human labour is *not* a commodity. This is, of course, of secondary importance compared with the fact that the selection of legislators is now—potentially, at any rate— in a great measure in the power of the working classes; but still it is a hopeful, significant, and noteworthy thing. In the speech from which the opening sentence of the present article is quoted, Mr. Gladstone classed among the great questions that " are within and beneath the political questions that are to be found upon the surface," and upon the solution of which " the well-being of England must depend,"—Mr. Gladstone classed among these, " How to secure labour its due honour; not only the labour of the hands, but the labour of the man with any and all the faculties that God has given him. How to bring the country to believe that in the sight of God and man labour is honourable, idleness is contemptible." That, with due allowance for oratorical amplification and roundaboutness, this was as good as an explicit assertion that labour is not a mere commodity, even those who argue that labour *is* a commodity will, we think, admit, and in that lies its practical importance to working men. The words may not have been specifically intended to have the meaning we attach to them, though they logically and necessarily involve it; but in any case they embody a most "healthy" sentiment. A far-reaching truth has seldom, perhaps, been more epigrammatically and axiomatically put than—"Labour is honourable, idleness is contemptible." Within a week or two of their utterance a Scottish Republican Association had adopted the words as their motto, and if they have not been added to the pieces of proverbial philosophy that are to be found doing twofold educational service as head-lines to copy-books, it is certainly not because they are not worthy of figuring in that capacity. The beauty or abstract truth of the sentiment few, we suppose, would question; and yet Mr. Gladstone might well ask, in an almost despairing strain, how are we to bring the country to believe it! The daily practice and action and tone of our social life and constitution reverses the sentiment. It is idleness that is regarded as honourable, that is honoured in the person of idlers; labour—and especially manual labour—that is looked upon as contemptible, especially by the idle. That those who work should be, speaking broadly, those who want; those who work not, those who have, is such a perversion of material justice, so great and glaring an outrage against the inner sense of right, as could not but result in the misery and discontent which we see around us. How to remedy this, "how to secure labour its due honour," is, as Mr. Gladstone so solemnly affirmed, a deeper and more serious question than any that are to be found upon the surface of politics. Had he asked, " How to secure labour its due *profit ?* " he would, to our thinking, have been going more to the heart of the matter; for we believe it may be safely taken for granted that the honour would follow, would be commanded by the profit. As, however, the due honour of labour includes its due profit, Mr. Gladstone's view of putting the point merely involves a difference of verbal expression.

That labour does not get its due profit—does not get such a share of the aggregate results of productive industry as, with all reasonable allowance for every other agent, is due to its absolute and relative importance and indispensability, is, in our opinion, a position that requires no demonstration beyond what we have already incidentally given. In fact, we take it as a truism that is sufficiently demonstrated in being clearly stated; that is impliedly taken as admitted and understood in the asking of the question, How is the due profit (or honour) of labour to be secured to it ? Rightly considered, this question is the all-inclusive problem of the age—a moral and social, as well a political problem. And, judging by the results of the many attempts at solution, it would appear to be as insoluble as inclusive. To this surpassingly important " How " no satisfactory "Thus" has been returned, nor did Mr. Gladstone upon the occasion to which we refer profess to offer any. Repealed Corn Laws, Free Trade, and extended Franchise may be steps towards it, but time has shown that they are not *the* answer. To one question, however, leading up to the great question, and settling what is perhaps not the least important of its many points, we think there is a tolerably definite and conclusive answer. If it is asked by *whom* the due honour of labour is to be secured to it, the obvious answer, in our opinion, is, by itself—by the working classes. It is they who *must* answer the sphinxal question, or perish. It is they who have perished, and *do* perish by thousands, because it has hitherto remained unanswered. It is they who must unloose the Gordian knot of policy that entangles the question, if it is to be unloosed; or cut it if it must be cut. It is they who are being strangled under the incubus weight of the *sic vos non vobis* principle, and it is they who must shake it off. Yes! with all their weakness and imperfections upon their heads, they must fight the great battle. Many will no doubt help them voluntarily and generously, and others will be compelled to do so more or less unwillingly, but in the main they must work their own deliverance —must themselves win the battle which is their battle, and fight it *because* it is theirs. This is the idea upon the subject prevailing among the working classes themselves—the idea upon which they are basing, and are likely to continue to base, their action. If it is asked by what means the working classes can hope to successfully fight such a battle, the broad answer is, once more, we think, tolerably obvious—by combination. And this again is the view taken and acted upon by the working classes. But that the fight is theirs, that they must fight it themselves, and that combination must be their weapon, is about all that they do see clearly. Upon or against whom, or in what manner to direct their operations, they are as yet at a loss—are divided and undecided ; and these are the points upon which we will venture to offer remark and suggestion. In the first place, it must be evident that as with its overwhelming strength in point of numbers, and, as we hold, preponderating indispensability in the work of production, labour has been unable to enforce its due, it must have great weaknesses in other respects. First, and perhaps, in its ulterior effects, greatest of these, is a want of comprehensiveness of view as regards " the situation " with which they have to deal. Even while they grasp the idea that combination must be their weapon—must be *the* lever, whatever may have to be the fulcrum, by which they will have to move the social world—they fail to carry it to its legitimate conclusion. Till within the last few years their practice in the way of combination did not extend beyond trade unions, none of which even included *all* the members of the trades they represented. Latterly international working-class combination has become an actual and operative fact, but as a power for working-class ends it is as yet only an extension of trade unionism. It is true that continental workmen have mixed up political talk with it, and among them it seems more likely than not to be turned to practical account for political purposes, but up to the present time it is substantially, and as regards England wholly, and likely to remain, a trade thing. It is chiefly the artisan and in England the trade-unionist classes that are the parties to it, and the unionists have a horror—and many shrewd judges think a very wise horror—of any unnecessary mixing up of trade with politics. When they became convinced that "foreign competition" was not wholly the bugbear they had on first hearing of it been inclined to consider it, the English unionists saw that with machinery playing the part of leveller in the mechanical industries, they could not hope to be successful in getting decrease of working hours or increase of pay if continental· artisans in the same trades were to continue to work long hours for small pay. They argued that in that case the foreign workmen would have a great inducement to come and take their place if they struck; or otherwise, if they (the English) succeeded in a busy time in obtaining such an advance for themselves as more than equalled the value of the superiority of English over foreign workmen, the foreign masters would be able to under-tender the English, and such a slackness be brought upon

English trade as would be likely to lead to the workmen losing whatever advantage they had previously won. It was the clear conception of this position that induced the English unionists to seek international relations; and it is barely justice to the continental workmen to say that they entered into such relations in a most cordial and elevated spirit, and truly and bravely played their allotted part when a time of trial came. But for the international combination among the artisan classes, the Newcastle masters in the nine-hours' strike would have been greatly more successful than they were in obtaining foreign workmen—would perhaps have been sufficiently successful to have worn out the men on strike. But for the same combination the gain of the nine-hours' movement in England would not have been immediately followed by the successful continental strikes for a ten-hours' day, without the establishment of which "the balance of power" in tendering for contracts would probably have been against England, and the permanency of the so hardly fought and greatly sacrificed for nine-hours' principle made a doubtful instead of, as it now is, an assured thing. So far as it has gone, international combination among the artisan classes has been a good thing—a decided step in the right direction. The same may be affirmed, though scarcely in so unqualified a manner, of English trade unionism.

That small unions have perpetrated the most diabolical

crimes in the name of unionism, is most painfully true. But the unions that so disgraced unionism and manhood *were* small and isolated; and we speak of what we know in saying that none regarded those crimes with deeper abhorrence than did the general body of trades unionists, and none—strange as it may sound to some people—were more *surprised* to find that such crimes had been committed, or at the ideas of unionism that led to their perpetration. Those who made use of the discoveries of the atrocities of the Sheffield saw-grinders as an argument against trades unionism in general, and implied that they were an ultimate result of, and in consonance with, the fundamental principles of unionism—those who argued in this circle were either guilty of a perversion of truth for interested or party purposes, or ignorant of the subject to a degree that excluded them from the right of expressing an opinion upon it, involving so serious a charge. That the larger and better unions—the really representative ones—sometimes enforce a control over the action of their members generally, which bears hardly upon individuals, making them act in opposition to their opinions, wishes, and interests, is most true. But they only exercise such control in regard to matters that a council freely elected by the members from among themselves have decided upon, and only enforce it by legitimate means—morally, by arguments, appeals to good fellowship, and community of interests; penally, by such fines and forfeitures as are

embodied in the rules of their constitution, which each
member upon entering his union takes upon himself as
binding. That a man should be compelled to leave an
employment in which he may have been for years, and is
desirous of remaining, being comfortable there and having
personally no grievance ; that with a wife and children
dependent upon him he should be forced to give up a
working pay of (say) thirty-five shillings a week, and
come out upon a strike pay of ten shillings per week, does
seem hard. To many we know that it appears an intolerable tyranny, and there are doubtless numbers who
would agree with Lord Shaftesbury's high-flown assertion
upon this point, to the effect that "all the single despots, and
all the aristocracies that ever were or will be, are as puffs
of wind compared with these tornados of trade unions."
But with all due deference to a honestly entertained difference of opinion—a difference of opinion for which there
is, on the surface, considerable justification—we contend
that for the interests of the working classes it is necessary
and *good* that the unions should have such power. Good,
that is, in principle, though every exercise of it would be
open to criticism upon its own merits, and might be either
wise or unwise. The principle is that upon which nations
are kept together ; which has won many great causes. It is
virtually the principle of the greatest good for the greatest
number—a principle that inculcates the virtue of individual
abnegation of self in the interests of what is commonly

held to be the common good. That the present personal interests of a few, or even of a many, must not be allowed to stand in the way of the accomplishment of a general and permanent benefit, is, we maintain, both a just and expedient principle. It is a principle by which the working classes have already wrought good for themselves, and they will have to extend, not to lessen, its action if they are ever as a body to rise to a materially better position than they now occupy. Before leaving the general proposition that the principle *is* a good one, it will perhaps be as well to give an exemplification of its working ; and as an illustration of its effects, where only a few individuals had to be brought under it, we will cite a case that came within our own experience. In a large iron works in the Black Country, employing about one hundred and fifty mechanics, the wages stood at two shillings a week less than the men thought they ought to do, considering the state of the trade, and the rates of pay prevailing in other districts. The workmen therefore asked for an advance of two shillings per week, and were met by a point-blank refusal. They then asked that they might have a rise of a shilling a week immediately, and the other shilling some months later, but this proposal was also met by an unqualified refusal. It was an union shop, and after due deliberation the unionists decided that they must strike for the rise. Well, there were some half-dozen hands who had been long in the employ, who had sons in the works, and lived in freehold houses of their own. Urging these grounds as a reason for their proceeding, they objected to come out. Seeing this, about a dozen of the more faint-hearted among the other men said that, if *any* stayed in, they too would stay. With nearly a score of men left in, it was evident that if the strike lasted for any considerable time, others would have a good excuse for also going in—was evident, in fact, that the strike could not take place with any reasonable prospect of success. Feeling convinced of this, the more determined unionists stood to their rule, and *compelled* the half-dozen reluctants to come out in spite of all evasive pleas, and of some of them assuring the masters that they personally would not have left work had not the union ordered them to do so. The strike was for the full two shillings a week rise, and at the end of five days the employers conceded it unconditionally; and in the following week conceded also a proportionate advance of wages to their unskilled labourers. And thus, by a timely and uncompromising pressure upon half-a-dozen of its own members, the union gained a substantial advantage for four hundred men—for the labourers brought the total of the hands to that number. The great Newcastle strike affords an illustration of how the principle we are advocating acts upon a larger scale. When the strike had lasted for some weeks without any definite sign of a settlement, and short commons were becoming more or less the order of the day among the strike hands and their families, the masters, wise in their generation, offered a tolerably liberal compromise, provided the hands should be allowed to vote by *ballot* upon the question of its acceptance or non-acceptance. They knew that while the union leaders were resolved to maintain their policy of " no surrender," the general body of the men would not be in the least likely to openly vote for compromise whatever their private opinions might be individually. But they believed that at the stage the strike had reached a large number, probably a majority, would, on a ballot, have voted acceptance of the compromise. And there was substantial grounds for the belief! Many of the more far-seeing and uncompromising unionists *feared* that such *might* be the case ; that with the sense of responsibility to each other and " the trade " taken away, numbers might, from personal reasons, or in despair of ultimately gaining their demand in its entirety, vote in favour of the proposal of the masters. Therefore those whose voices practically ruled the action of the union vetoed the idea of the ballot. Had the desired (by the masters) ballot taken place—and but for the attitude of the unionists it would have taken place —the principle of the nine hours' movement might have been lost; and would, at any rate, have been greatly jeopardised. Had even a respectable minority voted in favour of closing with the offer of the masters, the case of the men would have been so greatly weakened in many ways, that outright defeat would probably soon have followed. At the time there was some high falutin' talk about the ballot proposal being scouted on the ground of its being an insult to the men, but the real motive and meaning of the rejection was that which we have indicated. Nor do we see that an avowal that such was the case would have been an admission of weakness. On the contrary, it would rather have been an evidence of strength. It was probably not less by their moral and constitutional power to enforce unity and secure obedience to authority, than by their money resources, that the leading spirits of the Newcastle strike were enabled to gain the concession of the nine hours' principle for themselves and the working classes at large. That the establishment of the nine hours' system is a great *national* benefit is pretty generally agreed; and there can be no doubt whatever about its being a great benefit to the working classes; and this great good was won by, and could not have been obtained without, that trade unionism which people who know little or nothing about it are so ready to abuse. That the ruling of a trades union in its corporate capacity should be made paramount over individual interests or feeling is not necessarily tyranny. The union leaders—we are not speaking now of one or two individuals who seem to have constituted themselves a sort of agitators-general to the working classes, but actual workmen who are officers or active members of their lodges, and of whom Bunnett, the secretary of the

Nine Hours League during the Newcastle strike, is a grand example—the union leaders are, generally speaking, men of greater business capacity than are the rank and file of the members; they are men, too, who make a greater study than do others of the position, strength, and opportunities of " the trade " in relation to the possibilities of promoting its interests. Seeing this, and that they themselves share whatever of peril or sacrifice the mode of action they recommend may involve, it is but just that their views should be considered as being in the nature of laws. Their position is often a very unenviable one. In enforcing personal sacrifice, and the sinking of individual opinion, in the endeavour to secure—and the belief that by so doing they can secure—a common good, they are in much the same position to the general body of the unionists as tax-makers are to tax-payers. All may agree that the objects for which the taxes are levied will be generally beneficial to the community at large, but many would shirk the payment of their individual share of the tax if the powers that be did not compel them to pay. That the power practically in the hands of trade union leaders has, like the power of minstries, been unwisely used on occasion, there can be no doubt, but that is no legitimate argument against the principle of the leaders having or exercising the power they have. The principle, we repeat, is a sound one, and, upon the whole, it has wrought for good.

The so-called tyranny of trade unionism is the one

point on which a case can be made out against the unions, that looks plausible to people who do not take the trouble to consider the subject in all its bearings, or who are prejudiced against the unions. That in all other respects in which they are operative, trades unions are unqualifiedly beneficial to their members, none even of those who are opposed to them can honestly gainsay. They are trade registry, trade insurance, and general insurance societies. By means of a network of lodges, and an organized system of reports from lodge secretaries, they are enabled to give members who are out of employment special and reliable information as to where they are or are not likely to obtain work. While members are out of employment, or incapacitated by sickness from following it, they afford them an income which, though small, is certain, and sufficient to obviate any appeal to charity. They make superannuation allowances, and make a provision for members who, through accident or disease, may be permanently disabled from following their trade. And finally, by means of an adequate funeral benefit, they give their members the assurance, so dear to the heart of working men, that whatever ups and downs they may have in life, they shall, when the end has come, at least be laid decently in mother earth, no pauper grave or pauper coffin enclosing them. The amount of good work which the unions do in these respects would, we fancy, astonish some of those who, with the rashness of ignorance, set them down as crying and unmitigated evils. Specific figures will, we think, convey the best idea of this work, and by way of illustration we will take a few statistics from the transactions of the "Amalgamated Engineers," the largest of the unions. In order that all may judge for themselves as to the degree of significance to be attached to the figures, we will first state that the society consists of thirty-five thousand members, that the entrance-fee to it ranges from fifteen shillings to three pound ten, according to the age of the member at the date of his admission, and every member, *while in employment*, pays a fixed subscription of one shilling per week. That such being the sources and extent of its income, its benefits are :—

Firstly, payment to members who are out of work from circumstances over which they have no control, at the rate of ten shillings a week for fourteen weeks, seven shillings a week for thirty weeks following, and six shillings per week for as much longer as they remain out of work. Secondly, sick pay at the rate of ten shillings per week for twenty weeks, and five shillings per week for as much longer as members may continue ill. Thirdly, superannuation allowance at the rate of seven shillings per week for life to members who are fifty years of age or upwards, and who have been in the society eighteen or more years. Fourthly, the payment in one sum of a hundred pounds to any member who through accident, blindness, imperfect vision, apoplexy, epilepsy, or paralysis, is rendered incapable of following his employment. Fifthly, at the death of a member his widow or next of kin receives the sum of twelve pounds to defray his funeral expenses, or on the death of his wife any member on applying for it may receive the sum of five pounds, leaving seven pounds to be paid to his representatives at his own decease. With the payments to and benefits from it thus set forth, let us take the operations of the society during the long period of disastrously dull trade that succeeded the commercial collapse brought about by the joint-stock mania—1867, and the two following years. In 1867 its total expenditure under the heads of the five benefits enumerated was £86,067, made up of items as follows :—Out of work pay, £58,243 ; sick pay, £15,558 ; superannuation allowance, £5,982 ; grants of £100 each to members permanently disabled by accident or disease, £1,000 ; funerals, £5,282. In 1868 the total was £95,143, the items being—out of work pay, £64,979 ; sick pay, £16,992 ; superannuation, £7,123 ; grants to disabled members, £1,000 ; funerals, £5,049. The total for 1869 was £93,012, being out of work pay, £59,980 ; sick pay, £17,777 ; superannuation, £8,055 ; grants to disabled members, £1,600 ; funerals, £5,600. The grand total of the expenditure of the society upon these benefits during the three years, therefore, amounted to £274,222 ; and if such figures do not speak for themselves, no comment upon them is likely to make their teaching understood. The total outlay of the society during these three years was considerably in excess of its total income during that time. But those three years were, as we have said, exceptionally bad ones, about the worst the trade has ever known; as a rule its expenditure is considerably below its income, so that even after the unexampled drain of those three years it had at the end of 1869 a clear balance in hand of £76,176—a balance that has been largely increased during the period of good trade that has ensued since that time.

In short, trades unions do more than any other existing institution to secure the working men "the glorious privilege of being independent." Trades unionists are, generally speaking, the best respected and most self-respecting of working men; and it will invariably be found that the best situated trades—as regards the position of the mass of the workmen engaged in them—are those that have the strongest unions. Of trade unionism, therefore, we say even more emphatically than we said of recent international combinations among the working classes, that it is a good thing as far as it goes. It, however, goes but a small way towards a general combination of the working classes, while the present constitution of the unions, and ideas of their members, are rather adverse than favourable to such a general combination. The very name Trade Union conveys that it must be exclusive; but apart from the *necessary* exclusiveness that lies in the qualifications for membership, the unions are very sectional affairs. There is no systematic inter-association among them; while the ideas of each incline to the We-the-People-of-England order, their notion of the interests of the working classes being, generally speaking, the interests of "the trade," or at the most of the artisan classes, especially the trade unionists among them. They have but little regard for the unskilled labourers attached to trades, and are, above all other men, bent upon "keeping them in their places," upon seeing that they remain unskilled labourers, and do not "creep into the trade;" while whatever of pity they have for those most to be pitied of all human beings, the agricultural labourers, is largely mixed with contempt. After all, however, it is questionable whether when all things are considered trade unions could be much other or better than they are. But taken with the shortcomings which, like other mundane institutions, they undoubtedly have, the unions are upon the whole, as we have shown, highly beneficial things. They are the most striking example extant of working-class combination and what it can effect. They are a practical and satisfactory proof that combination *is* the best and readiest means by which the working classes can apply their power, and through what they have already achieved they point conclusively to its being the policy of the working classes to increase and strengthen trades unionism as much as in them lies. In this last respect there is room and need for a good deal to be done. There are still many trades without unions, there are trades again with rival unions, trades with unions that are not constituted upon the best models, and others with unions that number but a small minority of the trade as their members. All these are weak points; points upon which amendment is needed, in which amendment could be effected, and would materially benefit the working classes. If, for instance, there was a well-organized drivers' union, we would not, at the time when the trades with unions were rejoicing over the gaining of the nine hours' movement, have had philanthropic gentlemen writing to the *Times* to point out that tramway and 'bus drivers had to work seven days a week and fifteen or sixteen hours a day. No trade with a soundly constituted union would work such hours—no trade with a union does work anything like such hours. Another weak point in trade unionism as it stands is the want of a more general amalgamation of unions of trades that are more or less interwoven with each other—trades that are, in fact, under the prevailing subdivision of labour, practically joint trades, each being engaged upon productions which when finished are the work of all. The engineers is an amalgamated society, and much of its strength and success is attributable to its being so. Its full title is " The Amalgamated Society of Engineers, Machinists, Millwrights, Smiths, and Pattern Makers." All of those branches are engaged in what is generally called the engineering trade. Previous to the year 1851 each of these trades had an union of its own, into which only members of that trade were admitted; but coming by that time to see that as their trade operations were to a common end, their trade interests were also broadly in common, they in that year amalgamated, and at once became —and still remain—the most powerful trade union in the world. Now at the present time there is a stonemasons' union, a bricklayers' union, a carpenters' union, and a painters' union; but there is *not*, as there ought to be, an amalgamated builders' union. Wherever there are a number of trades employed in the production of a single article or class of goods, it is, we think, a self-evident proposition that it would be more to the advantage of each and all of those trades that they should be united in a single great union than that each should have a small separate acting one. That while the general strength that lies in' trade unionism should be fully recognised by the artisan class, there should be so little of union amalgamation among cognate trades, is to be attributed to that want of comprehensiveness of view which we have spoken of as a weakness of the working classes. The greatest opportunity of extending the trade union principle, however, lies in the formation of labour union among the unskilled and agricultural classes of labourers. Such unions could not, of course, afford their members the substantial money assistance that trade unions do to theirs, but they could be made to give the strength that is found in unity, and to be a means of inter-communication and concerted action for the general good. If we had such unions on an adequate scale, it would no longer be possible for a newly-appointed dock-master to arbitrarily break down the already miserable pay of the dock labourers, at a time when trade was more consonant with a rise than a fall of wages; nor should we see the agricultural labourers in Dorsetshire working for eight shillings per week, while the same class were receiving twelve shillings a week in Yorkshire. This last is per-haps a more important illustration of the good such unions could do than at a first glance might appear. We think it may be safely assumed that broadly the profits of farm-ing are equal in the two counties, and that therefore the Dorsetshire labourer is made to suffer either for an in-feriority of soil for which the landlord should pay, or a want of skill or energy upon the part of the farmers, the conse-quences of which should fall upon them. If, therefore, a labour union could bring Dorsetshire wages up to the Yorkshire rate, it would, in addition to effecting the rise of wages, be enforcing a most momentous principle—that the burdens or losses, that in equity should fall upon land-lords or capital, are really borne by them, not, as is so largely the case at present, by labour. In the organization of labour unions, self-help would of course be the best help; but, as the labouring classes are at present situated, aid from others would be of great service; and "friends of the working classes" could do no better thing for the interests of those classes than promote the establishment of such unions. In this work, trade unionists could greatly assist; and in brotherliness they should do so—should, if necessary, initiate the movement. There is certainly a good deal in the plea that trade unionists have enough to do to look after their own affairs; but with all due allowances made on that score, they, as the most influential and happily placed section of the working classes, have it in their power to do much for the advancement of the interests of less fortunate sections. Each for themselves is a sound enough doctrine in a general way, but it is not one that it is well to see carried to extremes as between the various divisions of the working classes. To those who look at the moral bearings of the question of the improvement of the condition of the working classes—and they are a more important phase of the general question than those who do *not* look at them may think—it is a discouraging thing to find working men indifferent to any comprehensive scheme for the good of their class, unless it can be shown to them that they personally are likely to benefit by it in a special degree, or that its general advantages are certain to become operative within their lifetime.

While, however, we think there can be no reasonable doubt that a general combination of the working classes would, if rightly used, lead to a general improvement of their condition, and of the condition of society at large, it is perhaps a piece of " the eternal fitness of things " to be thankful for that such a combination has not as yet been brought about. In conjunction with the existing opinions and ideas of the majority of the working classes upon some of the cardinal points of the broad question of the relations between capital and labour, the strength which a general combination would give them might prove an instrument of self-destruction. In the arguments brought forward in advocacy of the retention by capital of its present proportion of the whole profits and results of production ; in the assertions that such proportion is not merely a just but also a natural and necessary one, working men have detected so much of what they conceive to be specious falsehood, and intended bugbearism, that, without further examination, they have jumped to the conclusion that the whole case of capital is of the same character. When they are told that capital has no country; that working men, by combining to *enforce* higher wages than capitalists say they can afford to give, are adopting a suicidal policy, driving capital—in other words, their own means of livelihood — out of their trade or country ; when working men hear this sort of thing—and it is a doctrine that is being constantly dinned into their ears with a burden of " woe, woe to ye if ye listen not to us the preachers and prophets ! " — they set it down as an attempt to lead " the Proletariat upon a wrong scent."

They say that to a very considerable extent capital has a country—the country in which it is sunk. With all the resources of modern invention given in, buildings and "plant" are still in a double sense *fixed* capital. Practically they are irremovable from country to country, and in the case of being disposed of on the ground that the business in which their money cost had been sunk, no longer returned an adequate profit, they would only be convertible or realisable at a sacrifice that would be very little short of absolute annihilation. Again, working men argue, that seeing how fully stocked every trade is with capital as well as with labour, it would be impossible for the realisable and circulating capital of any one considerable trade to be suddenly invested in another trade * without having the effect of reducing the returns to capital to a point as low if not lower than that to which the demand of the men would have brought them in the trade which the capitalists had abandoned. Further, and finally, working men believe that with the power that they are now acquiring of putting a general and simultaneous pressure upon capital, they can effectually cut the ground from under it in regard to the power of migrating here or there or into this or that trade at will. To instance the Newcastle strike once more. Had only

* Of course it follows as a natural sequence of the theory of the prophets of woe that the capital forced by workmen out of one trade would *all* seek the one other which was reputed at the time to be yielding the largest return to capital.

the Newcastle engineers got the nine hours, the theory that their employers would be likely to lose trade, and to look for some other mode of investing their capital, would have been tenable; but, as we have seen, the nine hours' movement was generally enforced throughout England, and was closely followed by the Continental equivalent—a ten hours' movement. The broad result of the nine hours' movement in this country is, that the artisan classes have gained for themselves—and from the previous rate of profits to capital—an addition to their income equal to about a thirteenth of its former total.* The substantial question at issue in the struggle for the nine hours was, whether the profits of capital could stand this diminution without disastrous results following; whether the endeavours to subject it to such diminution was not in the nature of an attempt to kill the goose that laid the golden eggs. Capital, and those of its inclining, solemnly asserted that such a reduction would mean ruin; bankruptcy to masters, beggary to workmen; and that in battling against it they were really fighting for the true interests of labour. The working classes, however, were hard of belief on the point—so hard of belief that they fought out the issue to the end, and in the end won; but both they

* Many people are under the impression that the workmen have gained six hours a week by the nine hours' movement, but as under the nine hours' system the working week consists of fifty-four hours, and in the engineering and several other trades previously consisted of fifty-eight hours, the gain is only four.

and capital survive. Indeed, considering the gloomy prognostications put forward by and on its behalf, it is not a little astonishing to see how flourishingly capital gets on under the state of things against the idea of which it so fervently lifted up its voice. The event has demonstrated that capital *could* stand the reduction, and, taking the prophetic vein ourselves for a moment, we will not hesitate to say that it could and *will* stand one further reduction in the proportion of its profits, and still remain in robust health—be all the more robust by reason of the reduction. We will venture to predict that within another twenty years capital will still be in a very comfortable and desirable position under an eight hours' system.

But because a great deal of humbug, *that working men have found out to be humbug,* has been talked in support of the present position of capital, it does not follow, as many of the working classes conclude, that all that is said about the rights of capital, and the necessariness of capital to production, is humbug. Though it is somewhat surprising that they should do so, working men, as a body, think too much of capital in the abstract, are too much—or perhaps we should say too invariably—given to see in an employer a capitalist, and nothing more. They do not see that capital, as they chiefly come into relation with it, as engaged in productive industries, is practically *a tool*— as much a tool, though in a larger way, as a hammer or file. They make no allowance for capitalistic skill, do not understand that it is as palpably and specially a skill as is mechanical skill, and as fully entitled to remuneration. The number of instances in which working men who have had no particularly great skill in their trade, technically speaking, have risen to be masters and capitalists in it ; and the fact that, of men who have started with equal advantages in respect to mere money capital, some, though working hard, have come to ruin, while others have made fortunes, would, it might be thought, be sufficient proof to make the existence and importance of such a skill self-evident; but it has not had that effect with working men, and that is the chief cause of their estimating the natural rights of capital as almost *nil* as compared with those of labour. They can appreciate inventitive talent, and understand its often being entitled to exceeding great reward ; but the capitalistic talent, which is second only to the inventitive one, as a means of giving work and developing and applying material resources, they do not as yet appreciate at its proper value. They do not realise to how great an extent it is a motive power in carrying on the every-day life of the world ; how greatly instrumental it is in spreading the benefits of inventions, and encouraging inventors. For instance, when Brassey, the great railway contractor, died, leaving a personalty of upwards of three millions, and people were talking of his leaving such great wealth, many working men were led to exclaim in an injured tone, " Ah, he made that out of *us !*" On the mention of his name they muttered of bone-grinding, bloodsucking, and the tyranny of capital; and they spoke of him as though he had, as a matter of course, been an enemy of the working classes—an enemy who had wronged and injured them to an extent the greatness of which was to be measured by the greatness of his wealth; while the real fact was, he was one of the greatest friends the working classes of this country ever had, as well as one of the most striking examples of capitalistic talent that could be adduced. It was not as an engineer, but as a capitalist, that he was great. He had the faculty of using capital in its capacity of a tool, as a general uses his soldiers. In his way he was a general, the greatest general that England has ever possessed—the Wellington of our armies of peace. He has had upwards of fifty thousand workmen in his employ at one time, and he always led his armies of labour victoriously. In constructing railways in all parts of the globe, he showed that English capital and labour combined could do for foreign nations what those nations could not do for themselves. He conclusively demonstrated to the world the superiority of British labour, and in so doing appreciably raised its value. His works were of national utility; and in most of the great countries of Europe, with the exception of his own, he was titled or decorated as a man who had done the state some service. In making his own money he must have circulated millions and millions of wages among the working classes; and great as was the fortune that he left behind him, its total amount probably did not represent more than a *necessary* margin for such a business as his was at its highest point. That such non- or mis-apprehension upon so vital a point of the relationships between capital and labour, as the existence of a distinct capitalistic faculty, which is an essential element of production, does very largely exist among the working classes at present, and that *in its nature, and potentially,* it is the grave and destructive danger that the advocates of capital say it is, no observant and candid working man will deny. And that is why we say that great a means of good as a general combination of the working classes could be made, it is well we have not got it as yet! If with the weakness of the false views we have been speaking of was associated the strength of combination, there would be painfully good reason to exclaim,— " Let chaos come again ! " But with other things as they are, the danger lying in these views is for the most part only potential, not operative. However useless or little deserving working men may think capital, they know, as a matter of fact and experience, that if they would proceed against it successfully, they must proceed slowly. An eight hours' working day has been the fixed idea and aim of at least two generations of workmen, and though they were told that it was visionary, utopian, suicidal, and so forth, they refused to give credit to the prophets of failure and evil. They worked resolutely and unceasingly towards the desired end, and though they met with many heavy blows and much sore discouragement, they were not dismayed. They rallied from each immediate defeat and struggled on, borne up by an unshaken and unshakable confidence in ultimate success. After many years they have at length reached the last stage but one of their journey, and they, at any rate, have no doubt that in good time they will win the goal they have so long marked out for themselves. Now, the slowness of progress that characterizes their endeavours to place themselves in a better position relatively to capital has, as a set-off to its disadvantages to the working classes, this important advantage—it allows time for knowledge and education to spread amongst them to a degree that enables them to make a wise and moderate use of each successive advance towards their end. Taking the facts of the past from which to make deductions as to the probabilities of the future, there is every reason for confidently believing that the spread of knowledge and growth of intelligence which is leading to the extension of the combination principle among the working classes will, by the time it has led to such a development of that principle as would give labour anything like a dictatorial position, have enabled the general body of working men to see how erroneous are some of their present views, and to form a just conception of the fact that capital as well as labour has rights, and that the more easily understood than described faculty which we have called "capitalistic talent" is one of the most important of those necessary for production. Upon the whole, therefore, there is very little real ground to fear that labour, in pursuing its purpose of altering the relations between capital and itself to its own advantage, will act in the destructive manner which, in the existing state of its views, we have admitted would be potentially possible.

A number of the more thoughtful and better educated among the working classes do recognise the importance of the capitalistic talent, and see the danger. that lies in its non-recognition by the general body of their class, but these men are as firmly of opinion as any of the others, that labour should, and without any injustice to individuals, and with great benefit to society *could*, be in a materially better position relatively to capital. As the present views of these men are what the views of the labouring classes at large will be when they come to be better educated and more enlightened, it is well worth while to place them upon record, so that in case of their being demonstrably fallacious those to whom it is given to finally discriminate false scents from true may be enabled to come forth with their demonstrations. The views of these men are to this general effect :—That while the capitalistic operator in production is individually entitled to a much greater remuneration than is the individual manual labourer, the extent and rate of that remuneration must be regulated less by his and the individual labourer's proportionate necessariness to the work of production in which they are both engaged, than by its relation to the means of securing the greatest good to the greatest number. That rates of interest, returns upon capital, and other talk of that kind is—only talk. That though an employer who now makes fifty thousand a year may only be getting what at present is held to be simply a fair return upon his capital, it would be much better for society and for human happiness if his share of the profits of production were reduced to thirty thousand a year, and the other twenty thousand a year divided among his workmen in the shape of an increase of wages. These, broadly put, are the views of the more advanced thinkers among the working classes—the views that are likely to become general, and that at no very distant date there will be a determined attempt to practically enforce, unless in the meantime it can be shown that the possibilities of the case do not admit of their attainment, or that if attained for a time they are likely to ultimately prove injurious. By the time the great majority of working men have come to hold these views they will be open to reasonable conviction as to their being wrong. But they will not allow vague generalities or mere assertions to be *reasonable* grounds of conviction. Hitherto whenever labour has insisted upon any concession, capital has cried out that such demand, if granted, would inevitably prove to be the metaphorical last straw that would break its (capital's) back. In the course of years, however, many of these (allegedly) fatal demands have had to be granted, and yet, as we see, capital has *not* given up the ghost; it lives and prospers. If when labour makes further demands, as it undoubtedly will, capital raises the last-straw cry, it will have to be in some more definite form than any it has hitherto adopted. " Foreign competition," or any other generality of that kind, will not serve their turn. It would be treated as a cry of Wolf, wolf! where there was no wolf. If capital would dissuade labour from persistence in any demand for better terms on the ground that such demand involves a strain upon capital that it cannot bear without being prejudicially affected as an instrument of production, it must show plainly and precisely that such is the case. It must the secrets of its prison-house unfold—must produce its books, give exact facts and figures, and afford the means for their verification. If it does not do this, no last-straw cry of the general order that it may raise will be believed —by working men.

Large numbers of the working classes, and many among other classes, are of opinion that co-operation in production is capable of being, and destined to be, the solution of the difficulties in which the question of the relations between capital and labour is embedded. But this is a view of the matter in which the more thoughtful and observant few among working men do not coincide. Inside the working classes the idea is chiefly based upon that non-apprehension of a distinct capitalistic talent of which we have been speaking. It contemplates the abolition of capitalist employers and the dividing of the *whole* of the profits that now fall to them among share-holding workmen. This idea is, of course, regarded as impracticable by those who do recognise the existence of a special capitalistic talent, and comprehend something of its nature and rarity. They argue that not only cannot capitalist employers be abolished, but that the character of their talent is a *natural* bar to co-operation; a sign to those who read it aright that co-operation is not *the* solution of the modern sphinx. It must be evident upon the face of the matter that under co-operative conditions capitalistic talent would be in chains, and its immense usefulness to the world, including the working classes, seriously impaired. Some of the greatest achievements of this talent—achievements by which civilization at large have greatly benefited—have, *till they were sanctified by success,* been regarded by those who had not the capitalistic instinct as mere mad schemes—schemes the attempting of which a majority of any considerable association of working men whose interests would have been affected by failure would have emphatically vetoed. On the other hand, the knowledge that they did risk other interests besides their own, and that in case of failure a thousand angry men would consider themselves as having the right to cast the stone, would often give pause to capitalists, would make them timid and hesitating where alone they would be daring and decided. To our thinking, a little reflection upon matters of detail ought to make it apparent that the elements of production are not co-operative in their nature, in the sense we are now speaking of. We can understand those outside the working classes believing in the idea of co-operation in production, but that any working man who, with eyes to see and ears to hear, has been engaged in a large workshop should be found to have faith in it seems to us passing strange. "Jack is as good as his master," and "I'm as good a man as you," are principles that, to say the least of it, obtain as largely in workshops as other circles ; and jealousy, envy, ill-feeling, and talk of favouritism and back-stair influences, in connection with promotions in position or pay, are anything but unknown in them even now, when a master-mind can authoritatively say this shall, or that shall not be. What sort of a pass matters would come to if every envious or aggrieved workman was a partner in the concern, and had a voice in its management, is one of those things that can, perhaps, be more easily imagined than described. To those who have seen nothing of the inner life of workshops this may appear a far-fetched objection, but as a matter of fact it is a very important one, and in practice would be very likely to occur if not watchfully guarded against, while the necessity of guarding against it would be a serious restriction upon those who had to direct operations. One of the strong points of the capitalistic talent is to distinguish *fitness*, to see abilities in men that do not appear on the surface, and are not seen by others; to, in short, discern who are the right men for the right places. In the exercise of their discrimination in this respect, masters and managers often promote men to positions of authority whom nine-tenths of their fellow-workmen do not consider entitled or qualified to be so promoted; and if the dissatisfied majority were in the position of partners they would inevitably organize a meeting and "resolute" the promoted man, and perhaps the promoting manager, out of office. How injuriously the possibility of such proceedings would affect the operations of production need not be pointed out. Again, those of the working classes who believe in the idea of co-operative production look only at one side of it—the *rosy* side. They regard it simply as a means of immediately transferring the profits of the capital employed in production, and in time the capital itself, to their class. They never reflect that there are losses as well as gains in the operation of productive industries. The notion of working men as partners in a *losing* co-operative concern, working for reduced wages, or no wages at all, is undreamed of in their philosophy. When they come to realise the seamery side of the case, their faith in the potency of co-operation will be very much shaken, if not altogether dissipated. In the Brigg's Colliery and other undertakings, both in England and on the Continent, there have been arrangements between masters and workmen, by which the latter have been awarded a certain share of the profits of capital, in addition to their wages. These instances have been and are frequently cited as examples of the success of the co-operative principle in production. Strictly looked at, however, these cases illustrate, not the principle of co-operation, but the liberality and philanthropy of the individual employers concerned. The latter make the arrangements voluntarily, and can discontinue or alter them at will, while the workmen on the one hand have no voice in the management, and on the other no responsibility in case of loss. So far as we know, there has been no instance of successful co-operation in production; nor while the human character remains constituted as it is at present is it likely that there will be any such instance upon a considerable scale. To sum up on the point—and we think we have fairly led up to and given grounds for the conclusion—it is as workmen, employed, wages-receiving "hands" that the working classes at large must be benefited, if they are to be benefited at all. This the best men among them, that is the leading trade unionists, recognise as a natural law ; a fact that *must* be accepted. It is the *line* upon which their operations is based. Of *how* they are likely to attempt to work toward their end we have already spoken. In finally quitting this part of our subject we would for clearness-sake explicitly state, as we have throughout implied, that we do not confound co-operation in production with co-operation in distribution. The latter is within certain limits a perfectly practicable thing. It has already greatly benefited the working classes, and is capable of doing, and is in all probability destined to do, much more for them. Between the working-class consumer and the producer, or even the first buyer, there is, as things stand, and where co-operative stores do not intervene, an unnecessary degree of middleman-ism. Too many profits are got out of, too many adulterations got into goods ere they reach such small purchasers as individual working-class consumers necessarily are, and for remedying this co-operative distribution is undoubtedly the best means.

There is one point in connection with the general question of the relations between capital and labour to which, though they note it, the working classes do not give anything like the degree of attention that in our opinion they ought to do—that it would be wise and profitable for them to do—the point, namely, of emigration. When working men are told by political economists that overpopulation is the real cause of poverty and low wages, they answer that there is no over-population. But the doctrine that there is room enough for all, though it may be theoretically true, cannot be effectively true till there exists a systematic and readily applicable means of apportioning the " all " to the " room ; " that is, until such countries as England have, as part of their constitution, a well-organized and smoothly-working system of emigration for carrying off from them what, in reference to their space and capabilities of affording employment, is over-population. The working classes see in a general way that emigration would be a great benefit to them, and in times of special distress it is always one of the means of relief upon which they *would* fall back if they *could*—if it were available. To them, however—and to a good many other people, we should imagine—it has always seemed that the formation and direction of a system of emigration adapted to carry off an overflow of population, and accessible to such of the industrious poor as were suffering from the results of that overflow, was a self-obvious function of the governments of old countries, especially those which had colonies of their own. It has therefore always been to Government that the English working classes have applied for help when, on the ground of an overstocked home labour market, they have wished to emigrate upon any considerable scale. Governments, however, have on one pretext or another always declined to give the required assistance ; the unemployed more immediately concerned in each case have lingered on as best—a very bad best—they could, and the matter has been allowed to drop. But should it have been so allowed to drop? We think not. If Government won't help them, that is all the greater reason why they should try to help themselves in the matter. We believe they could do so. In times of dull trade, the trade-unions spend hundreds of thousands in out-of-work pay; the Amalgamated Engineers alone, as we have previously mentioned, spending fifty and sixty thousand a year in this way. In such times millions of working-class savings have also to be spent, while strikes, to gain concessions that in a less crowded labour market would have been granted for the asking, have likewise cost their millions. Speaking broadly, we should say that a tithe of what has been spent and lost by the working classes in these ways during the last twenty years would, under judicious management, have *bought* and established a colony as large as England. In this matter, as in most others, what is past cannot be recalled; but working men could scarcely set themselves to the discussion of a more important question than whether in future a portion of such moneys could not be applied to purposes of emigration. In times of ordinary briskness many of the artisan class are inclined to be lukewarm on the subject of emigration, by reason of a supposition to the effect, that in new countries the agricultural labourer is more important than, and classed above, the mechanic. On the narrow-mindedness of this view we will not comment; we will only say that we think it is greatly exaggerated as regards the substance of it. Where on new lands produce is being raised to a considerably greater extent than is necessary to supply those directly engaged in cultivation, there arises a necessity for artisan labour—roads, houses, implements, and a thousand and one other things are soon wanted. But apart from this there are often opportunities for artisans to emigrate to where there is a call for their craft, and a certainty of their bettering themselves. Emigration clubs upon a large scale might easily be started, and still more easily might a special emigration fund be associated with each trade union. Every grade of the working classes might well join in an emigration movement, if it was only on the ground of self-interest, for there is none of them that would not be benefited by emigration—benefited both in respect to the men who left the country and those who remained in it. Take even the engineers—the best situated of all the larger trades. The thirty-five thousand members of its union are the *élite* of the trade; men of approved competence, steadiness, and integrity; men who could command the pick of work were there a sufficiency of it in the country to employ all "the trade." That there is not such a sufficiency could not be more conclusively demonstrated than by the fact that in moderately good times there are always hundreds, and in bad times thousands, of these men out of employment. Some of them are out of work for weeks, months, aye, and—in the periods of reactionary dulness that follow flush seasons of trade— even years. The expenditure by the union of sixty-four thousand pounds in one year as out-of-work pay is a tolerably significant fact in this connection; but a few smaller more detailed figures, taken from the Transactions of the society, will more strikingly exemplify the straits to which the artisan class are liable to be reduced from want of work ; in other words, from over-population. In addition to its specified benefits, the Amalgamated Society of Engineers has an extra and discretionally granted one, in the shape of a "benevolent fund," for the relief of exceptional cases of distress among its members. The fund is raised by occasional small levies upon the members, and varies in total amount from about one thousand to about three thousand a year, according to the necessities of the time. This fund is administered in a manner that leaves very little possibility of its being either imposed upon or ill-applied, so that there can be no reasonable doubt of the distress that it relieves being genuine and unavoidable. The case of a distressed member is first brought before his branch in lodge-meeting assembled, and if it is satisfied as to his being truly needful and deserving, it appeals on his behalf to the general council of the society, who, if in turn satisfied concerning the application, make a grant ranging in amount from two to seven pounds. From July 1st, 1869, to June 30th, 1870, five hundred and eleven such grants were made, amounting to an aggregate sum of £2,007. Several of the cases relieved were those of men who had been out of employment upwards of two years; but by way of specimen we will take more *average* cases. In the society's report the names of the relieved members are given in full, but initials will suffice in this place. Here is one of fifteen appeals from a manufacturing town in Lancashire :— "R. N. S., who had been on donation" (that is, on out-of-work pay) "forty weeks, and during the twelve months previous sixteen weeks. He was receiving 7s. per week, with a wife and seven children dependent upon him for support, three of his children earning conjointly 13s. 6d. per week. Five pounds was granted. He had two previous grants—£5 in November, 1862, and £6 in December, 1863."

From upwards of a hundred appeals from the metropolitan district the following may be cited as an ordinary case, there being some not so bad, and others much more distressful :—

"A. S., who had been on donation thirty-seven weeks, and twelve months prior had been on benefit thirty-three weeks. During this time one of his children died and his wife was confined. He was in receipt of 7s. per week. Four pounds was granted."

This is how it is with the picked men of the best trade of the country, and any member of the union looking through the list of the benevolent fund grants, might with a sorrowful truthfulness say to himself, "This is but a picture of what I might be." It is a state of things to which men are reduced by circumstances beyond their own control—to which consequently any man in the trade *may* be reduced, since in slack times, when there is *not* work enough for all, some *must* be brought to it. When it is this way among the Amalgamated Engineers, it may easily be guessed how it is with other trades, and with those of the working classes who have no trades. These are painful facts, but like most evil things they have a lesson for good in them; and to us, we repeat, their lesson to working men seems plainly and emphatically to be—Emigrate. Carry into practice your own theory that there is room enough for all. Go ye to your mountain—the room—since it cannot come to you.

The lot of the working classes is, upon the whole, a very sad one, to many of them an utterly miserable one—a veritable death in life. That it can be amended we fully believe, but we are as fully persuaded that it is by themselves that the amendment must be wrought. It is to them that the hitherto unanswered question of the modern sphinx is directly addressed. It is they who pay the tremendous penalty of its remaining unsolved, and who in that seem to be marked as the appointed Œdipus. This is substantially how they have come to see the matter for themselves; and they accept "the situation," and, while recognising the Herculean character of the task, they are not dismayed. But while taking as their motto, "Self-help is the best help," they know that there are many able men of other classes who, *for their sake*, are devoting all the energies of their mind to the solution of the great question, and from these they will always gratefully receive advice, suggestions, or assistance; and in no better—we will even say in no holier—cause could any man give aid.

THE PRESS AND THE PEOPLE.

> " How shall I speak thee, or thy power address,
>   Thou God of our idolatry, the Press ?
> By thee, religion, liberty, and laws
> Exert their influence, and advance their cause;
> By thee, worse plagued than Pharaoh's land befell
> Diffused, make earth the vestibule of hell :
> Thou fountain at which drink the good and wise,
> Thou ever-bubbling spring of endless lies,
> Like Eden's dread probationary tree,
> Knowledge of good and evil is from thee."
>   COWPER.

" I KNEW a very wise man that believed that if a man were permitted to make all the ballads, he need not care who should make the laws of a nation." So wrote that bold and intelligent seventeenth-century politician, Andrew Fletcher of Saltown, in a letter to the Marquis of Montrose. The letter purported to be " An Account of a Conversation," but posterity has taken it for granted that Fletcher was himself the " very wise man," and the shrewd saying which is now a proverbial and oft-quoted expression is set down as his. How pithy a saying it was, what a knowledge it evinced of the salient characteristics of the many-headed, there is no need to point out here. Song has always been a power among the peoples of the nations,

and is so even now, when other means have, in a great
measure, superseded it in the most important of the
national functions that it once fulfilled; as witness the enthusiasm which, under certain circumstances, such songs
as "Rule Britannia," "The Watch on the Rhine," and
"The Marseillaise," still evoke. At the time when Fletcher
recorded his saying, ballads did for the people in things
political a great deal of that which is now done for them
by the press—formed a vehicle for the expression of
spontaneous ideas and wishes, and served as instruments
for arousing latent and creating new opinions among
them. Had Fletcher, however, lived at this day, and
been desirous of influence with the people, he would
have wished to be not a writer of ballads, but an "In-
spirer" of a working-class "Organ," an organ with
"Police Intelligence," "News of the Week," and "Accidents and Offences" as its stock tunes, and political
leaders and letters, and "Answers to Correspondents," as
its variations. A press organ is now an essential element
of power in the nation; who would obtain the latter must
possess the former as a means to the end. Each division
of society, and every "interest" of any considerable
magnitude or strength, has its press organ or organs,
without which it would be both absolutely and relatively
weaker. An acknowledged press organ is greater than an
individual law-maker, and the aggregate organism of the
press, if unanimous, is probably more powerful than the

whole body of our law-makers; for though most of us
deny the impeachment if brought against us personally, it
can scarcely be doubted that broadly the press in a great
measure creates, as well as expresses, that public opinion
to which even law-makers must ultimately bow. But while
an organ gives power to an interest or party, it in turn
receives power from their being powerful in proportion as
they are numerous, united, or strong. This being the
case, it may be considered natural that in things political
numbers of papers lay claim to being the organ, or, at any
rate, *an* organ of the working classes. If those classes
were to believe all that they are told in this connection,
they would be the best represented section of society; as
a matter of fact, they are—and that in more senses than
one—the worst. If the conventional, the toast-master,
the upper and middle class idea of the constitution and
extent of "the press" were a verity, the working classes
would be absolutely without press representation. Among
those journals which quote each other's articles as the
"Opinions of the Press," and which not only foreigners, but
the great majority of those outside the working classes at
home, regard as being the whole press of the country—
among these self-assuming, greatly believed in, and really
powerful journals, the working classes have not a single
special representative. That is to say, not a representative that they admit to be such, that does not assume an
unwarranted and unjustifiable authority, or make a false

pretence in professing to be such, or whose views go anything like far enough in the direction of their own to
please them. Indeed, it is a standing and most irritating
grievance with working men, that these journals, which
profess to combinedly express the total of public opinion,
not only sin in omission, but also in commission; that,
not content with not representing the working classes,
they wilfully and seriously *mis*represent them—take their
name in vain, and for political or class purposes attribute
to them opinions and feelings the very opposite of those
they really entertain. That this grievance is, to say the
least of it, founded upon fact, no person who reads the
newspapers, and has at the same time opportunities of
knowing what opinions really prevail among the working
classes, will for a moment doubt. Nor need the fact of
the press making a stalking-horse of "the working man"
overcome us with special wonder—it is only following the
fashion in doing so. There is nothing more wonderful or
tricky in the *Standard* creating (upon paper) a non-
existent being, and labelling it "The Conservative Working Man," and describing a gathering of members of
parliament, colonels, and squires, as a meeting of a
Working Men's Constitutional Association; or in the
Telegraph speaking in the name of the working classes,
with an implication, so strong as just to escape being an
assertion, of being their confidant, and the authorised
exponent of their opinions and wishes—there is nothing

more surprising or wrong in this sort of thing, of which scores of general and specific examples could, if necessary, be adduced, than there is in those who seek to legalise marriage with a deceased wife's sister, asserting, as they have done, that it is a working man's question, and a measure greatly desired by the working classes; or agriculturists seeking a repeal of the malt tax, affecting to be chiefly influenced by a desire to cheapen "the working man's glass of beer." We are not of those who think that the hand of every man is *against* the working man, but, as a matter of fact, it would appear that the hands of all manner of parties and interests are *upon* him when they want anything. There is evidently an impression abroad that his name is a tower of strength in demanding legislative concessions, and as a consequence it is used to back all manner of demands. If there are any outside the working classes who form a conception of them from the many and various things asked for in their names, they must certainly regard them as a very embodiment of greed and dissatisfaction. Working men have an idea that in some instances they are so judged, and this is one thing among others that makes them so sore in respect to this practice of taking them as a stalking-horse. The press being a permanent institution, and dealing with all public questions that crop up, is the most frequent offender in this way, and its offences are committed in a manner that makes them doubly aggravating. Occasionally a paper will definitively use the name of the working classes when "fathering" upon them some opinion which they do not hold; but in most instances they manage, so to speak, to evade making themselves liable. As a rule, the stalking-horse business is done by an all-inclusive generalisation, which takes in and uses the working classes without distinctly specifying them. Some opinion or feeling that may really be general among the upper or middle classes, or that, on the other hand, may merely be invented to suit the passing and special purpose of the minister, or party or interest whose organ asserts their existence, but which, in any case, is in opposition to views entertained by the working classes—some opinion or feeling of this kind is by a deft use of expressions of universality made to appear universal. It is spoken of as having entered into "the great heart of the nation,"—as a thing on which high and low, rich and poor are agreed,—upon which the voice of the people, from peer to peasant, is as one man, —concerning which there is unanimity from land's end to land's end, and much more in the same sweeping but safely general tone. There is never any attempt to argue up to or demonstrate this universality. It is taken as understood, and all argument and demonstration deduced from the position of its being *the* granted proposition. It is easy to understand how much this style of procedure annoys those who are opposed to the opinions thus put forth; who, so far as their opportunities permit, express that opposition, and have a feeling amounting to conviction that those claiming universal belief for the contrary views are perfectly aware of the existence of this difference of opinion. That by the plan we speak of the working classes are frequently "bowled out," are in a greater or less degree extinguished where the expression of opinion is concerned, none know better than themselves. But this "smart" journalism sometimes cuts backwards—does harm not only to the working classes, but also—and in a greater degree—to the cause or person it is intended to serve. We will give an instance of this which, to our thinking, is so significant and important as to justify its being specially selected as an illustrative case in point, notwithstanding that it involves the necessity of dwelling upon a subject which is scarcely a pleasant one for a writer to deal with—the subject, namely, of the *real* feelings of the working classes in regard to the illness of the Prince of Wales. It is a subject that, as a matter of taste, would perhaps be best avoided, but there is a higher thing than taste to be considered—truth. And it is in the interest of truth that we speak. We take this subject in preference to any other to illustrate the principle of the reflex action of the trick of journalism to which we are calling attention, because, independently of its affording a striking illustration, it has a distinctive importance, and further and more particularly, because when it was being discussed as the event of the day taste was allowed to, in a great measure, restrain and burke the expression of a truth which, however disagreeable it may sound to ears polite, is so important from a national point of view that it ought to be spoken.

That English Republicanism has no material power,—that the material powers, money and property, are wholly against it, may or may not be true, but that English republicans are " rare exceptions," as Mr. Gladstone in the course of the Louise-dowry debate asserted, and as many others opposed to republicanism affect to believe, is *not* true—is decidedly the reverse of true. It is a mere matter of fact—and as a matter of fact, not of opinion, we state it—that the general body of the working classes now hold republican opinions, and that those opinions have grown out of an objection to the costliness of monarchy and the preponderance of the sham element in its composition. To them a prince who is nothing but a prince, is simply " the accident of an accident," and a person who gets a large slice of the national revenue without making any return for it, but who does not and would not get it with their goodwill. The feeling of ill-will accruing from these opinions is directed *ultimately* against the institution of monarchy, but in the meantime a portion of it is visited—most unfairly, we think ; but, as we have just said, we are not now expressing opinions, but speaking to facts—upon the living representatives of royalty. This personal phase of the ill-feeling is not really very deep or malignant, but in some cases it is blusterous and outspoken, and when the Prince of Wales fell ill, some of the more pronounced and reckless-tongued among the working-class republicans began to express themselves as being anything but grieved, and to talk much more of the advantages of a reduction of the civil list by £40,000 a year, than of the probabilities of the Prince's recovery. The more moderate men, however —and they were an overwhelming majority—not only did not join in this tone, but they remonstrated against it. They were as much republicans as the others, they said, but still monarchy was as yet the order of the day, and the heir to the throne, no more than another man, could help being his parents' son. He was a husband and father as well as a prince, and it was wrong to be less wishful for his recovery, to have less of sympathy for his near relatives, than would have been the case with them in regard to any other public man personally unknown to them. The majority were disposed to think kindly of him as a suffering fellow-man; many went beyond that; and altogether the feeling evoked by his illness was *at first* of a character calculated to materially lessen whatever personal ill-will there had previously existed against the representatives of monarchy. That such a desirable result would have flowed from this feeling had the Press let well alone, there can be little doubt. Had it been content with publishing the bulletins and expressing a *manly* sympathy, it would have served the cause of royalty; by acting as it did, it injured it. As soon as it was known that the Prince's illness was of a serious character, the papers set up a daily song of lamentation pitched in a tone that palpably indicated either that human nature had suddenly and for the time-being changed, or that the overwhelming *intensity* (in words) of the grief of these weeping leaders was forced and insincere; was, in a word, manufactured. The Press as a whole gushed, broke out in that really idolatrous tone which has characterized its utterances in regard to royalty since it has been made apparent that among the "common people" there is a strong desire to cast it down rather than to worship it. Concerning the death of Nelson it was a truth as well as a figure of speech to say that "Britannia wept with silent grief oppressed." He had done the State a great service, had made his country really "mistress of the seas," and the envy and admiration of the world, and he died as he had lived, gloriously. But to represent Britannia as in the same state over the intimation that the Prince of Wales was ill, was "coming it too strong," and doing the Prince an injury. He had done the State no service, and they knew it, and his proceedings in the "Autumn Manœuvres" certainly pointed to the conclusion that he was not destined to become a second Black Prince, and cover himself and his country with military glory.

The most and best that could be said of him was that he was good-natured ; had the genial qualities usually associated with good nature ; had stood the temptation and adulation to which he had been subjected with as little of evil result as would have been the case with most young men, and less than would have been the case with many men ; and that we might easily have a much worse king than he promised to make. This, on first hearing of his illness, is what the bulk of the working classes did say of him, and that in a kindly spirit and in association with a wish for his recovery. But this tone of feeling was changed when the press began to put forth its hysterical leaders on the subject of the illness—leaders which were as hyperbolically and fulsomely flattering as the capacities of the English language would admit of their being, and which, by the use of the universal implication of which we have spoken, imputed to the working classes a participation in the exaggerated sentiments expressed ; when the working classes were told—in effect—that by the Prince's illness the gaiety of the nation was eclipsed ; that in every home, "however so humble," there was gloom and anxiety as though one of their own were ill ; that the spirits of every man rose or fell each day according as the bulletins were more or less favourable or unfavourable ; and that any who had previously imagined that they had in any way disliked royalty, now discovered that they dearly loved its representatives, and had never really understood how much they had been attached to them until they were threatened with the dire calamity of the loss of one of them.

When, morning after morning, working men saw column upon column of this sort of drivelling, and that too at a stage of the illness when the records of the gushing papers showed that the brother of the sick Prince at any rate was not so overcome by his grief but that he could go snipe-shooting, and "honour the theatres with his presence "—when they saw these things they were irritated and disgusted, and, reasonably enough, their resentment extended to the Prince as well as the press. There was more fuss being made about him, they said, than there would have been had a thousand poor men lay fever-stricken in Bethnal Green. They wished him no harm, but if there was to be all this sickening and lying palaver over the illness of one man just because he was Prince of Wales, then the sooner there were no Princes of Wales the better it would be for the country. In that case perhaps the press would devote a portion of its space and energy to advocate the necessity for the extension of sanitary improvements to those neighbourhoods in which the poor perish by tens of thousands for lack of them, instead of to suggesting and going out of its way to attempt to demonstrate that there must be some sanitary defect in the mansion or neighbourhood wherein fever had presumed to lay its prostrating hand upon a prince. That was the strain of remark into which the more moderate working-class republicans were stung by the attitude of the press, and, talking in this tone themselves, they were less ready and emphatic in checking their more advanced brethren in the exposition of their doctrine to the effect that a saving of £40,000 a year in the civil list was, as a personal matter, of infinitely more importance to the working classes than the life of a mere prince.

When the all but fatal relapse in the Prince's illness took place, there was among the working classes a strong revulsion of feeling in his favour. None were in a rational and natural way—in such a way as ordinary men could be expected to feel for one who was only known to them by name—more sincerely sorry to hear of the relapse, or more earnestly wishful that it might not prove fatal, than were working men as a body. None watched the battle for life that ensued with a more keen or kindly interest than did they. None would have done truer reverence to the fair young wife or widowed mother in that time of their heavy trouble than they would have done ; none would have been more disinterestedly willing to have done anything in their power to have served or consoled them than they would have been. But still, as we have said, their sorrow was a limited, a natural one. They were not of those who paid so ill a compliment to the royal family as to assert that their grief, that the grief of any outsiders, was as poignant as that of those of his own blood, those to whom the *man*, the husband, the father, the son, the brother, was near and dear. If, as the papers at the time alleged, the nation hung weeping and despairing over the Prince's sick bed, the working classes were for the time not of the nation ; and whatever may have been the case with others, the feeling excited in their breasts by the illness was not of so overpowering or all-absorbing a nature as to in any way unfit them for following their ordinary occupations, or thinking of their every-day affairs. Their grief on his account was not such as it would have been over one of their own relatives, was not even such as it would have been over some who were not their own. There would have been a deeper personal grief among them had the Baroness Burdett Coutts lay a-dying ; a greater sense of national loss had it been Gladstone's life that was despaired of. Such affectionate solicitude towards the Prince as was elicited by his relapse was, however, like that excited by the first news of his illness, neutralised, or more than neutralised —in regard to any permanent good feeling that might have grown out of it—by the slavish and offensive maundering of the press. Over the relapse it out-gushed even its previous gushing. It, so to speak, grovelled on the earth, tore its hair, clothed itself in sackcloth, and cast ashes upon its head. It wept, and would not be comforted ; cried, " Woe, woe is us if our Prince is taken away from us ; all life and light will be gone from us,

and our only desire will be to wrap our mantles about us
and die decently." During the time when it was feared,
almost expected, that each bulletin would be the one
announcing death, feeling and attention were so concentrated upon the hourly wavering question of life or death,
that the regulation daily howls of the press—howls
palpably even less sincere than the whisky-inspired
howls of an Irish wake—were but little regarded. But
when the immediate danger was past, this newspaper
drivel afforded grounds for some very odious comparisons
being made about royalty. The *Pall Mall Gazette* of
Dec. 16, 1871, in an article on "The Prince and his
Commentators," hitting at "the sighing, weeping, agonised
scribe of the *Telegraph*," observed that "the nauseating
horrors of forced and false sentiment" penned by the
agonised scribe in question were not, after all, meant for
the Prince, but "only intended to infuse into the minds
of gentle readers a feeling of melting admiration for the
good, the genial, the eloquent, pious, and pathetic writer;"
and it (the *Pall Mall*) emphatically protested against its
contemporary's leaders on the Prince's illness on the
grounds that they were "compounded like an American
drink," and made up of "maudlin reflections, sham tears,
and an affected agony of exhortations and piety." Now,
what the *Pall Mall Gazette* thought of the *Telegraph's*
writings concerning the Prince's illness is very much like
what the working classes thought of the writings of the

press generally upon that subject : they were very strongly
of opinion that if, in addition to being rank hypocrisy,
they were not arrant nonsense, they were worse—arrant
blasphemy.   If there was any one journal which they
regarded as worse than the other in this respect, it was
the *Times.* The leading journal was held to have delved
a yard beyond the rest when, by way of climax to its
"nauseating horrors of forced and false sentiment," it (on
the 11th of December, 1871) took the Prince's illness as
the text for a sermon leader, the burden of which was
Divine Right—divine right as a still extant thing, and a
natural instinct.   The fact that critical journals have
frequently asserted—and quoted chapter and verse in
support of their assertion—that the history of the *Times*
is often much more curious than true, may be cited as a
slight apology for the presumption of working men in
differing from its teaching upon this point.   They could
understand the realism of the doctrine of divine right as
put by Wordsworth into the mouth of Rob Roy—

> " That they should take who have the power,
> And they should keep who can."

The right divine of a strong arm, strong mind, and
unscrupulous conscience.   But they doubt whether
monarchical right divine was ever anything more than a
scholastic theory; and they do *not* doubt that, whether
theory or actuality, it fell with the head of Charles I.
They were therefore surprised, as well as disgusted, to

find the *Times* preaching of "how impossible it is for rulers or people to escape those momentous relations into which, without any will of their own, they were born," and giving vent to such utterances as, "The sentiment of the people would remind the clergy, if they need to be reminded, that their religion is good for very little if it cannot dignify, strengthen, and hallow the highest form of human association." . . . "There is no more natural or more sacred relation than that which subsists between the head of a great nation and those whose interests are entrusted to him. A religion which claims to explain our life to us should always, as in times past, have more to say on this cardinal subject than on any other human affairs." . . . "Whether he would or not, the Prince of Wales holds towards all of us an intimate relationship which it is certain we ourselves have not established. It has grown in long years out of the nature implanted in us, and the destiny impressed upon us." That the writer of this wonderful article knew the real meaning of what he wrote, or that, in writing it, he had any intention beyond that of surpassing the efforts in the way of "forced and false sentiment" of other "sighing, weeping, agonised scribes," we very much doubt. Still more strongly do we doubt that the article really expressed the opinions of even those whose views the *Times* is popularly supposed to represent, but in any case we can and *do* most decidedly and conscientiously assert that they are not the opinions of the working classes, and that those classes resent, and are irritated by, all attempts to include them—by the use of the universal implication method—as holding such opinions. The nature implanted in them does *not* lead them to accept the doctrine of divine right "whether they would or not," or prevent them from entertaining the heterodox belief that there *are* "more natural and more sacred relations" than those between Prince and People. If the *Times'* idea of "the nature implanted in us" is a correct one, the nature of working men must be very perverse, since it further leads them to be of opinion that if the highest function of religion is such as the *Times* asserts it to be, then that highest function is a very low one, and religion a very dear thing at the price we pay for it; a thing that could very well be dispensed with altogether. The working classes have an opinion of their own concerning the part religion played in the matter of the Prince's illness. More than one of the gushing journals asked, Could any more sad or piteously touching scene than the sick-bed at Sandringham be imagined? We answer emphatically that many more sad and touching scenes may not only be imagined, but seen. We will name only one such scene—a scene that is, alas! but too often to be seen under the sun in this England of ours— the scene, namely, that is to be witnessed, and once witnessed never forgotten, on the banks of a mine in which an explosion has taken place. The sight of the ghastly, horror-stricken faces of the mothers and wives, sisters and children of the miners, who have rushed from their homes on hearing the dull, heavy sound which they know *is* the death-knell of some and may be the death-knell of all who are in the mine. The sound of the voice of their woe, even in the first bitterness of which there mingles the thought of what they shall do if they have lost their bread-winner, if he should be already dead, or should not be got from the pit alive. The suspense of those who watch around the bed of a dear one who is sick nigh unto death is one of the most painful experiences of life, but still it can scarcely compare with the unutterable agony of those who watch, not by the well-tended bed, but by the black, bleak pit-mouth—watch, not knowing but that the loved ones are already dead, or whether even their bodies may ever be recovered. There have been cases in which scores of miners have been imprisoned in the bowels of the earth, and in which the question of the possibility of their being alive has had to remain undecided until workmen from above could cut their way through. The thing has been known throughout the land; and it has been known, too, that the exploring workmen would be engaged in their labours of mercy throughout the Sabbath; but the Primate who commanded the special prayers of the Church for the recovery of the Prince never called for public prayers that the entombed miners might be saved alive to their families. It may be that the Primate and the Church hold that the life of a prince is of more value, is more worthy to be prayed for, than the lives of any number of miners. So do not the working classes, however. They mark such things as these, and inwardly digest them, and the result is that they are surprised that clergymen should be astonished that they do not attend church ; that they have but scant respect for any formalised religion—but scant belief in the professors of them practising, or even really believing, what they preach.

The working classes as well as others understood the political importance and significance of the question of the Prince's living or dying, understood why when his death seemed imminent the funds should have gone down. That they took an immense interest in his illness and its fluctuations is most true, but interest should not be confounded with other feelings. If it necessarily meant affection or grief, the Tichborne " claimant" should be about the best-beloved or most-grieved-over personage in the country. That their feeling was anything like the one of overwhelming personal sorrow and despair which the papers represented as overcoming the whole nation, is not true. That it was so very little true, that since the time it has grown to be something rather the reverse of it, is wholly the fault of the papers.

It is in the manner we have been speaking of that the universal-implication phase of smart journalism sometimes

rebounds—does injury to those it is meant to serve. To
give a strictly pointed instance of this in connection with
the subject we have taken as our general illustration—the
subject of the illness of the Prince of Wales. On one
occasion one of the gushing journals had a head-line in
large capitals, " Devotion of the Duke of Edinburgh."
Looking down the columns of the paper the reader found
that the capitalised " devotion " in question was that the
Duke had one night sat up with his brother, not retiring
to sleep till six in the morning. Now, when the necessity
arises, working men will sit up all night with a sick mate,
and at six in the morning retire, not to sleep, but to work.
But the shopmates of a man doing such a kindness would
never dream of speaking of the " devotion " of Jim or
Jack So-and-so ; they would simply say that he was what
a mate ought to be. How men holding this view contrasted this picture and that, the simple natural act with
the adulatory high-flown heading, may be easily understood. Their comments upon the difference were the reverse of complimentary. Some of them extended to the
Duke as well as the paper, and very warmly expressed the
sentiment that if that was the royal idea of devotion, the
commentators were happy to think that their feelings
were not constituted upon a royal model. That such
remarks did injustice to royalty in general, and the Duke
of Edinburgh in particular, there can be no doubt. Without knowing anything more of the Duke than that he is a

young man and a sailor, we will venture confidently to
affirm that *he* would not have spoken of his simple act of
brotherliness as " devotion," and we feel but little less
confidence in expressing a belief that, did he think the
matter worthy of a moment's consideration, he would
despise the toadying scribe who had so written of it.   The
bulk of the working classes are as yet unused to drawing
fine distinctions, and so it comes that the papers that
beslaver royalty overreach themselves, and do royalty an
injury.   Over the illness of the Prince of Wales they
caused injustice to be done to him and the institution
with which he is so nearly associated, for of course neither
he nor monarchy was responsible for their high-flown
outpourings.   The Prince at any rate has good occasion
to exclaim, Save me from my friends—of the press.

To enter into any general discussion of the relative
merits of the Monarchical and Republican principles
would be foreign to our present purpose, but we may say
incidentally that, apart from the special matter of the illness of the Prince of Wales, the tone of the press in
defence of Royalty has done more to damage it and spread
Republicanism than a regiment of Dilkes or Odgers could
have done.   To imply and affect to believe that the working classes are among those who bow the knee to the Baal
of royalty (as they conceive it to be), embitters them
against it far more than does telling them—what they
already know—that it is an expensive thing.   Few work-

ing men attend political lectures, while the great majority of them read newspapers, not perhaps the papers which give vent to the unwise adulation of royalty, but others that make a point of extracting and calling special attention to the most fulsome and (to the working men holding Republican opinions) irritating passages in such royalty-worshipping compositions as we are alluding to.

Large numbers of the working classes are readers of the cheap daily papers, but they read them only as newspapers, not in the sense in which a paper is spoken of as an organ. In the latter sense the press, as it is generally understood, is not their press. They have another, but we regret to say that we can scarcely add a better press. Their press, in the political organ sense, may be said to practically consist of two of the penny weekly papers— *Reynolds's Newspaper* and *The Beehive.* Time was when the *Dispatch* was *the* organ of the working classes, but its day in that respect has gone by. Whether or not its circulation, as well as its price, has gone down of late years, we cannot say, but it is certain that its political influence has. *Lloyd's Newspaper*, the most extensively circulated and energetically pushed of the penny weeklies, is, like the cheap dailies, valued principally as a newspaper. Its leaders are well written, and, like every other paper of its class, it specially advocates working-class interests in connection with the social and political questions of the day, but politically it is held in greater regard outside the working classes than inside them, from the reason that many outsiders have a very natural impression to the effect that, having the largest circulation among the working classes, it is the most largely representative of their political views. This, however, is a mistake. The working classes generally delight in news; in police and criminal court intelligence, and the record of moving accidents by flood and field. But only a section of them take an active interest in politics, and this section take in, *as political organs, Reynolds's* and *The Beehive*. These two papers are accepted and looked up to by the political division of the working classes as their especial guides, philosophers, and friends; they believe in, admire, and are materially influenced by their political teachings. They are therefore the papers whose distinctive characteristics it behoves us to consider in dealing with the phase of the subject of the Press and the People at which we have now arrived. We will take *Reynolds's* first, as being by far the more important and influential of the two. Its advertised circulation is over 300,000, which is probably at least twenty times that of the *Beehive*. It is a general newspaper as well as a political organ, and a very good newspaper as regards the range and fulness of its news. It is well and watchfully edited, the eyes of its editor being evidently carefully fixed upon most other papers. Its political articles show knowledge and research, and are written with an immense deal of what their admirers would call vigour. They furnish working men with much valuable statistical and other information that they would not otherwise be likely to get hold of, and their reasonings and deductions from facts are often clever, bold, practical, and just. But their *style*, their *tone*, is thoroughly bad ; so much so as to more than counterbalance the good qualities of the paper, and make it, as a political organ, nearly everything that is undesirable; dangerous—so far as it is powerful—to society at large, and injurious to the classes whose interests it professes to serve. It does not, after the manner of some journals, adopt a motto ; but, practically, its motto is a paraphrase of the old pirate one, of "a friend to the sea, a foe to all upon it." It is "a friend to the working man, a foe to all above him." It makes a client of the working classes, striving when necessary to make the worse appear the better reason on their behalf, and abusing opponents when they have no case. And while it rails at all others, it habitually flatters and "knuckles down" to the working man, and not only does not admit, but combats the idea of such a possibility as his views upon any disputed question being wrong. He is the horny-handed son of toil, the only real creator of the country's wealth, and so forth ; those who hold different political opinions, or are in different grades of society, are fools, idlers, blood-suckers, bone-grinders, addle-heads, and the like. Its articles have, as we have said, their good points, but, taken through and through, they are—and it would be hard to say anything stronger —infinitely more unfair and one-sided than even the general run of political party articles, and are, beyond all comparison, more coarse, abusive, and personal. It is never tired of inveighing against class feeling and class legislation, and yet its own political teachings are as intensely and ruthlessly class as it is possible for them to be.   If those teachings could be carried into effect, they would result in all save the manually labouring classes being in a worse position relatively to those classes than the latter are now relatively to even the most privileged classes.   Indeed, its teaching upon this point is pretty much to the purpose that none but the working classes, in the popular acceptation of the phrase, have a right to be on the face of the earth. It has, of course, a perfect right to attack institutions, and measures, and public men in their strictly public capacities; and so far as it does only this, its condemnatory criticism is often as justifiable as severe.   But it so mingles its criticisms with base personalities and scandalous inuendos, that it is hard to separate the one from the other, and, unfortunately, those who accept its teachings at all accept them in their entirety—accept the application of the unwarrantable abuse as well as the warrantable criticism. It is, for instance, strongly opposed to the system of granting "provisions" for the children of the Sovereign; it has a right to be so, and to argue that the system is a monstrous injustice to the people; but the right to denounce the system, and the policy of the ministers who uphold it, could surely be exercised to the most full and effective extent without the use of such language as this in reference to the idea of the purchase of an Irish residence for Prince Arthur:—"That young gentleman has already cost us much more than he can be worth; and if further demands are made upon our purses for his behoof, we shall be inclined to wish that when he tumbled out of the billiard-room window at Marlborough House, after dinner, instead of spraining his ancle he had broken his neck." The general style of this journal—the style which makes it an evil and objectionable political teacher—will perhaps be best shown from its own pages, and we will therefore proceed to show it by means of a few illustrative quotations taken at random. Its political matter consists each week of three or four editorial leaders, and two other leaders in the shape of letters signed respectively "Northumbrian" and "Gracchus," and political homilies and denunciations are also frequently inserted in its column of "Answers to Correspondents." This Correspondents' column is one of its most important features; and as it is thoroughly redolent of its style, we may as well turn to it first for an illustrative example or two. Here, for instance, is a specimen of a hit at "a bloated aristocrat:"—

"DUCAL DONKEYISM.—It generally happens that at county agricultural dinners the louder a donkey brays the more uproaringly he is applauded. We can, therefore, readily comprehend that at the Badminton farmers' dinner the Duke of Beaufort was cheered lustily when he said that he should like to see the writers of newspaper articles who remonstrate against royal proceedings, 'tied up and flogged.' The dukes are decidedly a dull lot, and perhaps the Duke of Beaufort is the dullest of the bunch. His name is only known as associated with that intellectual game, 'Aunt Sally,' of which, at one time, he was an enthusiastic patron. Judging by the style of his after-dinner eloquence, we should say that the ducal head of Beaufort might, by reason of its wooden solidity, admirably serve the purpose of an 'Aunt Sally.' Nature apparently intended the man for a coachman; fortune made him a duke. The former denied him brains; the latter has given him wealth and a title. By such nonentities as himself the Duke of Beaufort would have England governed. But it cannot be. Let him crop the strawberry leaves from his coronet, and put asses' ears in their place. The bauble would then be a symbol of the ducal mind."

Here, again, is a bit of historical information which in its definiteness will, we think, be news to most people :—

"YOUNG REPUBLICAN.—It is perfectly true that the late Prince Albert was a believer in the coming deluge of republicanism in Europe. He constantly enjoined upon his family the necessity of economy, telling them that 'the time may come when the savings you lay by now will be the only resources left you.' We should think that the Queen has profited by this advice, for she does not spend very much of the money which is paid to her by this heavily-taxed country."

In this column it is rather fond of giving historical summaries reflecting upon monarchs. Thus, in one answer— too long to quote entire—it gives as historical facts all the old scandalous rumours against Queen Elizabeth which the Spanish ambassadors of her day tried so earnestly, but vainly, to prove to be more than spiteful inventions. The correspondent is informed that—"A worse woman than Elizabeth never existed. She was dissolute in her morals, a murderess, and a destroyer of the people's rights and free will of the worst and most implacable dye. . . . . As to her political life, her cold-blooded ministers and herself were engaged the whole of their lives, after she mounted the throne, in practices most dark, most detestable, and assassin-like."

The more private answers are sometimes very curious; such, for example, as the one in which "An Old Sub-scriber" is informed that—"In this country a man can have but one wife at a time."

But the most remarkable answer we remember ever having met with in its columns—an answer that showed a marvellous reliance upon the ignorance of its readers, and the very sublimity of impudence upon the part of the paper—was one having reference to the letter upon the Franco-German war which Carlyle wrote to the *Times*, and which ran thus:—"We presume you allude to the two columns of incomprehensible gibberish by T. Carlyle, published in the *Times*. It was mere drivel and twaddle."

The political articles in *Reynolds's* are headed, and their titles are generally a pretty good key-note to their style. Thus one on bishops is headed "Live Lumber;" one on the aristocracy is entitled "The Land Robbers of England;" and another, making an accusation of govern-mental jobbery, "Ministerial Grubbers and Aristocratic Cadgers." But the matter of the articles as well as the manner of their titles shall speak for their style. In an article on "The Republican Rulers of France," there is quoted, for purposes of comment, a portion of a letter by Sir Francis Head, and the quotation is introduced thus : —" Here is a specimen of ribald rubbish, penned by an antiquated, mouldy-minded, worm-eaten, bilious old Tory, named Sir Francis Head, and admitted into the columns of the *Times*." In the course of the same article the ex-Emperor of the French is spoken of as follows :—" The imperial liar, thief, perjurer, traitor, fool, and coward, is constantly brought forward, as though his opinions, his thoughts, and his sentiments, even if given in all truthfulness and sincerity, were worth a dump." And further on we have a reference to " The chicken-hearted, white-livered, dirt-eating press of England ; manipulated as it is by the black-hearted aristocracy, and the narrow-souled, money-grubbing middle classes of the country." In an article entitled " The Peers in the Pillory," called forth by the opposition of the House of Lords to the bill for the abolition of purchase in the army, it asks, " Who and what are the leaders of this crusade against the people ? " And it answers its own question in very characteristic fashion. " First," it says, " we have the Duke of Richmond, commander-in-chief by right of selection of the Tories in the House of Lords.' He is the descendant of the notorious and infamous Madlle. de Querouaille, concubine of Charles II., who ennobled her bastards and settled upon them the amount of a tax levied upon every ton of coal that entered the port of London." After giving some account of the ancestress of the Duke, the article goes on to say :—"The Lennoxes have never been remarkable for either their morality or intelligence. Most of them have been, and several still are, pensioners upon the people. As we are told that those who tend fat cattle should themselves be fat, so the present Duke of Richmond, not being a person of very bright and commanding intellect, is admirably suited to lead the 'stupid party' in the House of Peers." The Marquis of Salisbury is taken next, and is described as "A perfect type of the ancient Tory nobleman—arrogant, overbearing, insolent, and defiant." Earl Lucan is set down as the third leader of the Opposition, and he is spoken of as an "undistinguished" officer, giving utterance to "balderdash ; " and as he quoted General Canrobert in support of his opinions, the article in passing observes :—"Canrobert never was a soldier, but simply one of the murderous myrmidons of Bonaparte."

Passing to the rank and file of the peers who voted against the bill, it gives a list of a dozen of them who are in receipt of pensions, and classes them as "'Casuals,' actually receiving, in the shape of pension from the public purse, out-door relief from the public they have insulted and defied." "All these persons," it goes on, receive direct alms from the public, and yet have the audacity to assist in thwarting its views ! What would be said of a plebeian pauper who, while constantly receiving relief at the hands of the relieving officer, insulted and defied those who gave it? These unruly 'casuals' should behave themselves better. It is neither graceful nor grateful to receive alms with one hand, and slap the donor in the face with the other." "In fine," the article asks in conclusion, "are nine-tenths of the people of England to be ruled by a few men—some descended from prostitutes, others obfuscated by old-fashioned feudal notions, or by military failures, or by a lot of pensioners and so forth? It cannot and must not be. These blatant peacocks, who boast of their lineage, which is traced back to the lifetime of a French harlot, and are proud of the strawberry-leaved coronet which has descended to them from the stews—these blunder-headed boobies must be taught that fighting against the people's will is battling with the inevitable."

There has been some talk of having working-men M.P.'s paid from State funds; it may be guessed from the above style of reference to pensions, how any such member who ventured to differ in the slightest degree from the popular view of any question would fare at the hands of *Reynolds* and its admirers. What base insinuations would be levelled at one so situated may be inferred from some remarks we are going to quote from this notable organ, aimed at a man very differently situated —a man, too, who throughout his life had devoted the

energies of a greatly talented mind to the service of the
people—John Bright. In an article on " Mr. Bright's
Return to Public Life," this journalistic friend of the
working classes writes as follows :—

" We hope and trust that Mr. Bright will not renew his political
career from the point it had attained when he retired into private life, but
make a fresh start as a tribune of the people, rather than as the hanger-
on of the Court, the apologist of jobbery, and colleague of some of the
most incorrigible jobbers. We much prefer John Bright in Quaker
broadcloth, than attired in even the Court costume as modified to suit his
views and convenience. When Mr. Bright went into retirement his
popularity was rapidly on the decline ; in short, he was realising to the
letter in his own person the truth of the well-known adage, that the
descent of the downward path is rapid indeed. People were pained to
find the man who had once so boldly and unreservedly denounced out-
door relief to the aristocracy, in the shape of pensions, places, sinecures,
&c., associated with a Cabinet that was bestowing, with lavish hand, the
people's money upon those who neither earned nor deserved it. It was
piteous to hear of the once outspoken John Bright remaining a dumb
dog upon the Ministerial benches whilst measures for the cruel coercion of
Ireland were being brought forward by the Cabinet of which he was a
member ; and it was sad to read of him constantly dancing attendance at
Court under the chaperonage of Lord Granville. Truly, no one who
knew the John Bright of ten years back could have recognised the same
man in the silent and submissive President of the Board of Trade in
1869."

Here, by way of conclusion to our extracts from its
political articles, is a specially characteristic sentence :—

" The fact is, that with a bone-grinding, blood-sucking millionaire
middle-class on one side, a rapacious, tyrannical, liberty-hating, and, as a
body, a murderous-minded aristocracy—composed as it mostly is of men
who would rather behold a dozen poachers shot stark dead upon the sward
than that a single pheasant should fall by their guns—on the other side ;
between this merciless mammon-worshipping middle-class, and the
hereditary curse of the country, the millions of toilers have been and will
be duped, betrayed, and crucified."

These are examples of its habitual style of political

discussion, or rather of the swash-buckler abuse that it substitutes for what ought to be discussion ; and a volume might easily be filled with such specimens. It is, however, in replying to criticisms upon itself that *Reynolds's* comes out in the fullest glory of its Billingsgatish style. A noticeable and very undesirable feature of the paper is, that it inserts advertisements which no respectable journal would admit, and which it is a discredit to Government should be allowed to appear in *any* publication ; and in reporting certain classes of police cases, gives details which other newspapers usually pass over as "unfit for publication." For this, and especially for the latter offence, it has often been censured by other journals, and by none more frequently or severely than by the *Saturday Review*, to whose criticisms in particular *Reynolds's* replies in its choicest strains. In a leading article it calls it "the Saturday skunk of Southampton Street," and goes on to say that "Not unfrequently, but indeed very often, the turning over its pages is as unsavoury a proceeding as the successive opening of a range of stink traps, so foul is the stench coming therefrom." Under the guise of "Answers to Correspondents," it returns to the attack, styling the *Saturday* "that polecat of the press," and comparing it to a "filthy frowsy old harlot" and "a dung fly," in language fully in keeping with the epithets. "Censure," says this particular answer to a correspondent, which is headed "The Saturday Stench"—"Censure

coming from such a source is pure, or rather impure, com-
mendation. We have already lifted the *Saturday Review*
out of the gutter with a pair of tongs, slapped its face
and dropped it into its native mire, and we now do the
same for the last time; as a paper like *Reynolds's*, which
circulates hundreds of thousands weekly, cannot care to
give gratuitous advertisements to one that only publishes
a few paltry hundreds."

It does, however, incidentally mention the *Saturday*
again in connection with this matter. In another leader,
entitled "The Age of Hypocrisy, Cant, and Humbug,"
it observes :—" Last week we had to answer the attacks
of a lion of the press, the *Saturday Review*, for publishing
the full details of the notorious Bow Street police case;
this week we are assailed in a similar manner by a louse
—the *Echo*; that halfpenny hypocrite, which, if it
snuffs an unsavoury odour from afar, is the first to dive
its nose into the cesspool, and rake up the filth deposited
therein."

Such is the style and spirit of *the* organ of the bulk of
the politically inclined section of the working classes—a
style which they admire, but which is, nevertheless, injurious to them. It persistently flatters them, and panders
to their ignorance, prejudice, and passion. It creates and
fosters class animosities in their minds, and leads to their
turning a deaf ear to any political teachings or opinions
which are restricted to the political questions on which

they bear, and are not mingled with, and to a great extent overshadowed by, highly-seasoned personality. If there are any who doubt that this paper really has influence among the working classes, they have only to go into almost any large workshop on a Monday morning, and they will speedily be convinced that it has. They will find men gleefully dwelling upon such "hits" as we have been quoting, and they will further find that these men are very emphatically of opinion that "*Reynolds* is the boy for them"—"them" being the upper and middle classes in general, and the government and royalty in particular. The believers in *Reynolds* — and their name is Legion—have caught the style of their organ. They are intolerant, and therefore intolerable. They make not only other divisions of society, but also the best men of the working classes, chary of co-operating with them for political objects; and this is in a great measure why it falls out that the working classes, while so violent in the expression of their political opinions, are found to be so helpless to give practical effect to them. The violently talking party, like its favourite journal, arrogates to itself not only all true political knowledge, but also all honesty of political purpose. It will tolerate no opinions but its own, will not reason upon points of difference, and disdains compromise, seeking only to over-throw and crush those who may differ from them. Thus it forces even those who are in some greater or lesser degree agreed with it, to hold aloof from it—sometimes to oppose it.

The second accepted organ of the working classes— the *Beehive*—has not, as we have already mentioned, anything like the circulation of *Reynolds's*. For this circumstance there are three chief reasons to account: firstly, it does not season high, after the fashion of *Reynolds's;* secondly, it appeals to a higher degree of intelligence than that which leads a man to admire *Reynolds's* can be; and, thirdly, because it does not, except in a very limited degree, combine the functions of a general newspaper with those of a political organ. Nor has it the same influence with those among whom it does circulate as has *Reynolds's* with its readers, simply because its circulation is among men who think and reason for themselves—men who, while accepting the paper generally, do not accept it blindly, and who, though mostly agreeing with its opinions, differ from them at times, and only allow themselves to be influenced by them after critically weighing them and arriving at a conviction that they are right. The *Beehive* may be described as the organ of that fraction of the politically inclined section of the working classes whose organ *Reynolds's* is not. It is more theoretical than most other papers. It aims at a widely philosophical tone, and evinces a preference for dealing with grand schemes of universal regeneration rather than with parliamentary or other measures of limited scope. Though it discusses such measures, it is rather in a style that makes texts of them for sermons of its own, than in one of detailed, or strictly relevant, criticism. Occasionally it deviates into a somewhat *Reynolds*-like style, as, for instance, when, in objecting to some criticism upon Professor Beesley that appeared in the *Pall Mall Gazette*, it attacked the editor of that journal by name, and indulged in such talk as—" In the old duelling days, Mr. Greenwood might have been called off to Chalk Farm at the risk of being perforated with a pistol ball. . . . . Professor Beesley may be satisfied to treat him with contempt, but some man of more angry disposition and rougher manners may some day make him smart where he is more sensitive than he appears to be on the moral side of his nature. . . . . Lies are lies under all circumstances, and a mean denial of justice to escape the consequence of lying cannot be excused even in the columns of the *Pall Mall Gazette.*" As a rule, however, its tone in dealing with politics, and politicians in connection with them, is tolerant, moderate, and manly to a degree that many journals of far greater pretensions might imitate with advantage to the interests of good feeling and taste. As an illustrative example of this, we would point to the moderation of its tone in replying to some of the anything but moderate criticisms upon the parties to the " seven points" of the Committee of Workmen and Peers. Those who " slated " the seven points were not content

with denouncing them as short-sighted or utopian ; they
stigmatised the men who drew them up as quacks, traitors
to radicalism, self-seeking schemers, humbugs, officious
meddlers, and the like. Now, the leading writers of the
Beehive were among the men thus branded ; but in replying in their own paper to the comments with which
such vituperation was mingled, they respected the personal courtesy, and allowed that liberty of difference of
opinion which others had in a great measure withheld
from them. Several articles upon the subject appeared in
the *Beehive*, one of the best and most characteristic being
by Mr. George Howell, in the issue for November 4th,
1871, and in that article the severest thing in the way of
personal reflection was a retort founded upon Mr. Gladstone having spoken of the framers of the seven points as
quacks. "Mr. Gladstone himself," said Mr. Howell, "has
swallowed many of the pills of these quacks, and is a
more robust politician in consequence, and he will have
to swallow many more if he is to continue as the leader
of the Liberal party." This was a perfectly legitimate
and admissible repartee, and one, too, in which, whatever
there was of personality, there was certainly something of
truth. The chief leader writer of the *Beehive*—it should
be mentioned that most of its leading articles are signed
—is Mr. Lloyd Jones, a gentleman well known as a
speaker at meetings convened for the purpose of fur-
thering working-class views of political and social ques-

tions, and as having an extensive knowledge of statistics bearing upon such questions. The fact that he and other writers on the paper are regarded as being in a greater or lesser degree professional agitators, and that in that capacity they are generally to be found associated in the same "movements," has given rise to a belief among some portions of the working classes to the effect that the journal is made subservient to the individual purposes of the writers *as professional agitators ;* that it is nothing better than a journalistic mutual-admiration society. But though we certainly find one contributor enthusiastically exclaiming that the articles of five other contributors whom he names "are an honour to Englishmen, and should make us feel proud of our country ;" though we find this in one instance, the mutual-admiration idea—in the ignoble sense in which it is entertained—is in a general way unjustifiable. It is not an idea deduced from a study of the ordinary manner and matter of the paper, but a jumped-to conclusion from the fact we have adverted to above. Again, as it is mostly taken in by active trade unionists, others—non-unionists and unskilled labourers —say that the paper is a thing of clique ; that if it can further the interests of the unionists, it does not care what becomes of others. But this, too, is a mistaken view—a view that an unprejudiced examination of the columns of the journal would disprove. It certainly makes a special feature of "Trades Intelligence," but as a political organ it advocates the interests of the working classes generally, and, as between the various sections of them, impartially. Its great weakness, in addition to the smallness of its circulation, is rather the reverse of cliquism, since it consists in dealing with the generic question of the improvement of the condition of the working classes too much at large. It indulges over-much in that widely philosophic, or would-be philosophic, tone of which mention has already been made; and in what is, for any journal intended for general reading among the working classes, an unwise and self-injurious dilettanteism of idea and expression. Much of what is written in it is, in homely phrase, " over the heads" of average working-class readers, while it furnishes others with grounds for saying that the paper is impracticable, and its writers men who, with the arrogance of ignorance, or of that little learning which is a dangerous thing, rush in where better men fear to tread. It deals too much in abstractions and " grand ideas "—deals with them, too, with a self-satisfaction and assurance, and an assumption of finality of political knowledge and insight, that is anything but becoming. "The Positive Solution " and " Comtism *v.* Christianity " are doubtless important and interesting subjects, but they can scarcely be effectively discussed in the compass of a short newspaper article, while, even if they could, it savours much more of a vainglorious desire upon the parts of the writers to show their

knowledge, than of either sound wisdom or policy to dis-
cuss them in the pages of a journal which seeks a circulation among classes not one in ten thousand of whom have
read Comte, and comparatively few of whom know who
or what he was.   In the present state of education among
the working classes the general body of them look upon
such subjects as too " flowery " for them, while the better
educated among them, who take an interest in the discussion of social and political problems, go for their
reading on these abstruser points to sources where they
are more fully discussed than they can be in a newspaper.

A glance at one or two of the *Beehive* articles will serve
to show how the paper plays into the hands of those who
argue that the working classes are altogether unfit to be
entrusted with the real work of government; that as yet
they have no adequate idea of what is and what is not
possible in the way of government and social organization.
We will take as an example a leader upon " The Seven
Resolutions." It opens by saying :—" The Council of
Skilled Artisans has not gone far enough by a great deal
in drawing out its seven resolutions ;" and goes on :—
" In the seven resolutions three essential requirements
are omitted.   They are—

" 1st. That the working classes should have provided for them
permanent and well-paid and well-regulated employment.

" 2nd. That they should have not merely the means of acquiring
' elementary education,' and ' practical knowledge,' and ' technical skill,'

but also, for old as well as young, such an Education of their Moral Nature, under the influence of the Knowledge of the Causes of Evil and of Good to man, as is necessary for the highest happiness of all. This will be an Education which will so develop the good feelings of human nature in each individual, that men will require nothing but the promptings of their spontaneous impulses to induce them to adopt the undeviating practice of 'doing to others in all things as we would have others to do to us.'

"3rd. That those who are to receive this Education and to have this Employment should be so *Placed* as to be surrounded, as far as possible, with favourable influences only, and to be enabled to act in accordance with their rightly educated Moral Nature."

The great bar to our obtaining these three requirements is, the leader proceeds to say, the competitive system in buying and selling, and in the relations between capital and labour. This system is to be done away with, and then—

"Arrangements must be formed—New Self-Sustaining Villages—in which a limited number of families may unite, under competent guidance, to supply as far as possible their own wants of every kind, each person doing a fair proportion to the required work, and all participating alike in the resulting advantages. And when men have acquired the Knowledge of the Causes of Evil and of Good, and all will agree to observe in all their proceedings the Great Precept of Social Religion, there will be no difficulty in forming and carrying out such arrangements."

That most people would set down this as visionary talk; that some might even go the length of calling it nonsense, the writer seems to be aware; for he adds, that " Men imagine that it will be difficult or impossible to form such arrangements, solely because they do not understand the subject." And so far he is quite right. Men, generally speaking, do *not* understand the subject of social reconstruction founded on moral regeneration, especially ordinary working men. We are not of those who think that the discussion or propounding of such great ideas is mere waste of time, but we do say that it is out of place in a paper like the *Beehive*—that it is a weakness in it. Speaking not only from general knowledge, but also from observation specially directed to the point, we can safely assert that the average working-class reader of newspapers turns away from such articles when he encounters them. On the other hand, as we have already intimated, such articles furnish those who already monopolise the actual legislative power with arguments in favour of their still exclusively retaining it; enables them to say of the working classes, See, they know not what they want.

In an article on Political Economy, by Mr. Christopher Nevile, a writer whom we do not remember to have met out of the *Beehive*, and to whom at any rate it will be doing no injustice to say that he is a lesser authority upon the subject of which he treats than Stuart Mill, we find a definition of political economy somewhat at variance with Mill's, given with an unquestioning and unqualified decisiveness such as Mill does not venture upon. " What is political economy?" the article commences. "Is it a science with certain absolute unchangeable facts to be ascertained, such as astronomy, chemistry, or mechanics? Certainly not. Political economy is that science which most promotes the welfare and happiness of a community. It varies with all the changing circumstances of a nation."

Now, it may be that this is *the* meaning of political economy; but seeing that the assertion is followed by very slight and not very conclusive exposition, and that most of the received authorities upon the science allege that it does embrace "certain absolute facts," which do *not* "vary with all the changing circumstances of a nation"—seeing this, we think that the assertion might very becomingly have been made with less of axiomatic certitude; that Mr. Nevile might have given *his* definition as such, not as a settled and incontrovertible law. This dogmatism of definition in matters hard to define is a characteristic of the political articles of the *Beehive,* and forms another of the paper's weak points.

That the *Beehive* allows its columns to become an asylum for some of the most halting and pointless amateur attempts at versification that it is possible to imagine *out* of a collection of Seven Dials' ballads is perhaps a small matter, but so far as it goes it tells against the paper—puts a weapon into the hands of those outside the working classes who are desirous of ridiculing the pretentiousness which certainly characterises the journal in dealing with things political.

Though in discussing the important subject of the relations (or want of relations) between the press and the people we have wrought by way of illustration rather than argument, we trust that our illustrations have pointed as conclusively as any arguments based upon the matter of them would have done, to the deduction which we think they support—to which at any rate we have intended them to lead. And that deduction is, that notwithstanding the self-allegation of innumerable journals to the effect that " the working man " is of all others the person whom they most delight to honour ; that his views are those which they are best pleased to expound, and which they *do* expound—that notwithstanding this, the working classes are virtually without press representation. There is no paper that represents them in the same sense that the *Standard* represents the Conservative party, or the *Morning Advertiser* the interests of the licensed victuallers. In the Fourth as in the Third Estate they have no specially representative member—no member whom they wholly trust, or whom it is wise or safe for others to take as wholly trustworthy when they speak in the name of the working classes. In the matter of the press, the people are between two stools, and are in consequence metaphorically upon the ground. Of the two papers which do come nearer to being political organs of the people than any others, one is a mere panderer to their prejudices ; the other overshoots what should be the functions of a journalistic political organ, and is moreover weak by reason of the smallness of its circulation. A penny weekly paper, which, while a good newspaper, made a special and prominent feature of politics from the working-class side ; which in politics confined itself to a

practical discussion of the questions of the day, but discussed them with the courtesy of tone characteristic of
the *Beehive*, would be the best "organ of the people."
But as yet the time is not ripe for such an organ to be
—what in order to live, and become a power, it ought to
be—a commercial success. Owing to the defective state
of general education among the working classes, and still
more owing to the manner in which the taste in political
discussion of the politically inclined division of the working classes has been vitiated by the toadying, pandering,
and high seasoning of *Reynolds*, and of agitators whose
holdings-forth are ever in King *Reynolds's* vein, such a
paper as we speak of could not be commercially successful in competition with journals that would continue to
toady simply with a view to commercial success. The
one hope of improvement in this respect lies in the spread
of a higher education among the working classes; and
in the matter of education there does happily seem to be
some prospect of advancement. What a weakness the
want of an accredited and influential press organ is to
the working classes as a political party in the State need
scarcely be pointed out. It leaves them pretty much in
the position of an army without artillery.

Of the manner and the means by which the journals
usually spoken of as "The Press" misrepresent while
professing to express the opinions and feelings of the
working classes, we have already spoken, and in conclu-

sion we will only say upon this point that it is to be hoped that legislators do not take these expositions as the reliable gospel they profess to be. If they do, and act upon them, startling consequences may some day ensue. We have already stated our opinion that the universal implication method is a matter of policy, not of ignorance of the existence of conflicting views ; and we here repeat that it is a most dangerous policy—a two-edged policy —a policy that would be best left well alone, and that writers who valued the tranquillity of the country before the interests of political party would leave well alone.

THE TWO RACES OF POOR.

THE poor we have always with us. While civilization and science, the spread of education, and growth of commerce, have each and all vastly increased the aggregate wealth of the country, they have not in anything like a corresponding degree decreased its aggregate poverty. The great army of the poor, as Longfellow styles it, grows greater with the general growth of civilized communities—grows greater, while the smaller army of the rich waxes richer and still more rich. For though there may be some clap-trap, there is also substantial truth in the assertion that the tendency of the times is for the rich to become richer, and the poor poorer. That England's contingent of the great army is an extremely numerous one is but too well known. But there is an important feature in regard to the elements of it which is by no means so generally understood, or appreciated, as it would be well for both rich and poor that it should be. It is not sufficiently borne in mind that "the poor" are divided into two leading classes, having altogether different characteristics, and requiring to be dealt with upon entirely different principles. The majority of people, when they speak of the industrious poor, have but a vague sense of contra-distinction—some no sense of it whatever. They do not fully realise the fact that there is a very large class of pauper and semi-pauper poor who are also a wilfully *idle*, and a more or less scheming and professional poor. It is in distinction from this class that the industrious poor are so called. This idle section, from being open, bold, and persistent in its attacks upon charity, has become the best known division of the English contingent. Indeed, by its energetic self-assertion it has brought those who take things for granted, or only examine them superficially, to believe that it is the whole rather than merely a part of the contingent, and it certainly manages to secure the great bulk of both the public and private relief intended for the general body of the poor. As a matter of fact, however, it is not even the most numerous division, and it is most undoubtedly not the one in which will be found the most trying phases of poverty, or those most worthy of consideration, or best entitled to help. Between it and the industrious poor a great gulf is fixed, and by far the largest proportion of the suffering incidental to poverty is to be found on the industrious side of it; that is, it is to be found there by those who search it out, or are acquainted with the inner life of the industrious poor—for being borne Spartan fashion, its existence is often undreamt of by the kind but easily satisfied observers who are most readily moved by the lighter ills which are paraded and traded upon by the idle poor. By the latter morally thick-skinned class the proverbial coldness of the hand of charity is not felt; while to the industrious poor its touch is icy cold—colder, sometimes, even than death—the bitter lingering death by starvation which is not unfrequently preferred to it. The idle poor go to extremes in searching out charity and making prey of it; not so much because they need it, as from their knowing by experience that by canting, scheming, and a persistence untrammelled by any shade of self-respect, it is to be obtained—even by the most worthless. The industrious poor, on the other hand, shrink from an appeal to charity even in the direst extremity—not so much from innate reluctance to acknowledge failure in the battle of life, as because the proceedings of those who habitually batten upon it have brought charity to be regarded as synonymous with shame, so far as the recipients of it are concerned. A working man, if compelled to seek charity—especially the charity of the State—con-

siders himself, and is considered by his fellows, as degraded. This is, of course, a healthy sentiment, and
conduces to the maintenance of an independent and self-
reliant spirit. But though, broadly speaking, the feeling
is a commendable one, there can be no doubt that it
sometimes becomes an evil when adhered to too un-
swervingly. It is a wrong and morbid feeling when in a
time of utter need, arising out of uncontrollable circumstances, it restrains a man from seeking the aid which in
such a crisis nature prompts him to ask, and the community at large are prepared to give, and to which,
moreover, the law of the land, and perhaps the still more
self-satisfactory law of payment—in the shape of poor-
rates contributed in the days of such prosperity as may
have previously fallen to the lot of the man—has decreed
something of the character of a right as well as of a
charity. To obtain the occasional charity of which, in
specially hard times, he may come to stand in need, and
to afford which is the legitimate and *intended* aim of State
relief, a working man has to associate with the pitchy
professional poor, and he is regarded as defiled by the
contact, for none hold this class in greater aversion than
do the working classes, and none know them more
thoroughly.

Apart, too, from this matter of class sentiment, the idle
stand practically in the way of the industrious poor where
charitable assistance is concerned. The elaborate lying

and plotting to which they resort has led to the adoption
of an equally elaborate and complicated machinery for the
award and distribution of charity. And though such
machinery is comparatively powerless to keep the habitual
charity-hunters at bay, having but little chance against
their versatility of invention and shameless fervour of
assertion, it is a sore stumbling-block to any occasional
applicants who do not know "the ropes." Such applicants find themselves beset with formalities and delays to
an extent that, but for their knowledge of what the idle
class *do* get, would lead them to suppose that the object
of the official dispensers of charity must be how not to
give it. But with their knowledge of what is given, and
to whom it is given, they come in the bitterness of their
feeling to conclude that "poor relief" is not for the industrious poor who seek it perhaps once in a lifetime,
but for idle schemers who prey upon it all the year round,
and year after year. That those entrusted with the distribution of poor relief are actuated by principles that
justify such conclusions, others beside the industrious
poor sometimes assert ; as, for instance, when it is discovered that a death by starvation might have been
averted but for some blunder or neglect upon their part.
But, generally speaking, we think that the severe censure
incidental to such occasions is more or less unfair. Dis-
tributors of poor relief have a very difficult task to per-
form. As a rule it is the idle poor they have to deal with,

and as applied to that class their general method and practice cannot be condemned as harsh, though it unfortunately becomes cruelly so when brought to bear upon the industrious poor. But then it is equally true and unfortunate that, with only such grounds for forming a judgment as are afforded to charitable officials, it is a very hard matter to distinguish between the worthy and unworthy poor. The latter are generally artists in their way. They are, as has already been hinted, thoroughly conversant with the formalities of application, and the nature and extent of their " rights." Their tales of woe are always " pitiful, wondrous pitiful," and at the same time wondrously well fitted to the requirements of the rules and regulations bearing upon them. They are glibly told, and generally admit, of a certain amount of superficial proof as to their being true in the letter, and where the exigencies of the case require a " get up " upon the part of the applicants, or scenic effects in their homes, those accessories are managed with professional skill. Loop'd and window'd raggedness of attire, a shivery-shaky-ness of manner, and " 'umbleness " of tone, are effective weapons in their hands; while with a few artistic touches they will give an appearance of desolateness and squalor to their households that will seem heartrending to any one unacquainted with the fact that it has been put on for a purpose.

With the industrious poor the reverse of all this is the

case. If compelled to seek charity, they scarcely know
how to set about it. If at length they succeed in getting
through the barriers with which it had become necessary
to guard the approaches to it, they appear shamefaced,
tell their tale falteringly, and rather try to speak hopefully of than exaggerate their necessities. Moreover,
they strive to the last to appear as clean and tidy as possible in their person and household ; and uncleanliness
and untidiness being amongst the readiest passports to
charitable relief, this, of course, tells heavily against
them. So much of the poverty brought under the notice
of the charitable is associated with slovenliness, that the
possibility of poverty existing in conjunction with neat
and cleanly habits of life seems to be regarded with suspicion. That a person with well-washed skin and well-
mended clothes may be actually suffering from hunger,
and in every way be in greater need of assistance than
one with a dirt-begrimed face and tattered garments, appears to be scarcely comprehensible to the philosophy of
guardians and givers of charity. From these causes it
usually happens that it is the industrious rather than the
semi-pauper poor who are taken to be the impostors—the
people who apply for charity of which they really do not
stand in need. If relief is granted to them at all, it is
generally of such an insufficient character—of a character
so utterly inadequate to the wants of those who have only
applied for it when in desperate straits, and as a last re-

source of all—as to be practically only a bitter mockery. Sometimes a rebuff of this kind, or a refusal of any help whatsoever, coming as a crowning climax to long previous suffering, proves too much for the victim, who lies down and dies under it. Then comes investigation, and the discovery of the painful truth. Burning indignation is roused that one should so perish in our midst, while the relief that should have saved them was withheld by its almoners. On the heads of these almoners the storm, in the shape of comments in the public prints, spends its force. But are those who censure on such occasions quite sure that they would have acted with greater discernment and humanity *under the circumstances?* Do they consider what the circumstances are? That those whose *business* it is to dispense the public alms are engaged in a constant struggle with schemers, and are bound in self-defence to look with suspicion upon the statements of applicants; that in numerous instances they have found more woeful and better-told tales than those that call forth the newspaper strictures, to be wholly untrue; and that they know that if they allow themselves to be too easily trapped by such stories, newspapers will be indignant with them upon that score, while fiery ratepayers, smarting under a sense of large and increasing taxes, will accuse them of being something worse than merely indiscreet? Do the censurers consider these things? Can they feel certain that *they* would instinctively distinguish between the story of the true man and that of the well-graced actor ? Are they perfectly assured that *their* hearts would not be hardened and made strong in unbelief by daily contests with the lying, lazy, fawning beings who form the bulk of the seekers after charity ? For some miscarriages of charity officials are doubtless in a measure responsible ; but in a general way, the chief cause of such miscarriages lies in the fact that the organizers and recipients of charity belong respectively to halves of the world which know nothing of how each other live.

In the working-class districts of our great commercial and manufacturing centres thousands of idle and industrious poor are to be found mingled together—sometimes even occupying apartments in the same house. To casual visitors to such districts there appears no difference between the two classes. To them the district is simply a poor neighbourhood, and its poor broadly " the poor," while such differences as come under the notice of visitors calling for purposes of charitable investigation are in favour of the idlers. The latter are always aware of charitable visitants—it is their business to be so. They know their days and ways of calling, and prepare for them, generally with the desired (by themselves) effect. They, their children, and household are all made to appear artistically wretched, while the industrious poor, striving to hide or make the best of their poverty, seem comfortably off by comparison. But to those who, like the present writer, has lived in such districts, and had the opportunity of watching their inhabitants when "off guard," the differences in the modes of life of the idle and industrious poor are as palpable as they are great. The industrious poor are, for the most part, unskilled and only casually employed labourers, members of trades that have been superseded, or of branches of existing trades that have fallen under the sway of sweaters—needlewomen, charwomen, and washerwomen. The earnings of such people are small and precarious. They have to live hardly and from hand to mouth even at the best of times, and when evil times come—when employment cannot be found, or, through sickness, cannot be followed—they suffer terribly in the struggle to keep body and soul together. The hungry stomach, the scantily-clad back, the fireless grate, the foodless cupboard, and, worse than all, in many instances the cry of their children for the bread they cannot give, becomes familiar to them. To keep themselves alive at all, at such times, they have to part with their little belongings, and get into debt with petty tradesmen, and thus they are encumbered when what is to them prosperity returns again, and their whole life becomes a heartbreaking struggle with the bitterest poverty.

Nominally, the charity-hunting poor belong to the same class as the industrious poor, but only nominally. The men, though calling themselves labourers, are really loafers. Most of their time is spent in public-houses, or

hanging about public-house corners. They will only work
in a holiday kind of way. They will perhaps go " hop-
ping " for a few weeks in the season, or in fine weather
they will invest in a little fruit or a few bottles of ginger-
beer, and attach themselves as a sort of camp-followers to
out-door pleasure seekers. Or they will engage as banner-
bearers in processions, or to play " the mob " at elections,
or any other occasions requiring actors in that line. Even
such work as this, however, they look upon as extra—
things the doing of which entitles them to special credit,
and to spend the money earned in a "spree." And in a spree
they usually do spend it. They have no need to think of
home, or take heed for the morrow. Among the idle
poor it is the women who are the lion's providers—the
foragers of the army. It is they who hunt up and hunt
down the charities that are laid under contribution to
supply the commissariat department. It is they who beard
boards of guardians and relieving officers in their dens.
If " 'umbleness " and whining fail them, they will assert
their "rights" (?) with aggressive valour. Strong in
those rights, they will, if brought to bay, snub minor
officials and face higher ones defiantly. Their husbands,
they will say, are out of work, and have no prospect of
obtaining fresh employment ; there is consequently nothing
coming in to support them and their families ; they cannot starve, they belong to the parish, the parish is *bound*
to maintain them, and they are there to exact their bond.

If they are widows, they are by so much the stronger in their claim. Other poor widows may

> "Stitch ! stitch ! stitch !
> In poverty, hunger, and dirt ; "

or they may go out charing, or labour at the wash-tub ; but so will not they. They have no husband to work for them, they cannot get work themselves, their children can neither work nor want, and as before they cannot starve, and the parish is bound to keep them. And the parish finds to its cost that it has at any rate to help to support them. Out-door relief has to be given to them by way of compromise, as the lesser of two evils. The alternative of having to go into "the house" does not drive them away as it does the industrious poor. Indeed, in the winter months they will often "take a turn in the house" from choice, coming out again, like the birds, in spring.

In charging upon charities that are not "bound" to support them, these amazonian foragers cannot show so bold a front; it would not be their tactics to do so. Where they have no "rights" to use as weapons of offence, such boldness would be rashness; so, acting with the discretion which is the better part of valour, they trust solely in these cases to their skill in manœuvring; and though cases could doubtless be cited in which they have failed to "draw" their intended victims, their stratagetical powers are, as a rule, all-sufficient. If they go before boards or committees, they are prepared for a much more searching fire of cross-examination than they are usually subjected to; while, when the agents of charity call upon them, their victory is easy and assured, since they are then in an entrenched position.

In the homes of the idle poor there is plenty of dirt, squalor, and raggedness, but no lack of creature comforts. So far as eating and drinking go, they may, by comparison with the industrious poor, be said to fare sumptuously every day. They are often in receipt of relief in kind to an extent that necessitates their selling a portion of it, many and many a parish loaf being bartered by them for a pint of ale or glass of gin, or the price thereof. They are prepared for all times and seasons. The industrious poor must be very ill indeed before they will adventure upon so expensive a proceeding as that of sending for a doctor, but to the others a doctor is no cost; they lay claim to the services of the parish doctor whenever it seemeth good to them, and in this connection it is curious to note how well versed they are in the symptoms of those vague " sinkings " and weaknesses for which " nourishment " rather than medicine is prescribed. In the households of the industrious poor the prospect of an addition to the family is seldom an altogether pleasant one, the preparations for it involving considerable outlay, but to the idlers it gives no anxiety on that score. The

parish doctor, as we have just said, is their doctor, and
with their extensive knowledge of things charitable they
have no difficulty in securing a "Dorcas" bag. Nor does
the idea of "another mouth to fill" at all alarm them.
The child will be born in the parish, and the parish will
be "bound" to keep it. There, according to their comfortable logic and *practice*, the matter ends. Again, the
industrious poor fear the winter with its cold, wet weather
and long dark nights, but so do not the idle section. They
know how to get themselves on the books of societies
that lend blankets, how to get tickets for coals and soup,
and they can rely upon securing a large haul of season-
able benefactions during Christmas and New Year
times.

In all material matters the same sort of difference between the two divisions of the poor is to be found, but
the most striking difference is perhaps, after all, in their
personal air. Let any one contrast the groups of men
who in slack times congregate around workshop-gates in
the hope of obtaining employment, with the groups who,
alike in busy and dull times, hang about public-house
corners in poor neighbourhoods. In the first there is a
saddened quietness; those who enter into conversation at
all speaking in a subdued tone, and ever on the one subject—work, or rather on the want of it; the length of
time they have been out of it, their adventures in search
of it, and chances of finding it. Many of the faces are

unmistakably hunger-pinched, and all of them wear an anxious, self-engrossed expression. In the other groups there is, on the contrary, a general disposition to noisiness —drinking, fighting, and wife-beating exploits are being boisterously and blasphemously discussed, and there is an evident inclination to indulge in horse-play and the hustling of respectable passers-by. Most of the faces are heavy, lowering, and more or less drink-besodden, and all bear an expression of don't-care-ishness, the only variation being that some are stolidly, others recklessly don't-carish.

Among the women of the two classes there is an equally marked difference. The women of the industrious poor are seldom to be seen save by their neighbours. Though they strive to make the most and best of things, they have often

> "Only the ghost of garments on,"

and are always poorly clad and poorly fed, and more or less haggard in appearance, and with true womanly instinct they shrink from the public gaze. The women of the idle poor, on the other hand, have neither the cause nor disposition for such shrinking, and in any case they have to come before the outer world in their pursuit of charity. If any person taking an interest in such matters as we are treating of would like to see what manner of women these be, let them take up their stand

within view of a relieving office on a morning when the
parish loaves are being given out. Such a spectator, even
though he may not be in a position to contrast these
poor with their industrious compeers, will at least be
able to convince himself that, as regards the majority
of them they are not the *suffering* poor. He will see
that these are comfortably dressed, and the fleshy figures
and faces of many of them bear sufficient testimony to
their both eating and drinking well. The looker-on will
further be able to note that they have one and all a
" countenance of demand," and will see them lightly
laughing and gossiping among themselves in a manner
that shows that the crushing cares of poverty at any rate
have not fallen to their share. They are of the fortunate
type of poor, of whom it may truthfully be said—

> " They sleep in peace by night,
> Secure of bread as of returning light;
> And with such firm dependence on the day,
> Their need grows pampered and forgets to pray—
> So sure their dole, so ready at their call,
> They stand prepared to see their manna fall."

To some it may appear that we have spoken harshly, and
to others personally unacquainted with the classes who
are the recipients of charity what we have said may
sound strange ; but it is strictly true, and is rather under
than over-coloured. As wonderful and incongruous things
are done in the name of Charity as were ever perpetrated
in that of Liberty. If always twice blessed in spirit, it

is often twice cursed in effect. If it covers a multitude
of sins in those who give, it but too often, in another and
worse sense, covers a multitude of sins in those upon
whom it is bestowed. To the worthless scheming poor
of whom we have been speaking it is a cloak for and
incentive to the sins of idleness and lying; and though
they, of course, do not see it in that light, it is a curse to
them in that it does incite them to those sins—it makes
their lives morally degraded, prevents the development
of any germ of human nobility or a spirit of independence that might be in their nature, and at the same time
puts curses into the hearts of the industrious poor to see
it so ill, so wrongly applied.

Police court records occasionally show instances of the
successful prosecution of people for obtaining *parish* relief, though proved to be in possession of means or receipt
of incomes amply sufficient for their maintenance in their
degree. But the cases of this kind legally punished or
otherwise brought to light are a most infinitesimal proportion of the number of such that actually exist. The
chances of being " dropped on " for obtaining charity by
false pretences are in the present state of affairs, and are
known in charity-hunting circles to be, so exceedingly
small as not to be worth taking into consideration by
those who are not restrained from imposition by higher
motives. This, and the fact that to obtain charity is, to
those who are sufficiently unscrupulous and pauper-

spirited, literally as easy as lying, has led to many who
are not poor at all making prey of charity, while genteel
paupers and charity-hunters are quite a class. When,
some three years ago, it came out, in the course of a
metropolitan county court case, that a man summoned
for the non-payment of the fees of his daughter's music
master was in receipt of parochial relief, the disclosure
gave rise to no little surprise, and afforded subject-matter
for sundry newspaper leaders, in which the writers tried
to account for such a phenomenon, as they conceived it to
be. But in working-class circles the only surprise excited
in connection with the matter was at others being so surprised at it. It is true that there was a certain farcical
anti-climax in the association of such ideas as those of
parish relief and private music lessons. The case *was* a
striking one of its kind, but it was only one of a kind—
only striking, not exceptional. The principle of such a
difference between parents and children as that indicated
in the music lesson case is one of the curiosities, though
not one of the rarities, of charity. Very often young men
and young women living under the same roof with their
parents, and living wholly or in part upon charity
hunted out by the elders, will in public present a widely
different appearance from that of the parents—an appearance more suggestive of music lessons than of dependence
upon charity, and so wholly superior to that of the parents
who play jackall for them, that you are not surprised that

these elders should tell you that they "know their place too well" to think of speaking to or in any way recognising their children before any who do not, by some means beyond the reach of either parents or children to control, know that the relationship exists. Many a smartly-dressed young lady (as she will call herself), who, perhaps, as an occasional hand at the dressmaking or millinery, or in some other " genteel " business, earns about as much as will pay for her hats, or who, on the other hand, may be altogether an idler—many a young lady of this stamp, who talks about her pa and her ma, " walks out " with her " young gentleman," and attends dancing classes, is the daughter of a frowsy, dirty, ragged charity-hunter, who may be seen going through the streets ladened with parish bread, or flitting about whining and lying wherever there is a chance that alms may be had. As a rule, it is in connection with a daughter that this particular curiosity of charity is to be witnessed, though occasionally a son, who is genteelly as well as loafingly inclined, is one of the parties to it, and in that case the point of non-recognition in the presence of strangers is sternly insisted upon—by the " young gentleman."

We have often heard it asked—have ourselves often been asked—why the industrious poor, who see so much of the abuse of charity, do not expose, and by exposing end it. The brief answer to this would be, that those who ask the question do not know the charity-hunters, and the industrious poor do. The men of the charity-hunting set have more or less—generally more *than* less —of the rough, the women of the virago, in their composition; and if any decent neighbour "rounds" upon them by giving information as to their true character, they will retaliate by "rounding" upon him in their fashion— which is a decidedly unpleasant one. They will make the neighbourhood "hot" for him, will assail him with the vilest abuse whenever he chances to come within earshot of them, seek to fix quarrels upon him, and perhaps break his head. Moreover, such an attempt to interfere between them and their prey stands very little chance of being successful. As we have said, their stories generally admit of a certain degree of proof of being true in the letter. They *are* out of work, and have been for a long time; and though the person seeking to expose them may be morally certain that they need not have been out so long, and would not have been but that charity had given them the means of living without work, he cannot demonstrate that such is the case; nor can he prove that it is *not* to see men who they think can "put them on to a job" that they go into public-houses, or that it is *not* "kind gentlemen," touched by their broken-hearted appearance, who treat them to the drink which, with an affectation of humility and candour, they will perhaps admit *might* have got into their poor heads a little, through being taken on an empty stomach. Again: a great deal of charity is awarded through clergymen and others having a professional interest in religion, and with these the worthless seekers after charity are wondrously canting, "'umble," and pliant, and have an equally wondrous aptitude for seeing and admiring the beauty of any religious teaching the moral of which is pointed by a relief ticket. On the other hand, the industrious poor, being of an independent spirit, are very often brusque with ladies and gentlemen who ask questions that are inquisitorial and impertinent put to any except those who have *solicited* charity, and who, moreover,

> " Twit them with a godly tract
> That's turned by application to a libel."

For it is worth while to note in passing—and many of the respectable poor do note it and resent it—that the great majority of the tracts so largely distributed in poor neighbourhoods have no application whatever if it be not that they are specially intended for the perusal of habitual drunkards, or brutal godless ruffians. This has the effect of disposing religious almoners of charity to regard the charity-hunters with greater favour than the industrious poor, and to believe the canting assertions of the former class to the effect that anything the latter may say against them is uttered in all hatred and uncharitableness, and in a spirit of disparagement to their "'umbleness" and inclination to godliness.

We once attempted to expose a rank case of charity-hunting, and as our experience upon that occasion was really of a generally illustrative character, we will record it as a general illustration of this part of our topic. We were living in the East-end of London, in a court that was inhabited—as many courts in the crowded parts of the metropolis are—by a combination of the well-off and ill-off working classes and the non-industrious poor, the difference between the more prosperous and poorer families being marked by the former having houses entirely to themselves, while the others lived two and three in a house. The charity-hunting division mustered pretty strong, and among them was one noteworthy individual known as the "Father"—not from anything patriarchal in his appearance, but from a cause that will presently be stated. At one time the Father had been a working man—a dissipated, lazy, time-losing one certainly, but still a working man in the ordinary acceptation of the term. But during a time of great distress, which turned the stream of public benevolence upon the district to a special extent, he found that it was possible to live wholly by charity, and had turned the discovery to the fullest practical account. At the period when it was our fate to be his neighbour he had given up work, and was settled down as what working men call a "forager," and a forager, too, of the very worst type, since he made his wife and children do all the foraging, while he battened upon the proceeds, and crowned the measure of his iniquity by starving and ill-using those by whose degraded exertions he lived. He did not frequent public-houses, but he would sit boosing in the house all day when he could get drink, and would thrash his miserable wife when she either could not or would not procure it for him. His family presented a most charity-exciting appearance, and got a good deal given to them, but with very little benefit to themselves. Any food beyond what would keep body and soul together in them was disposed of to find drink for the insatiable father; clothes were by his command pawned; and while he drank the money obtained by that means, his wife had to go and hawk the pawn-tickets about to raise the wherewith to find him a fresh supply. One of his two children was old enough to go out as an errand boy, but whenever he managed to get himself a place in that capacity, his hopeful parent would so badger his employer to pay his wages before they were due, that to avoid the annoyance the boy was discharged; whereupon the father would proceed to kick him, his idea of the whole duty of man in respect to his family being to live on and kick them. Sometimes when he was ill-using his children, neighbours would interfere by crying "Shame!" upon which the father, virtuously indignant, would come out and inform them that he was the father, and would be the father, and act as the father—and hence the title by which he was known in the neighbourhood. This was the Father as we saw him—the Father in his true colours; but to ministers and other charitable visitors the villanous wretch seen by his neighbours was not (on the surface) visible. To them, who but the Father was a meek, religiously-inclined man, bowed down by misfortune? Who but he would not care on his own account—would be quite resigned, since it had pleased the Lord to afflict him, were it not for the sufferings of his dear wife and little ones? Who but he had a racking cough, and suffered from distressing pains in the head and back, resulting from a (mythical) accident which he had met with years before? Who but he was regarded as a superior and much more deserving being than the rough characters around him? Who but the Father, in short, was a consummate hypocrite, as well as a thorough scoundrel?

We lived right opposite this fellow, and perforce saw a good deal of his proceedings. There was something, or rather so much about him specially obnoxious that we were soon imbued with an ardent desire to expose him, and were only restrained from doing so by a wholesome dread of consequences, and a doubt of being able to act successfully against his lying and canting, and the gullibility of charitable visitors. Before long, however, our mind was made easy on the first and more formidable point. We knew that the charity-hunters were strongly clannish; that if you tried to interfere between any one of a set and their prey you would bring the whole set about your ears; and that they were about as unpleasant a kind

of people to be at enmity with as could well be imagined.
This knowledge, as we have just hinted, made us pause
until we saw that the Father, though well known, was anything but much respected even by the charity-hunting
set in the court. His extreme cruelty to his children
caused him to be heartily disliked. The women in particular regarded him with a burning indignation, and it
seemed very much upon the cards that they would some day
mob him, and had they done so ill-health would no longer
have been a fictitious plea with him for some time after-
wards. Concluding from the estimation in which he was
held that the others would not make his cause their own,
I decided to take action for the accomplishment of my
desire to expose him. A little of the charity on which he
lived was received from the parish, but the bulk of it
came from more or less private sources, and a good deal
of it through a clergyman of the district. The Father
had " got on the right side " of this gentleman, who gave
the family tickets or recommendations for all sorts of
charities, assisted them from his private means, and as a
special perquisite made over to them the bread and cake—
usually a very considerable quantity—left from tea parties
and school treats in connection with the place of worship
to which he was attached. This gentleman we selected as
the fittest person to be enlightened as to the true character of the Father. We told him respectfully, but
pointedly and unequivocally, that his *protégé* was a lazy,

drunken, scheming fellow; that physically he was much fitter to be at work than thousands who were working hard every day; and that he need not be constantly out of work, and would not be only that he found it so easy to live by charity. Having listened to our story, he very justly answered that he would not condemn without judging; he would investigate for himself. Accordingly he went over to the Father, who, however, as the event showed, proved too much for us, and maintained— probably strengthened—his position on the "right side" of the clergyman. When the latter came back to us he pretty plainly hinted that he was afraid we were a very unneighbourly neighbour, and sadly lacking in the charity that thinketh no evil. Were we quite sure, he asked, that the beer-can we had spoken of as going into the Father's house so frequently had beer in it? Were we aware that so poor were the family that the beer-can was the only utensil they had fit for carrying liquids, and that, as a consequence, tea, coffee, and soup given to the family by good people in the district had to be brought home in it? Well, we had occasionally noticed a head on the contents of the can such as is seen on beer, and is never found on tea or coffee or soup; and we had further observed that on the days upon which the can was most frequently backwards and forwards the Father was most uproariously drunk, and most frequently and mercilessly ill-used his unfortunate children; but at the same time we could not say that what the clergyman suggested was *not* the case, and we had to admit as much. Had we ever known Mr. ——, the clergyman went on, mentioning the Father by his name, to refuse work, or to say that he would not take work if it was offered to him ? We ventured to remark, in reply to this, that it was scarcely possible that we could have such knowledge ; that nowadays men very rarely had the chance of refusing work ; that it was not offered to them ; that they had to look for it, and compete for a share of it. This the clergyman evidently regarded as an evasion that was not worth noticing, and with increasing severity of manner he went on to ask whether we could not conceive that a man might be driven by distress to ask for his boy's wages before they were exactly due, or did not understand that it was the duty of a parent to chastise his children if he found them disobedient, or inclined to associate with evil companions ? We of course admitted that we could readily conceive the one thing and understand the other ; and the upshot of this part of the business was that the clergyman left us impressed with the idea that we had attempted to malign a worthy and unfortunate man.

The clergyman could scarcely have got out of earshot when the Father came forth to his door-step, and in a harangue, largely made up of curses loud and deep, informed the neighbours generally, and the charity-hunting section in particular, that there was a sanguinary spy and informer in their midst; that the atrocious character in question had tried to put "a spoke in his wheel" with the parson, but that he (the Father) had soon talked the parson over, and made the spy out a sanguinary liar. From this he proceeded to darkly hint that the informer had better look out, that there would be "blood for supper" some fine night, and that no person need be greatly surprised if he (the informer) were found "corpsed." To our chagrin, too, we found that, alarmed at the idea of one who lived among them letting the light in upon them, the charity-hunting set made common cause with him as against us, and among them they made the court so "hot" for us that we were fain to quit it, and shake the dust of it from off our feet.

Among the charity-hunting set in this same court was an old beldame known as "Granny," a brief account of whom and her mode of life will afford so good and general an illustration of a common practice in connection with the genteel pauperism of which we have spoken, that we think readers will prefer to have the practice exhibited by means of such illustration rather than by mere dry description. A weird, wizened, dirty-looking old lady was Granny. She would have stood a bad chance in the witch-burning days, and even at the time when we were her neighbour she was regarded as somewhat of a sybil by servant girls, for whom she sometimes "cut the cards." But though she occasionally picked up a shilling or two by fortune-telling, it was upon charity that she lived and supported a great hulking son, whom she perhaps really believed to be the unfortunate innocent she represented him, and not the idle vagabond he was. She had lived upon charity for many years, and had long banished anything in the shape of a sense of shame in connection with seeking or receiving it. She was regarded as a sort of poor-law attorney to the neighbourhood, as she was thoroughly acquainted with the constitution and mode of procedure of all kinds of charitable boards, and could instruct people how, with very little trouble to themselves, they might secure parochial and other charitable relief. Her capability in the last point she turned to most pro fitable account. She had an extensive acquaintance among the sort of people of whom the worthy summoned by his daughter's music master was a type—people who, though not above accepting charity, and lying and scheming to get it, are too proud to be seen waiting among a crowd of paupers to receive it, and not so pressingly in need of it but that they can afford to forego part of it to save their sorry dignity. When it occurred to Granny that any of these were qualified in the letter, though not in the spirit, to make application for some sort of charity that was given partly in money, partly in kind, she would go to them, and suggest that they should " go in " for the charity; that they might as well have a share of it as any one else; that if a husband was out of work for the time being, there was no need to say more than that—no necessity for mentioning that he had been continuously in work for years before, and had saved money ; that if a widow's relations *did* assist her to such an extent that with doing a little work she could live decently, there was no occasion for her to say anything about the relations—she could simply plead widowhood. Well, they could do very well with the relief, and they didn't see why they shouldn't have a share of it, would say the parties to whom the suggestion was made; still they should hardly like to be seen hanging about a relieving office, or bringing home charity loaves or coals or the like. O, that needn't be a hindrance, Granny would answer ; they had only got to go before the gentleman and get their order, and she would take it for them, and bring their relief when she brought her own, and of course, as they were not very badly off, they would not mind giving her the bread as long as they got the money. On this understanding the bargain would be concluded. Sometimes the proceedings would be so far reversed that the genteel paupers would seek out Granny, but the agreement come to would be of the same character. In this way our particular Granny used to habitually get a large supply of bread, and occasionally—notably about Christmas time—of meat, tea, and other things. These goods Granny sold at reduced prices, and thus obtained money wherewith to supply her son and herself with gin and other luxuries. Her prices for the food that came into her possession in this way were considerably below shop prices, and so far the industrious poor who were her customers benefited; and very often this secondary benefit is all that the industrious poor ever derive from charity.

It was rumoured, too, of our especial Granny—and whether or not the thing was true of her, it is undoubtedly true of some of her kind—that when she was persuaded that she had got hold of clients whose miserable pride would be certain to prevent them from going before boards to make inquiries, she would occasionally take the liberty of intercepting their money relief for a week or so, saying that the authorities had been compelled to stop it for that time owing to extraordinary pressure upon their resources. By thus directly and indirectly preying upon charity, Granny managed to get a much better living than falls to the lot of most poor families who support themselves by hard work. And the Grannies are many, and their clients are a class.

Sometimes when this last phase of the abuse of charity has been under discussion, we have heard it said in very off-handed fashion—"Oh, the remedy for that is very simple: make every able-bodied person receiving outdoor charitable relief come for it personally." But that could not be done. Such a rule would prevent any of the honest poor, who might be receiving partial or temporary relief, from looking for work, and of course the other kind of poor could and would make use of the plea.

There is now a general impression that anything like promiscuous charity is a mistake, but it is only those whose way of life brings them into habitual contact with the charity-receiving classes who can fully realise how great a mistake it is. So utter a repugnance have the really working classes, and the truly industrious poor, to seeking charity, that the mere fact of charity being solicited should suggest doubt of those asking it belonging to those classes, and lead to a strict inquiry as to the truth of whatever allegations are made. If a private individual gives charity in any case with the merits of which he is not personally acquainted, or has not been assured of by some one on whose independence and judgment he can rely, the chances are much more in favour of his having played into the hands of an undeserving person than of his having assisted a deserving one. We think it may safely be said that the largest half of all our charity is secured by people who are neither truly needful nor worthy of it

To the intervention of the cormorant traders upon poverty, of whom we have been speaking, must in a great measure be attributed the fact that the enormous—and probably in itself amply sufficient—total of English charity fails to fulfil its mission ; that the law of the land, that no member of the community shall perish from want, is practically a dead letter. The ultimate object of charity is, we take it, to afford maintenance to the helpless poor, and give adequate assistance to those whose own utmost efforts at self-help fail to secure them a sufficiency of the common necessaries of life. This purpose English charity does not accomplish, though it can scarcely be doubted that its resources are equal to carrying it out to the fullest extent—if they were rightly administered. How to administer them rightly is a question to which only years of experimental trials can give a satisfactory answer; but the time has unquestionably arrived when "something should be done." There is one point in the required reform, however, concerning which we think there could be but little difference of opinion : the necessity, namely, for concentrating charity—for, if possible, confining its distribution to a single channel. In the face of such watchful, active, and unscrupulous enemies as the charity-hunting poor, diversity is a weakness. As matters stand, it is the point which more than all others favours their operations. The agents of each charity are led to infer that they alone are solicited for aid, and while the assistance that each may give may be all too small to meet the alleged wants, the gifts of a number will combinedly make up a very comfortable livelihood. If the exact total amount that each person or family was drawing from charity could be known, many of the idle poor would not be able to draw a tithe of what they do now; would be able to draw so little that the game would cease to be worth the candle to them, and, disgusted and desperate, they might be driven—to work for a living.

Centralization in charity would be a tower of strength against the attacks of the worst kind of poor—an undoubted benefit to the best, and to the public at large. Its tendency would be to extinguish the mere idle poor as a class, lessen the mass of full-blown technical pauperism, and ameliorate the condition of the industrious poor, who, from the causes we have spoken of, find charity as at present administered only vanity and vexation of spirit.

FINIS.